Writing and Language Handbook

Macmillan
McGraw-Hill

New York   Farmington

Macmillan/McGraw-Hill

A Division of The **McGraw-Hill** Companies

Copyright © 1997 Macmillan/McGraw-Hill, a Division of the Educational and Professional Publishing Group of The McGraw-Hill Companies, Inc.

Macmillan/McGraw-Hill
1221 Avenue of the Americas
New York, New York 10020-1095

Printed in the United States of America

ISBN 0-02-181468-6-8
1 2 3 4 5 6 7 POH 02 01 00 99 98 97

WRITING AND LANGUAGE HANDBOOK

PART 1: **Writing**

PART 2: **Reading**

PART 3: **Speaking, Listening, and Seeing**

PART 4: **Study Skills**

PART 5: **Grammar, Mechanics, and Usage**
Grammar and Usage
Capitalization and
    Punctuation

PART 6: **Vocabulary and Spelling**

PART 7: **Resources**
Writing Models
Glossary of Literary Terms
Index

PART 1: WRITING 1-31

1.1 The Writing Process 2-14

Prewriting 4-8

   Get Yourself Going

   Starting a Writing Folder

   About Your Topic

   Who's Your Audience?

   Brainstorming and Freewriting

   Graphic Organizers: See Your Ideas

Drafting 9

Revising 10-11

Proofreading 12

Publishing 13

Reflecting 14

1.2 Types of Writing 15-19

Narrative Writing 16

Descriptive Writing 17

Expository Writing 18

Persuasive Writing 19

1.3 Purposes for Writing 20-23

Write to Reflect

Write to Explain

Write to Describe

Write to Entertain

Write to Persuade

Write to Learn

Write to Understand

Write to Analyze

Write to Synthesize

Write to Evaluate

1.4 Using a Writer's Journal 24-31

Getting Started
Journal-writing Ideas
   Personal Thoughts and Experiences
   Learning Notes
   Reading Reactions
   Dialog Journals

PART 2: READING 32-67

2.1 Reading Strategically 34-47

Active Reading 36-37
   Make a Connection
   Ask Questions
   Write a Response
   Form a Group
Critical Reading 38-39
   Point of View
   Fact or Opinion?
   Faulty Logic
Before Reading 40-41
   Preview It
   Judge a Book by Its Cover
   The KWL Strategy
During Reading 42-45
   Ask Questions
   Determine Author's Purpose
   The SQ-3R Plan
   Mapping

After Reading 46-47
   Summarize It
   Talk it Over
   Reflect on It

2.2 Reading Nonfiction 48-53

Main Idea/Supporting Details 49

Classification 50

Cause/Effect 51

Compare/Contrast 52

Problem/Solution 53

2.3 Reading Literature 54-67

Reading Fiction 56-59

   Setting, Characters, and Plot

   Theme in Fiction

   Fiction Techniques

   Fiction in Action

Reading Poetry 60-65

   Poetry Forms

      Haiku, Villanelle, and Free Verse

   Poetry Techniques

Reading Drama 66-67

   Characters

   Script

   Structure

   Other Elements

PART 3: SPEAKING, LISTENING, AND SEEING **68-101**

3.1 Speaking and Listening 72-87

One-on-one Discussions 72

Group Discussions 73-74

Oral Presentations 75-82

   Preparing a Speech

   Making a Speech

   Purposes for a Speech

   Be a Critical Listener

Interviews 83-84
    Before You Begin
    During the Interview
Debates 85-87
    How to Get a Debate Going
    Before the Debate
    During the Debate

3.2 Seeing 88-101
Symbols 89
Creative Seeing 90
    Paintings and Drawings
    Sculpture
    Photography
    Illustrations
    Cartoons
Television 98-99
Advertising 100-101

PART 4: STUDY SKILLS **102-133**

4.1 Using the Library 105-122
4.2 Study Strategies 123-131
Using Computers .123-125
Taking Research Notes 126-127
Outlining 128
Study Strategies 129-131
4.3 Test-taking Strategies 132-133

PART 5: GRAMMAR, MECHANICS, AND USAGE

PART 5: GRAMMAR, MECHANICS, AND USAGE **134-211**

5.1 Grammar and Usage 136-197

Sentences 138-147
- Types of Sentences
- Subjects and Predicates
- Phrases
- Clauses
- Compound Sentences
- Complex Sentences
- Sentence Problems: Fragments and Run-ons

Nouns 148-153
- Concrete/Abstract Nouns
- Singular/Plural Nouns
- Possessive Nouns
- Collective Nouns
- Compound Nouns
- Appositives

Pronouns 154-161
- Personal Pronouns
- Pronoun/Antecedent Agreement
- Possessive Pronouns
- Reflexive and Intensive Pronouns
- Indefinite Pronouns
- Interrogative and Demonstrative Pronouns

Verbs 162-177
- Action Verbs
- Linking Verbs
- Using Linking Verbs:
  - Predicate Nouns and Predicate Adjectives

Direct Objects

Transitive and Intransitive Verbs

Indirect Objects

Active/Passive Verbs

Helping Verbs

Principle Parts of Verbs

Verb Tenses

Present-Progressive and Past-Progressive Verbs

Perfect Tenses

Irregular Verbs

Singular and Plural Verbs

Subject/Verb Agreement

Adjectives and Adverbs 178-187

Comparing With Adjectives

Definite and Indefinite Articles

Proper Adjectives

Avoiding Double Negatives

Prepositions 188-191

Prepositional Phrases

Conjunctions 192

Interjections 193

Clauses 194

Verbals and Verbal Phrases 195-197

5.2 Capitalization and Punctuation . . .198-211

Capitalization 198-201

Punctuation 202-211

Punctuation

Periods

Question Marks

Exclamation Points

Commas

Apostrophes
Quotation Marks
Italics/Underlining
Colons
Semi-Colons
Hyphens
Parentheses

5.3 Answer Key 212-219

PART 6: VOCABULARY AND SPELLING . .**220-247**

6.1 Vocabulary Strategies 222-237
Context Clues 224-225
Word Parts 226-229
Homophones and Homographs 230
Idioms 231
Etymology 232-233
Using a Dictionary 234-235
Using a Thesaurus 236-237

6.2 Spelling Strategies 238-247
Basic Spelling Rules .241-245
Spelling Bugs 246-247

PART 7: RESOURCES **248-317**

7.1 Writing Models 250-297
Story 250-251
Poem 252-253
Script 254-255
Personal Narrative 256-257
News Article 258-259
Feature Article 260-261

Editorial 262-263
Persuasive Essay 264-265
Descriptive Essay 266-267
Summary 268-269
Book Review 270-271
Observational Report 272-273
Research Report-Science 274-275
Research Report-Social Studies 276-277
Compare/Contrast .278-279
Cause/Effect 280-281
Problem/Solution 282-283
How-to Guide 284-285
Autobiography 286-287
Biography 288-289
Interview 290-291
Character Sketch 292-293
Business Letter 294-295
Friendly Letter 296-297

7.2 Glossary of Literary Terms 298-307

7.3 Index 308-319

PART ONE

Writing

CONTENTS

The Writing Process 2–14

Prewriting 4
Drafting .9
Revising 10
Proofreading 12
Publishing 13
Reflecting 14

Types of Writing 15–19

Narrative Writing 16
Descriptive Writing 17
Expository Writing 18
Persuasive Writing 19

Purposes for Writing 20–23

Using a Writer's Journal . .24–31

THE
WRITING PROCESS

Express Yourself

Writing is one of the most powerful forms of expression. Through writing you can bring your thoughts, ideas, and feelings to life—and you can share them not just with one or two people, but with many.

There's no special trick to writing well. It just requires some energy, some imagination, and a little persistence. Most of all it requires a knowledge of **the writing process**.

There are several stages in the writing process. Although the stages may vary somewhat from writer to writer, they generally go something like this:

Prewriting

This is the planning stage. You choose a subject, brainstorm, take notes, and think about who would be interested in reading your work.

Drafting

This is the writing stage. You don't need to worry about order or correctness —right now you're just trying to get all your ideas down on paper.

Revising

This is the rewriting stage. Look at what you've already written. You might decide to add, delete or rearrange sections. You might also brainstorm for new ideas. Share your writing with some friends to get advice and other opinions.

Learning how to write well is like coming upon a fantastic city, with unexpected discoveries around every corner. It's a long road and sometimes the going is slow, and the ride may get a little bumpy, but it's definitely worth the trip.

On the following pages you'll find a lot of ideas, suggestions, and strategies to help you make your way through the stages of the writing process. They're your maps for your journey.

Reflecting

This is when you take the time to think about what you've written. Consider what you like and what you don't like about what you wrote. You can also start planning your future writing projects!

Editing

This is the polishing stage. Once you're satisfied with what you've written, check it for errors in grammar, usage, and spelling. Correcting these errors will make your work clear and professional.

Publishing

This is the stage when you share your work with others. There are so many ways to do it. You might read your work aloud, submit it to the school newspaper, or give it to a friend to read.

Writers TALK

"I have rewritten—often several times—every word I have ever published. My pencils outlast their erasers."

—Vladimir Nabokov

✔ *You don't always have to use each of these strategies. The kind of writing you're doing will determine which you choose. You'll probably find that some writing comes very easily to you, and you may only have to use a few of these strategies. Other writing may be more difficult, and you may want to use more.*

GET YOURSELF GOING

It may sound strange, but one of the most important stages of the writing process happens before you ever put pen to paper. In the **prewriting** stage you start thinking about what you're going to write. The planning you do during this stage will help your later writing, so leave plenty of time for it.

Here's a list of strategies you might use during prewriting:

Prewriting Strategies

- Choose a topic
- Explore the topic
- Focus the topic
- Consider your purpose and audience
- Brainstorm and freewrite
- Use graphic organizers

Starting a Writing Folder

Many writers find that writing folders are very useful. They can help you generate ideas, keep track of current projects, and store finished projects.

▶ Let one section be for future writing ideas. Fill it with notes about your experiences and your reactions to them, favorite quotes and song lyrics, interesting articles and photographs, and topics you'd like to write about.

▶ In another section of the folder, keep your works in progress. You might want to make room for different genres, such as one section for poetry and another for prose.

▶ Keep your published works in another section.

4

ABOUT YOUR TOPIC

Choosing a Topic

Before you begin writing, you need something to write about. To find a topic, start with the resources around you. Make a writer's folder if you don't already have one. Try to think like a writer. Keep an eye out for interesting things, and take notes about them. You can also brainstorm about ideas with friends and classmates.

Exploring Your Topic

After you pick your topic, get a general overview by reading up on it and taking notes. As you begin to explore, ask yourself questions about your topic and discuss your ideas with others. Figure out what you already know and what you want to investigate further.

Focusing Your Topic

Once you have a general overview of your topic, focus in on a writing idea. Narrow your topic step by step. Work from the general to the specific, like this:

keep in mind

Choose a topic that interests you. Make it something **you'd** like to read about.

• • •

Explore your topic widely. You can only write about what you know.

• • •

You can't do everything. Stay focused on what you most want to write about.

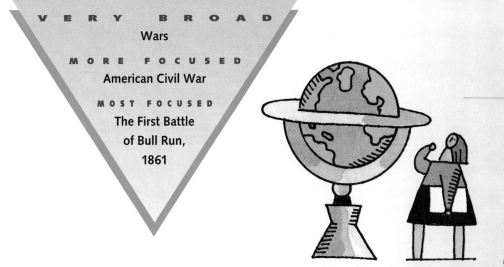

VERY BROAD
Wars

MORE FOCUSED
American Civil War

MOST FOCUSED
The First Battle of Bull Run, 1861

WHO'S YOUR AUDIENCE?

As you prepare to write, think about your **audience**—the people who will read what you write, or listen to a presentation of your writing. It's important to keep your audience in mind when you write, so you can decide on the best way to reach them.

You might try to imagine someone actually reading or listening to the words you write. Picture your teacher, a family member, classmates or friends reading your work. What would grab their attention? What questions might they have? Can you answer those questions now, in what you write?

Try to tailor your writing to fit the audience you will have. You'd write much more simply for a young child than you would for your school newspaper, for example.

Here's a checklist you can use to help you think about your readers:

Audience Checklist

✔ Who is my audience? How old is my audience?

✔ How will I get them interested in my topic? How will I keep them interested? . . . Excite them? . . . Make them laugh?

✔ What kinds of knowledge and experience might I have in common with them?

✔ Are they likely to be familiar with my topic? Or not? How detailed do I need to be?

✔ What questions might they have? Can I answer them as I write?

✔ Is my audience likely to have an opinion about my topic already? Are they likely to agree or disagree with my opinion?

IDEAS ARE EVERYWHERE

The more ideas you can generate during prewriting, the more you will have to work with when you write your first draft. **Brainstorming** and **freewriting** are tools that can get your ideas flowing.

Brainstorming

When you **brainstorm**, you gather ideas about your topic. Imagine a storm of ideas in your head. Think of as many ideas related to your topic as possible. Don't worry about whether each idea is usable. The object is to come up with all kinds of things. Keep a list as you go. You may even want to draw some pictures about your topic ideas. You can brainstorm by yourself, with a partner, or with a group.

Freewriting

Another way to get ideas together is to **freewrite**. Freewriting entails writing quickly, without stopping to think. It's a way to "free up" ideas that are already in your mind. Write down whatever comes into your head. Don't worry about how things connect. Just let the words flow.

keep in mind

The object is to gather as many ideas as you can. Later you can decide which ones to use.

• • •

When you freewrite, don't stop to think about whether your work is "good" or whether it's in the right order. Just let your ideas loose. You may surprise yourself!

Writers **TALK**

"My ideas come from everywhere—from things I read, from things people tell me about, from things I see about me, from things I experience."
—*Patricia Lauber*

GRAPHIC ORGANIZERS: SEE YOUR IDEAS

keep in mind

Diagrams *and* clusters *are just two kinds of graphic organizers. Feel free to make up different ways to sketch out your ideas.*

• • •

If you can see your idea before writing, your reader will be able to see it, too.

See the paper written from this diagram on pages 266-267.

• • •

See what a cluster map looks like on page 45.

• • •

See other kinds of graphic organizers on pages 49-53.

Graphic organizers are like drawings of your ideas. They can help you see your ideas and how they connect. Graphic organizers offer you an opportunity to sketch out your ideas without worrying about exact wording or connections between different parts of your work.

There are any number of ways to sketch out writing ideas. You can use visual images such as **diagrams** and **clusters** to help you brainstorm new material, to firm up ideas you already have, and to organize your material.

Diagrams

Diagrams can help you keep ideas organized as you brainstorm. The kind below, with overlapping circles, is called a Venn diagram. Venn diagrams are especially useful when you're preparing for a compare/contrast paper.

Alligators and Crocodiles

CROCODILES
• up to 23 feet long
• meaner, bolder
• 14 kinds

BOTH
• among the largest reptiles
• large jaws, lots of teeth
• good swimmers

ALLIGATORS
• about 12 feet long
• less likely to attack
• only 2 kinds

Clusters

You can also try **clustering**, or mapping. Write your main topic in the middle of a piece of paper. Then put writing ideas around it, trying to keep related concepts near each other. Draw lines to map out how each new concept connects to your topic. Your cluster can be simple or complicated, depending on how complex your topic is.

PUT IT IN WRITING

Now you're ready to write. Shaping your ideas into your first draft can be exciting, especially since you've already done much of the planning work.

Write your first draft quickly, getting all your ideas down on paper. Keep your original plan in mind as you write, but if you get swept up by a new idea, be flexible enough to investigate it. You'll have the opportunity later to rework and reorganize your first draft.

Once you've finished a draft, you may want to read parts of it aloud to a partner. You might also want to get some feedback from a member of your target audience.

CHECK it OUT!

✔ *Show, don't tell. If you want readers to be able to picture what you're writing about, use descriptions and images that make your ideas come to life.*

✔ *Take time to explore your material. Try different arrangements of your main points. You might want to try cutting and pasting sections in different ways.*

✔ *When you revise later, you'll need room to make notes and corrections, so leave wide margins. Make sure there's plenty of space between the lines by writing or typing on every other line.*

First Draft Strategies

- Keep your prewriting ideas nearby, and refer to them often.

- Make the tone of your writing fit the topic. If your topic is serious, a light, chatty tone won't set the mood very well. If your topic is informal, a conversational tone might work.

- Don't worry too much about grammar, wording, organization, or sequence; you can fix errors and rearrange sections when you revise.

- Imagine your audience. Keep them in mind as you write. If you're interested in your writing, others probably will be, too.

GETTING IT ~~WRITE~~ right

Here's one of the most important rules you'll ever learn about writing: nobody gets it right the first time. Everyone—from the beginning writer to the most successful author—has to revise.

To revise means *to see again,* and that's what you're doing when you're revising: you're trying to see your writing with new eyes, to figure out what works and what doesn't. The best way to do this is to put your work away for a while, so that you can look at it fresh when you start revising.

Writers revise in very different ways. Some change so many things it's almost as if they started over; others tend to make only a few changes. However you do it, it's helpful to keep a few strategies in mind:

Revising Strategies

- **Get some distance.** Allow time for a break to clear your mind before you revise. Go for a walk, play with a pet, eat dinner, or just sleep on it.
- **Remember the big picture.** You'll stay on target if you keep your main idea, your purpose, and your audience in mind.
- **Get feedback from others.**
- **Make sure your ideas are fully developed.** Have you remembered to include all your key points? If there's important information hiding in your notes or in your head, now is the time to get it into your draft.
- **Make your own revision checklist.** You can make a customized checklist for each piece of writing. Check out the one on the next page for ideas.

A checklist often comes in handy for keeping track of the revising process. Here's a checklist one student made; you might want to use it as a guide for making your own. Feel free to modify it to suit your writing style and needs.

Revising Checklist

✔ Do I need to rearrange my work?

✔ Should I do any cutting?

✔ Do I need to add any sections?

✔ Do I need to rewrite anything?

✔ Is every main idea supported by details?

✔ Are my lead and closing sentences strong?

✔ Do I need to clarify any sections?

✔ Is my style right for my audience?

✔ Is my purpose clear?

keep in mind

Double-space your writing. Leaving plenty of space will make revising much easier.

• • •

It can take several revisions to get it just right.

• • •

Keep a revising checklist handy, so you can refer to it easily.

Writers TALK

"The beautiful thing about writing is that you don't have to get it right the first time—unlike, say, a brain surgeon. You can always do it better, find the exact word, the apt phrase, the leaping simile."

—Robert Cormier

THE FINISHING TOUCH

Proofreading may not seem as important as drafting or revising, but remember this: if there are too many errors in your *form*, your reader won't be able to concentrate on the *content* of your writing. Errors in grammar, usage, or spelling are a big distraction.

Proofreading will be a snap if you can keep these strategies in mind:

PROOFREADING MARKS

∧   *Insert*

ℓ   *Take out*

≡   *Make a capital letter*

∕   *Make a lower-case letter*

⌐   *Indent the paragraph*

⑄   *Check the spelling*

∿   *Reverse the order*

⊙   *Add a period*

⋏   *Add a comma*

⌄   *Add an apostrophe*

⌄⌄   *Add quotation marks*

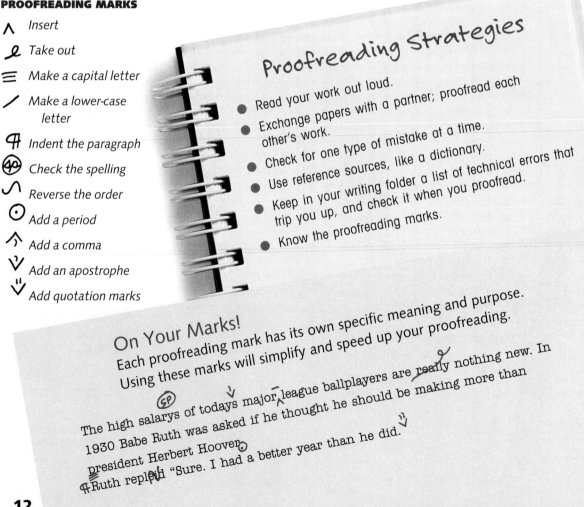

Proofreading Strategies

- Read your work out loud.
- Exchange papers with a partner; proofread each other's work.
- Check for one type of mistake at a time.
- Use reference sources, like a dictionary.
- Keep in your writing folder a list of technical errors that trip you up, and check it when you proofread.
- Know the proofreading marks.

On Your Marks!

Each proofreading mark has its own specific meaning and purpose. Using these marks will simplify and speed up your proofreading.

The high salarys of todays major league ballplayers are really nothing new. In 1930 Babe Ruth was asked if he thought he should be making more than president Herbert Hoover. Ruth replied "Sure. I had a better year than he did."

YOUR PUBLIC AWAITS

Publishing can be one of the most satisfying stages of the whole writing process. After all, once you've devoted so much energy and creativity to a piece of work—once you've written and rewritten and polished it until it's done—you may want to share it with an audience.

There are plenty of great ways to publish your work. Here are just a few suggestions to consider:

▶ **Do a Reading**
Organize a group reading. Ask other writers to participate. Invite parents and guests.

▶ **Make an Anthology**
Collect various pieces of your work under one cover. You might divide it by type of writing, or by topic or theme.

▶ **Give a Performance**
If you've written a play, you might stage it. Assign each part to an actor. Try adding music and sound effects.

▶ **Draw a Cartoon**
You might turn one of your stories into a comic strip and submit it to a school newspaper or magazine.

▶ **Submit to a Magazine**
Read magazines that publish student writing; see if your work is suitable for them. If so, submit it in the form requested by the magazine.

▶ **Write for a Newspaper**
Have you written an editorial or essay that might be of interest to your community? Your local paper probably has a column devoted to readers' viewpoints.

CONSIDER THIS...

Once you've finished your writing, take some time to reflect on the process. How did it work for you? Was it harder than you expected? Easier? Was there anything you would change next time?

Writers spend a lot of time thinking about writing. They're constantly searching for new strategies to improve their work and asking themselves questions about their writing process.

Here's HOW to...

THINK LIKE A WRITER

Ask yourself:

1. What do I like best—and least—about the last thing I wrote?
2. What topics am I most interested in now?
3. What new ideas or experiences do I want to write about?
4. What stage of the writing process do I find most difficult?
5. Is there another form of writing I'm interested in experimenting with?
6. When was the last time I tried a new prewriting strategy?
7. What did I find out about myself from my last writing project?

TYPES OF WRITING

4 WAYS TO TRAVEL THE WORD

Most of the writing you'll ever do can be divided into four main types:

Narrative Writing

tells a story–whether it's fiction (made up) or non-fiction (factual).

Descriptive Writing

paints a picture with words. It uses the five senses–seeing, hearing, touching, tasting, and smelling–to make writing come to life.

Expository Writing

is nonfiction that explains things. It gives readers facts and information.

Persuasive Writing

tries to influence readers to agree with the writer's viewpoint. It uses convincing facts and ideas.

In the coming pages, you'll read about these four types of writing. You'll also learn some strategies for writing each of them effectively.

For more on narrative writing, *see the model on pages 292-293.*

TELL A STORY

Narrative writing tells a story. (*Narrative* is really just another word for *story.*) The story might be fictional, as in a novel or a short story. Or it can be a real-life story, the sort you find in a biography or autobiography, or in a narrative essay.

If you're writing a fable or a science-fiction story or a murder mystery; or writing a report describing how John F. Kennedy became president or how your grandmother came to America from Italy; or writing an essay about the time you locked yourself out of your house and tried to come down the chimney like Santa Claus—then you're doing narrative writing.

Narrative writing

- ▶ tells a story
- ▶ has a beginning, middle, and end
- ▶ has a setting and characters
- ▶ is usually told in time-order (though some fiction may have flashbacks)
- ▶ often starts with a problem and then includes a series of events that lead up to a solution

One Woman's Journey

For a long time I have tried to imagine the boat that brought my grandmother here from Italy when she was young. At first I pictured one of those grand steamships, the kind they're always smashing champagne bottles against just before they set off for sea ...

PAINT A PICTURE WITH WORDS

Descriptive writing paints a picture with words. Whether you're describing a person, place, or event, try to include a lot of *sensory details*—details that appeal to the five senses. Sensory details help your readers to see, hear, touch, taste, and smell what you're describing, almost as if the scene was right there in front of them. Figurative language, such as similes and metaphors, also helps to create a vivid image in your reader's mind.

If you're writing a character sketch of the most interesting person you know; if you're writing a poem about the beautiful foggy beach you walked on last winter; if you're writing an essay detailing the sights and sounds of the World Series game you attended—then you're doing descriptive writing.

Descriptive writing

- ▶ paints a picture in words
- ▶ uses details that appeal to the five senses
- ▶ uses figurative language, such as similes and metaphors, to help create vivid images

For more on descriptive writing, *see the model on pages 252-253.*

The Foggy Beach
the fog descends like a white screen
so that I can no longer tell
where sky ends
and water begins

a seagull calls overhead ...

TELL IT LIKE IT IS

Expository writing is any writing that explains or informs. When doing expository writing, keep your focus specific and organize information in a logical order. That way, the reader will have no trouble following your explanation. Also, try to keep your language clear and precise, and be sure to include all the facts you'll need to make your points.

If you're writing a research paper about the history of women's basketball or the life of penguins; if you're writing a summary of the Kurt Cobain biography you just read; if you're writing an article about your school's new computer lab; if you're writing a set of instructions, or even a recipe—then you're doing expository writing. In other words you do expository writing all the time.

Expository writing

- ▶ explains or informs
- ▶ is focused on a specific topic
- ▶ organizes information logically
- ▶ includes all necessary facts
- ▶ uses clear, precise language

more
INFO

For more on expository writing, *see the observational report model on pages 260-261.*

On Line to Go On-Line

Students were lined up in the hallways last Monday, waiting to try out the new computer lab that has been built in what was once just a row of empty shelves in the library. The lab boasts some twelve computers ...

IN YOUR OPINION

Persuasive writing presents the writer's point of view and tries to influence readers to agree with it. When doing persuasive writing, include facts that support your point of view; also, make sure your language is clear and your argument proceeds logically. Before you start writing, spend time thinking about your audience—what kinds of facts and arguments would best convince them to agree with your point of view?

more
INFO

For more on persuasive writing, *see the model on page 251.*

If you're writing an editorial for your school newspaper about why eliminating the school band is a bad idea; if you're writing a review of the latest best-seller or big-budget action movie; if you're writing a letter to the editor supporting your town's new recycling plan—then you're doing persuasive writing.

Persuasive writing

- ▶ presents a clear point of view
- ▶ tries to influence the reader
- ▶ uses convincing facts
- ▶ presents an argument in a logical order
- ▶ requires a clear understanding of your audience

Let's Band Together to Save the Band

Is school only a place we go to learn facts and figures, dates and places? Or should it also provide opportunities for us to explore a wide range of interests, learn new skills, and maybe even learn something important about ourselves?

If you answered the latter, then you should be concerned ...

PURPOSES FOR WRITING

What's your TARGET?

Your **purpose** is your reason for writing. Your purpose will affect the content, the form, the style, and the tone of your writing. If you were going to shoot an arrow, you'd look first at the bull's-eye on the target. Just as seeing the bull's-eye would help you aim, knowing your purpose will help you reach your writing target.

Each piece of writing begins with a purpose. The purposes for writing can be divided into these five main categories:

Write to Reflect
We all need time for deep, personal thought, or reflection. We might reflect about the world in general, about things that happen around us, about our experiences and our hopes and dreams. Writing can provide a wonderful opportunity to reflect. If you keep a journal, you've probably recorded many of your own reflections there. Journal writing, poetry, and essays are some of the forms you can use to turn your reflections into writing.

Write to Explain
When you want to give readers facts, instructions, or other information, you are writing to explain. As a student you are frequently called upon to do explanatory writing—every time you do a book report or a research paper, for example.

Write to Describe

When you want to paint a picture with words, you are writing to describe. As an artist uses paint to convey a subject, a writer can use a palette of words to describe events, people, places, or objects. Descriptive writing—such as poems, character sketches, or personal essays—helps you to bring your experiences to life for your readers.

Write to Entertain

Writing that makes you laugh out loud, or gets you so engrossed that you miss your bus stop, is entertaining you. When you write to entertain, you're trying to grab your readers' attention and take them on an adventure of some kind. You can entertain with writing that is funny, suspenseful, or even scary. Novels and short stories are written to entertain; poems, essays, and comic strips can also be entertaining.

Write to Persuade

Language has power. When used effectively, words have the potential to persuade people to do almost anything, from ending a war to buying a certain brand of blue jeans to voting for one candidate instead of another. You can use persuasive writing to convince readers to share your opinions or to do something you find important. Editorials, letters to the editors of newspapers and magazines, and reviews of books, movies, and concerts all use persuasion.

With Your Target in Mind

You can, of course, mix these different forms in your own special blend to suit the purpose you have in mind. For example, many writers know that using entertaining stories can keep readers involved in a serious piece of persuasive writing. Many use descriptions of people and places to make their explanatory writing more vivid. Can you think of a way to blend reflection with description? How about combining explanation with entertainment?

WRITING TO LEARN

You've no doubt used writing countless times to record thoughts you've already had and things you already know, but writing is more than simply the end product of the thought process.

Here are some things the writing process can do for you:

Write to Understand

You may not know exactly what you think about something until you write about it. Maybe you've had the experience of thinking you know all about your topic, but when you begin to write, you realize you've got more thinking to do. Writing can be an opportunity to increase your understanding of what you read and hear. Here are some kinds of writing that can help you to demonstrate, develop, and refine your **understanding:**

- ▶ journal entries about events in your life

- ▶ essays stating your opinions

- ▶ reviews of books, plays, movies, or lectures

Write to Analyze

When you analyze something, you probe its meaning. Writing can help you examine a topic deeply, to consider its meaning—to you personally, to a larger group, or even to the world. As a student, you've probably been asked to write a compare/contrast piece or an essay about the pros and cons of an issue. If so, you have already analyzed something in writing. You can use these kinds of writing to sharpen your ability to **analyze:**

- ▶ outlines of the chapters in a book

- ▶ cause/effect essays

- ▶ compare/contrast essays

Write to Synthesize

When you synthesize information, you sift through what you've learned from several sources and blend it together to form a new whole. To synthesize effectively, you need to read your sources and decide what information is important enough to include in your own piece of writing. Sometimes you find the same information in two or more different sources, and you need to decide which source suits your purposes best. The second part of synthesizing is organizing—figuring out how to fit together the pieces you've chosen. Writing can help you to order material from your sources. These are some kinds of writing that may require you to **synthesize:**

- ▶ research reports

- ▶ informative essays about current events

- ▶ feature stories

Write to Evaluate

When you evaluate something, you judge its worth. If you've ever made a judgment about a movie, a flavor of ice cream, or a book you've read, you have experience with evaluating. Writing can strengthen your evaluating skills. You can use writing to take a stand on something and to defend your opinion with strong, solid reasons. Since evaluating things is a basic part of our experience, there are many kinds of writing that **evaluate.** Here are a few:

- ▶ journal entries that give your reaction to concerts, fashions, or parties

- ▶ book reviews

- ▶ newspaper editorials

"I write entirely to find out what I'm thinking, what I'm looking at, what I see and what it means. What I want and what I fear."

—Joan Didion

USING A
WRITER'S JOURNAL

Now that you know about the writing process, you're ready to do some serious writing. But where are you going to keep all the writing you'll be doing?

As you've seen, a writing folder is a good place to store your finished work and work in progress, as well as interesting articles and photos. But for keeping a record of your ideas, thoughts, feelings, and observations, nothing works as well as a **writer's journal**.

This section will tell you everything you need to know about keeping a writer's journal—from tips for getting started to suggestions for possible journal topics.

Tips for Journal Writing

1. Buy a special notebook to use as your writer's journal—one that appeals to you. The notebook might be bound or loose-leaf. Alternatively, you can use notecards and a file box.

GETTING STARTED

The most important thing to remember about keeping a writer's journal is this: *No one else ever has to see it.*

A writer's journal is for you. It's a place for you to explore ideas, think through problems, tell stories, record your observations, describe your experiences, compose imaginary letters, sketch, doodle, or just write about anything that catches your fancy. If you want to share it with someone else, that's fine. But you don't have to. A writer's journal is a very personal book, and you should never have to worry about what someone else will say about what you're writing there.

The hardest thing about keeping a writer's journal is beginning it—once you get going, you'll probably find it's easier than you think.

more
INFO

For more on starting a writing folder *see page 128.*

2. If you prefer, you can use a computer as your writer's journal. You might want to use different disks for each kind of journal writing or use a separate file for each day's entries.

3. If you can, find a quiet place to do your journal writing.

4. In your special journal-writing place, be sure to have lots of supplies on hand— pens, pencils, markers, erasers, and anything else you'll need.

5. Pick the same time every day to do your journal writing. This will help you get into a regular writing routine.

6. Don't worry about what you write. Just put down whatever comes into your head. Remember, no one else has to see it.

JOURNAL-WRITING IDEAS

✔ *As you go through your day, pay attention to the sensory details around you—the smell of the air after the rain, the sound of a passing motorcycle, the feel of a new pair of sneakers. Can you find the right words to describe all these things?*

✔ *Try to write every day. Your writing ability is like a muscle: the more you exercise it, the stronger it will get.*

A writer's journal is a great place to jot down writing ideas—if you're ever stuck for a writing topic, you can just consult your journal. What are some possible writing ideas? They're all around you! How about:

- ▶ records of your dreams
- ▶ jokes, riddles, poems
- ▶ interesting facts, quotations, song lyrics
- ▶ your favorite and least favorite books, movies, TV shows, CDs
- ▶ bits of conversation you've overheard
- ▶ descriptions of interesting people and places
- ▶ letters you'll never send, to people you know or wish you knew
- ▶ things you've always wondered about

• Last night I dreamed I was riding on a bus in Mexico. I was minding my own business, and the old woman in front of me turned and said, "I know where you're going." I got scared and woke up.

• All my life I've looked at words as though I were seeing them for the first time.
—Ernest Hemingway

• I read the other day that there are 137 different kinds of deodorant in America. What does this mean?

• Q: Fishing?
  A: No, drowning worms.

● I can't believe this! Mom just refused to let me walk over to Mike's house. She says it's too cold and rainy out. (Yeah, like I'll melt from the rain, like the Wicked Witch.) But I know the real reason. It's because she doesn't trust me.

● The man in the laundromat, carefully folding a little girl's clothing. The clothes looked tiny in his hands. He was taking the time to fold them all. No matter how small they were, he wasn't going to let any of her clothes get wrinkled.

● I think Ari is interested in Gail. Yesterday he touched her arm, like they were close. I've never even seen her talk to him, so I was quite surprised. I don't really like Ari. I'll tell Gail that when I get the chance. I'd like to see her reactions. The time is getting closer, I can feel it.

Personal Thoughts and Experiences

Consider this idea for a moment: you're the only person who's ever going to live your life. There's never going to be another person exactly like you. Your life is unique—why not keep a permanent record of it?

With a writer's journal, you can do just that. You can record the day-to-day events of your life, as well as your thoughts, feelings, and observations about them. Doing this will not only give you more writing ideas, it will probably also help you to figure some things out—sometimes writing about things can give you a new perspective on them.

If you keep a journal regularly, someday in the future you can reread it and see what it was like to be you now!

Learning Notes

Your journal is a place where you can connect one-to-one with your school subjects. Learning Notes can help you better understand your classes. The notes you take in class are probably content oriented; learning notes are more like notes about your own learning process. You might want to keep a separate section for each subject. You can record new facts and ideas you've learned about or progress you've made in a class. If your homework for a particular subject is confusing, you can keep track of questions you want to ask your teacher the next day; you may even be able to answer your own questions later on.

Something in history class has me confused right now—we talked today about the League of Nations. Ms. Ginsberg says the League of Nations was supposed to have been like the United Nations is today, but the League of Nations was defeated. The United Nations has been going strong for years, so why did Wilson have a hard time getting people behind the League of Nations? I want to nail down an answer on this—could be a good paper topic. Or I could write about why I'm a pacifist, but I need a better definition of pacifism. I should ask Jess what she's going to write her paper on.

PSST!

You can use your journal to blow off steam about a difficult assignment, or to brag to yourself about how well you did on a quiz.

My Notes on Autobiography of a Face
by Lucy Grealy

When my Aunt Lupe gave me this book, I
wondered why—it's about a girl who gets
cancer and has to have lots of operations,
which change the way she looks over and
over. As soon as I started the book, I could
barely put it down. The author writes
about her experience in a way everyone
could relate to . . . there's a bunch of
stuff about how your appearance affects
things—I got the feeling that every single
teenager in America could get into this
book, because we all go through our own
version of having our appearance change
and worrying about it and having people
react differently to us all of a sudden. I
bet even kids who everyone seems to think
are gorgeous get insecure about their
looks from time to time.

CHECK it OUT!

✔ *Journal entries are for your own use; they're not book reports (though your journal may come in handy if you are asked to write one), so stay loose!*

✔ *Some discoveries you may make:*

What kinds of stories do I like best? What kinds of characters do I relate to best? What can I learn from the characters? How do they change over the course of a story? Who are my favorite authors?

Reading Reactions

Reading reaction journal entries are for exploring ideas and feelings about what you read. You can record anything you like—thoughts that strike you about your favorite character, predictions about what might happen next, your opinion of the writer's style. You can also summarize the story. You may even want to relate what's going on in the story to events in your own life. Write as if you were having a conversation with yourself about what you're reading. Keep track of whatever interests you most or of things that anger you, puzzle you, or amuse you as you read.

MORE JOURNAL-WRITING IDEAS

You've read about many kinds of journal entries, and tips for how to get a journal started. If you still need ideas, here are ten things you might want to write about in your journal:

1. The best thing and worst thing about you
2. Your earliest memory
3. The funniest joke you ever heard
4. Your most embarrassing moment
5. The nicest thing anyone ever did for you
6. A description of a science experiment you conducted
7. Your favorite movie and why you liked it
8. A list of all the contents of a room in your home
9. Three things you know about another country
10. Your wildest predictions about the future

You might want to sit in a quiet spot and brainstorm other journal entry ideas—the possibilities are infinite. What are you dying to know about someone else? Take the opportunity to write and find these things out about yourself. Who knows what kinds of writing ideas, discoveries, or inspirations will come to you when you do?

You're the writer, the reader and often the subject of your journal—so you can design it in whatever way will be most helpful to you. As a personal, private record of your thoughts, observations, and feelings, your journal will be unique to you. Perhaps best of all, you can look back and read your journal as often as you wish.

WRITE BACK SOON!

A **dialog journal** is a special kind of writer's journal in which you and someone else—a friend, a teacher, a parent—write to each other. Your entries are like a written conversation, or dialog. You and your journal partner can have a written dialog about many things—a book you've both read, a movie you've seen, experiences one or both of you may have had, questions you'd like to ask each other, ideas you want to explore. Again, the terrain is wide open. It can be fascinating to watch ideas develop as you respond to your partner's entries and see your partner's reactions to what you've written.

Here's a dialog journal between a student and a teacher:

✔ *You and your writing partner can pose questions for each other to answer.*

✔ *More than two partners can communicate in a dialog journal—try passing it around a small group.*

Dear Ms. Jesenka: March 11

I just read a short story I really liked: "The Circuit" by Francisco Jimenez. It's about a family that moves a lot because they pick crops for a living. The mom has a pot that she brings wherever they go—it's dented and old, but it's precious to her because she bought it when her son was born. It made me think of my mother's quilt. Her aunt made it. It's faded and a little bit ripped at the corners, but she acts like it's a treasure. I bet people who move a lot like to have things they can hold onto. It was a great story. I bet other students would like it too.

　　Your favorite student (just kidding),

　　　　Fran

Dear Fran: March 13

I'm glad you liked "The Circuit." It's a favorite of mine, too. I enjoyed what you had to say about your mom's quilt. Just as the pot in the story signifies all the meals and good times the family has had together, I'm sure the quilt your aunt made symbolizes your family history to you and your mom. If you'd like to read other stories by Jimenez, I have a whole book of them you may borrow. The library also has a few copies of his story collection.

　　　　　Sincerely,

　　　　　Ms. Jesenka

PART TWO

Reading

CONTENTS

Reading Strategically 34–47

Active Reading 36
Reading Critically 38
Before Reading 40
During Reading 42
After Reading 46

Reading Nonfiction 48–53

Main Idea/Supporting Details 49
Classification 50
Cause/Effect 51
Compare/Contrast 52
Problem/Solution 53

Reading Literature 54–67

Reading Fiction 56
Reading Poetry 60
Reading Drama 66

READING STRATEGICALLY

Travel in a world of
IDEAS

Through reading you can travel to places you've never been, see things you've never seen, meet people you would never otherwise encounter. Just as you would plan for an important trip—buying your tickets, making your reservations, deciding what you most want to see—you can plan your reading to make sure you get the most out of it.

Here are some strategies to help you along the way:

Active Reading
When you're an active reader, you ask questions about what you read, make personal connections, respond in writing, and talk about what you read.

Critical Reading
When you read critically, you analyze what you read so you can make informed decisions about it. You identify the writer's point of view, differentiate between facts and opinions, and watch out for faulty logic.

Before Reading

You can tell quite a bit about a book before you sit down to read it. When you preview, you make educated guesses about the book—is the topic right for you? Is the information current? If there are illustrations, do they look interesting or useful? How much do you know about your topic already? What do you want to learn?

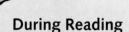

During Reading

As you read, it's a good idea to direct your many thoughts and reactions. How? Asking yourself questions about the material to make sure you understand it, trying to determine the author's purpose, talking about what you read, and summarizing parts of it in writing or out loud with a partner are all good ways.

After Reading

Active reading doesn't end after the final page. You can deepen your connection with what you've read even after you finish reading it. Summarizing and reflecting can help you think creatively about the material. Putting your thoughts into words can help you clarify your ideas—whether or not you like what you've read.

Writers TALK

"It is not true that we have only one life to live; if we can read, we can live as many more lives and as many kinds of lives as we wish."
—S. I. Hayakawa

LET READING BRIGHTEN YOUR LANDSCAPE

You read hundreds of things in passing every day—cereal boxes, street signs, newspaper headlines, billboards, signs at the store. Think about all the information you get from these little groups of words. Now, think about how much information is inside a whole book *full* of words.

How can you get the most out of what you read? Become an **active reader**. When you're an active reader, you get involved. You think about and respond to what you read.

Here are four useful strategies for becoming an active reader:

Make a Connection

Make a personal connection with what you read—even if you're reading about someone whose life is very different from yours. See if you can put yourself in different characters' places. Try to understand why they act the way they do. Think of the characters as real-life people whom you have come to know. Form opinions about what you read.

Ask Questions

Try asking yourself questions as you read:

- ▶ How do I feel about what I'm reading?
- ▶ Do the characters' actions make sense to me?
- ▶ Do the characters remind me of any people I know?
- ▶ Do I understand the events that are happening?
- ▶ Could similar things happen to me?
- ▶ What do I hope will happen next?
- ▶ What would I most like to ask this author?

What other questions would you want to ask yourself?

Write a Response

Another great way to get actively involved in your reading is to keep a response journal. In your response journal you can write thoughts, ideas, feelings, and reactions to what you read, as well as questions you might have. You might also want to note interesting facts, quotations you really liked, or passages you thought were particularly well written.

Form a Group

Sometimes you don't know exactly what you think about a book until you talk with someone else about it. Reading discussion groups can make your reading more interesting than you ever imagined.

How can you start a reading group? Here are some pointers:

- ▶ Assemble a small group of interested readers. The number of members is up to you. Try to include enough people to make the discussion interesting, but not so many that the group is hard to manage.

- ▶ Pick a book that you all want to read. (Make sure everyone in your group can find a copy!)

- ▶ Allow time for everyone to read it (a week or so, depending on how long the book is).

- ▶ It's a good idea for every member of the group to write down a list of questions and ideas before the meeting.

- ▶ Meet to discuss your reactions to the book. You may want to pick someone to lead the discussion when you meet. Try giving each member a turn to be the leader.

- ▶ Pick another book and start all over again!

more INFO

For more on keeping a journal, *see pages 24-31.*

Keep an open mind. There's more than one correct response to the book you've read— everyone will probably have a slightly different interpretation.

BE A READING DETECTIVE

Should you believe everything you read? Just because someone writes something, does this mean you have to agree with it? Absolutely not. Some writing will probably seem fair and sensible, and some won't. But how can you really tell the difference? The best way is to become a **critical reader**—someone who carefully analyzes what he or she reads in order to make informed decisions about it.

Here are a few tips to help you become an expert critical reader:

Point of View

All writers have a **point of view**—a set of personal opinions which influence the way they write about a particular subject. It's important for you to recognize a writer's point of view and figure out how it might have affected his or her writing.

If you're reading a news story, for instance, notice what sources the writer quotes. Are they all from one side of the issue? Or are they equally balanced?

VOL.CXLVI. . . No.47,901

GOVERNMENT WINS PEACE IN SUCCESSFUL TALKS

Government Forced Into Deal, Gives Away Our Land

Take a look at these two newspaper headlines, written about the same news story: one country has decided to give some of its territory to another in exchange for a peace agreement. Can you tell the differing points of view from the tone of the headlines?

When you're reading, ask yourself: What is the writer trying to say? How is this point of view supported? Do I agree with it? Why or why not?

✔ **Try to identify the writer's point of view.**

Fact or Opinion?

A **fact** is a statement that can be proven to be true. An **opinion** is a belief or a judgment—you can't necessarily prove it in a way everyone will agree upon. It's important to be able to tell the difference between facts and opinions because writers sometimes present their opinions as facts.

You can tell the difference between facts and opinions by asking yourself these questions: Can this statement be proven? Can it be generally agreed upon? Might someone disagree? Are these opinions supported by facts, or only by other opinions?

✔ **Differentiate between facts and opinions.**

Faulty Logic

When reading, check to make sure the writer's **logic** makes sense—that his or her arguments are reasonable and supported by evidence. Here are some examples of faulty logic:

- ▶ **Faulty Cause and Effect.** This is when a writer claims one event leads to another but doesn't show any clear connection between the two. For instance, the statement: "He won the tennis match because he was wearing his favorite shirt." Might there be better reasons why he won that match?

- ▶ **Either/Or Thinking.** Be cautious when a writer suggests there are only two ways to think about a situation; there may be more. For instance, the statement: "The government must shut down all polluting factories, or else we will have an environmental disaster." Might there be other options (such as making factories pollute less)?

- ▶ **Overgeneralization.** Sometimes a writer makes a statement that goes beyond what the evidence supports. Look out for generalizing words such as *all, none, always, never,* and *must.*

✔ **Watch carefully for faulty logic.**

LOOK BEFORE YOU READ

There are a lot of strategies that can help you become an active reader. Some of them you probably use naturally—without even having to think about it. In the following pages you'll learn some strategies to use while you're reading and after you finish reading. Here are a few tips you might find useful before reading:

Preview It

It might sound hard to believe, but you can tell a lot about a book or a selection before you read a single word. By previewing—looking at certain pieces of the book or selection ahead of time—you can get a good idea of what you're going to read. Here's a checklist to help you with your previewing:

Previewing Checklist

✓ Look at the title. What does it tell you about the topic?

✓ Who is the author? What do you know about him or her? What kinds of books does he or she write?

✓ Is there an illustrator? Are you familiar with his or her work?

✓ Look through the book. If there are illustrations, what can you learn from them?

✓ Is there a table of contents? Does it list chapter titles? If so, what can you tell from them?

Predict It

As you're previewing, you're probably already making **predictions,** or educated guesses, about the book or selection. You can't help it—previewing and predicting go hand in hand. In fact, predicting is a strategy that can help you understand what you're reading. Based on your previewing, make some predictions about what you will read, then revise your predictions as you read based on the new information.

KWL

The **KWL** strategy can be a useful tool before reading nonfiction. The letters *KWL* stand for:

K	=	What I **Know**
W	=	What I **Want** to Know
L	=	What I **Learned**

Before you read something, try making a **KWL** chart in your writer's journal or in a regular notebook. In the **K** column, list what you already **k**now about the topic; in the **W** column, list what you **w**ant to find out about the topic. Then, once you've finished reading, in the **L** column, list what you **l**earned. Here's an example of what a chart might look like:

K = What I <u>know</u>
W = What I <u>Want</u> to Know
L = What I <u>Learned</u>

K	W	L

✔ *If you were offered a chance to read someone's mind, wouldn't you take it? Reading others' writing is the next best thing.*

✔ *If a piece is difficult, try rereading—get the general idea of the piece first, then read again to catch details.*

✔ *If there are many words you don't know, jot them down, and look them up later. Then be sure to go back to reread so you can put your new vocabulary to work.*

AS YOU READ. . .

Just as certain strategies help before reading, there are strategies you can use **during reading** to get the most out of the material. Your mind already has a dialog with words—dozens of thoughts and reactions no doubt occur to you whenever you sit down to read. To get the most from your reading, the trick is to *direct* your thoughts—not just sit back and watch them.

It helps to have a clear idea of what you want out of reading. Here are some ways to get the most from what you read:

Ask Questions

As you read a book, story, poem, or essay, try asking yourself some of these questions. (You'll probably find your mind has been working on them already!)

▶ What did I just read? Did I understand it?

▶ What images do I see as I read?

▶ What might happen next? What makes me think so?

▶ What information can I get from the title and any subheadings?

▶ Do the characters remind me of anyone? If so, what characteristics do they share with people I know? What makes the characters unique?

▶ Are there any words I want to find definitions for?

Determine Author's Purpose

Writing begins with a **purpose**. While writing can be fun, it's also hard work—so an author must feel he or she has something important to share with you. Ask yourself as you read: *What does the author want me to get from reading this?* Trying to determine the author's purpose is a good way to figure the meaning of a piece of writing. Here are some clues to lead you to the author's purpose and some things to look for as you read:

▶ Is the author trying to convince you to share an opinion? If so, the author's purpose is to **persuade.**

   Look for supporting facts and statements that are strong and convincing.

▶ Is the author trying to share knowledge with you? If so, the author's purpose is to **explain** or **inform.**

   Look for logical order, and information that supports the main claim.

▶ Is the author trying to share an experience with you? If so, the author's purpose is to **reflect** or **entertain.**

   Pay attention to vivid details that make the writing come to life. You may be able to read more quickly than when an author gives you lots of facts.

keep in mind

Authors often have several purposes at once—perhaps to entertain and persuade, or to both reflect and explain.

• • •

The motive for writing each piece of nonfiction can usually be boiled down to a single sentence. Try to compose a sentence that explains the author's main idea. Pretend you're the author, writing a sentence about your own work.

THE SQ-3R PLAN

The **SQ-3R** plan will be especially handy when you read nonfiction. The name *SQ-3R* stands for: **S**urvey, **Q**uestion, **R**ead, **R**ecite, and **R**eview. It's a system for getting the information you need out of factual writing. This chart will give you the basics:

keep in mind

Rather than trying to get everything you need to know the first time you read, try rereading once or twice —you may find something new on each reading.

THE SQ-3R PLAN

Survey	When you survey, you scan the book or article to get a feel for the material you're reading. Look at titles, headings, subheadings, photos and illustrations, and captions.
Question	Ask yourself questions as you read. Jotting down the answers can help you stay involved in what you're reading.
Read	. . . and reread. If you don't understand something, go back and reread it. If you find a word you're unfamiliar with, take the time to look it up.
Recite	Talk about what you read to be sure you understand it.
Review	Summarize your reading, either out loud to a partner or in writing.

After you've tried the **SQ-3R** plan a few times, your mind will naturally begin the process. For now, try to memorize what **SQ-3R** stands for, so you can use it whenever you read nonfiction.

CLUSTERING

Clustering is a way of taking notes in a visual way. This is helpful when you're reading textbooks and other information-packed writing. Write the subject in the middle of a blank sheet of paper. Then write details you want to remember all around it, drawing lines between ideas as you find connections in what you read. When you're done, you'll have a "map" of your ideas.

Here's a cluster map one student made while reading a history textbook about Great Britain:

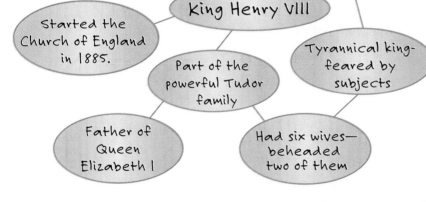

This cluster map will give the student a quick visual image of the reign of King Henry VIII.

✔ *You might want to work on a map with a partner, or in a small group.*

✔ *Each cluster map will look different, depending on the subject and degree of complexity.*

PSST!

A cluster map is a graphic organizer—a way to *see* your ideas. If you can see your ideas before writing, you'll be able to help your reader see them too.

keep in mind

Rewriting isn't the only way to summarize what you've read. Try retelling the story in your own words or acting it out for an audience.

WHEN YOU'VE FINISHED READING. . .

You've probably found that when you really love a book, you keep thinking about it long after you've finished reading. Active reading doesn't end after you turn the final page. Here are a few strategies to help you deepen your personal connection with a book, article, or story once you've finished reading it:

Summarize It

Summarizing is a great way to make sure you understand what you've just read. When you summarize, you find the main ideas in what you've read. Choose the most important information, then rewrite it briefly in your own words.

For summarizing articles it's helpful to focus on the opening and closing paragraphs, and the headings and subheadings. These will often help direct you to the main ideas.

A **story pyramid** can help you to summarize fiction. The pyramid can help you choose the most important information.

STORY PYRAMID

Name of main character
_____

Two words describing the main character
_____ _____

Three words describing the setting
_____ _____ _____

Four words stating the problem
_____ _____ _____ _____

Five words describing one main event
_____ _____ _____ _____ _____

Six words describing a second main event
_____ _____ _____ _____ _____ _____

Seven words describing a third main event
_____ _____ _____ _____ _____ _____ _____

Eight words stating the solution to the problem
_____ _____ _____ _____ _____ _____ _____ _____

Talk It Over

Have you found that when you read a really great book, you can't wait to tell someone else about it? Like summarizing, **talking it over** is a great after-reading strategy because it helps you to understand what you've just read. Putting your thoughts into words—by talking with a partner or a discussion group—helps you to clarify your ideas. And this is true even if you *didn't* like a particular book—talking it over with someone else can help you to understand why.

Reflect on It

Did you know that you can actually improve your abilities to think deeply about what you read? Just like shooting jump shots or playing the guitar, **reflecting** is a skill you can develop through practice. To get you started, keep these pointers in mind. They'll help you to think creatively, and from different perspectives, about what you read:

► Ask "What if?" Imagine what might have happened if one of the plot events had been different. How would the rest of the story change?

► Think in opposites. Imagine that the main character is a totally different type of person. How might this affect the story?

► Change the ending. Could there be another ending to this story? What might it be?

► Now you be the author. Imagine how you might have written the book differently. What would you keep? What would you change?

For more on speaking and listening strategies, *see pages 68-87.*

"A book is like a garden carried in the pocket."
—*Chinese proverb*

READING NONFICTION

FINDING PATTERNS OF INFORMATION

Main Idea/Supporting Details
presents an idea and backs it up with facts.

Classification
organizes material into groups
with similar characteristics.

Cause/Effect
shows how one thing leads to another.

Compare/Contrast
focuses on the similarities and differences
between things.

Problem/Solution
starts with a problem, then suggests
a way to solve it.

Most nonfiction is organized according to a certain structure,
or **pattern of information**. Becoming familiar with these
structures will help you discover meaning in nonfiction.

On the following pages you will find out about the most
common information patterns in nonfiction. You'll also learn
strategies to help you gather information from what you read.

HOW TO SUPPORT YOURSELF

An information pattern you already know from your own writing is **main idea** and **supporting details**. The writer presents an idea and then backs it up with factual evidence. When you write your own paragraphs, you probably try to include enough details to support your main idea. See if you can identify the main idea and supporting details here:

> New York City is home to a remarkable array of cultural offerings. Theater fans will find Broadway and off-Broadway plays, and dozens of smaller productions around the city. If you enjoy dance concerts, you can choose from ballet, Latin dance, modern dance, and others. New York's dozens of museums and galleries host a huge range of art shows, from ancient art to contemporary. You can hear many kinds of music around the city—from jazz to punk to hip-hop to opera; there are musicians everywhere, from Carnegie Hall to your local subway stop.

STRATEGY: Outlining will help you to see the main points at a glance. Use the main ideas as headings and the supporting details as subheadings in your outline.

New York's cultural offerings

    Drama

    Dance

    Art

    Music

more **INFO**

For more on outlining, see page 128.

CATEGORICALLY SPEAKING. . .

Some nonfiction pieces are organized by **classification**—that is, organized into categories or groups that share certain characteristics. The following passage is organized by classification. As you read, see if you can identify the categories and the characteristics that distinguish them:

A forest is a dense growth of trees and underbrush covering a tract of land. There are three major types of forests throughout the world.

Deciduous forests thrive in moderate climates; they are made up of seasonal trees and plants that shed their foliage, or leaves, each year. Coniferous forests grow in cold, northern climates. Coniferous forests are made up of conifers (evergreen trees and bushes that bear cones and do not drop their leaves or needles). Rain forests, lush evergreen woodlands with an average rainfall of at least 100 inches a year, are found in both tropical climates and cold northern regions.

STRATEGY: Charting important information from what you read will help you see the categories graphically and remember their distinguishing traits more effectively.

FORESTS		
Dense woodlands and underbrush covering a tract of land		
DECIDUOUS	**CONIFEROUS**	**RAIN FORESTS**
• seasonal foliage	• conifers	• lush, evergreen
• moderate climates	• evergreens	• tropical/cold
		• at least 100" of rain per year

THE REASONS WHY

When writers need to explain a chain of events, they often organize their material to show **cause** and **effect**. The cause is the reason something happens. An effect is what happens as a result of the cause. Try to find cause/effect relationships in the paragraph below:

> My dog Bowzer ran away last week. After looking all over the place, I cried my eyes out, then figured I should do something useful. I made signs that said when and where I'd seen him last, and described Bowzer: his black and brown markings, and his strange ears, one of which sticks straight up while the other flops over. After reading the signs, my neighbors said they'd keep an eye out for Bowzer. A few even offered to join my search. The next afternoon my neighbor Sylvie found Bowzer playing with her little brother outside the elementary school three blocks away. I was so happy! And I think Bowzer was too.

STRATEGY: By making a **diagram** like this one, you can present the cause/effect relationship graphically.

For a cause/effect writing model, see pages 268-269.

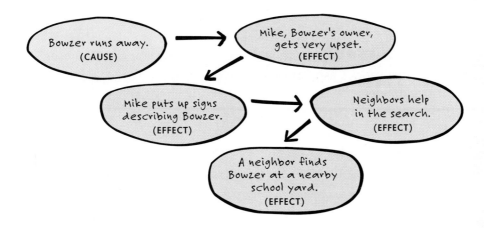

WHAT'S THE DIFFERENCE?

If what you're reading emphasizes similarities and differences, it has been organized according to **comparison** and **contrast**.

When comparing subjects, writers use words and phrases such as: *similar, like, the equivalent of,* and *the same as.* Writers show differences, or contrast, with words and phrases such as: *unlike, in contrast to, however, but,* and *on the other hand.* In a compare/contrast piece, a writer usually describes both similarities and differences. Read this travel brochure:

more INFO

For a **compare/ contrast** *writing model, see pages 266-267.*

• • •

For more on **Venn** *diagrams, see page 8.*

Both Paris, France and Lonely Lodge, Arizona overlook water— Paris is located on the Seine River and Lonely Lodge is on Skunk Creek.

Lonely Lodge

Both have famous towers— the Eiffel Tower in Paris and the broken clock tower at Lonely Lodge. Best of all, for both places, admission is free— although parking is up to $3.00 a day at Lonely Lodge.

STRATEGY: With a **Venn diagram** you can easily see how various aspects of your two subjects are alike and different.

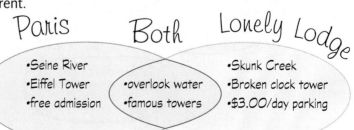

Paris — Both — Lonely Lodge

- Seine River
- Eiffel Tower
- free admission

- overlook water
- famous towers

- Skunk Creek
- Broken clock tower
- $3.00/day parking

AND THE ANSWER IS. . .

The **problem/solution** information pattern is very common in newspaper articles, and in science and social-studies texts. The writer begins with the statement of a problem, then presents various solutions, or ideas for solving the problem. This newspaper editorial is organized according to the problem/solution pattern. How many solutions can you find?

more
INFO

For a problem/ solution *writing model, see pages 270-271.*

• • •

For more on clustering *see page 45.*

How to Stop Lewis Park Litter Hazard

Litter in Lewis Park is becoming an eyesore and a health threat. One solution would be the addition of large trash cans at all the park's entrances. Adding another maintenance person would also help the situation. And enforcing no-littering laws might make Lewis Park's litterers clean up their act. Not many people would toss a food wrapper on the ground if they knew it would cost them $100 to do so.

STRATEGY: A **cluster map** will help you remember more effectively what you read.

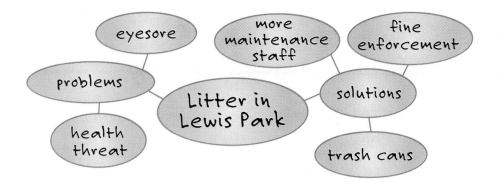

READING LITERATURE

Writing as ART

You read nonfiction in order to learn more about a particular subject. Reading **literature**, though, is a very different process. Literature is about *creativity*, not information. It can excite us, move us, maybe even help us to understand other people (and ourselves) more deeply than we ever have before.

Literature is writing as art. Just as you would look at a painting differently than you would a subway map, you read literature differently than you do nonfiction writing. When you read literature, you're not trying to identify or memorize facts; instead, you're reflecting and imagining, as well as exploring ideas and feelings in a personal way.

Fiction

Fiction (which is really just another way of saying "imaginary stories") is the most widespread and popular of the branches of literature. It's impossible to imagine a world without stories. Fiction ranges from short-short stories of just a page or two, to novels of a thousand pages or more. All fiction has three basic elements: setting, characters, and plot... but each story combines them in a unique way.

Fiction, poetry, and drama are the main branches, or genres, of literature. In the following pages you'll find out more about each of them. You'll also get some tips to help you read literature—and maybe even inspire you to start writing some of your own.

Poetry

Poems can create many different experiences for the reader—powerful emotions, musical language, and vivid sights and sounds. Like fiction, poems can tell stories, but they don't have to. Many poems simply convey ideas and feelings through carefully chosen language and images. Poets use rhyme and rhythm to create the structure of a poem, and to influence its mood. Some poems follow forms, like haiku or sonnet, that have been used for centuries. In modern times many poems are written in free verse. A poet who writes in free verse creates a new form for each individual poem.

Drama

Drama—another word for plays—is a form of literature that's meant to be performed before an audience. LIke fiction, plays tell stories. Drama also has characters. In drama, however, the characters are actually presented to us by actors. Settings are shown with scenery and props. Most plays are divided into acts, which are somewhat like the chapters in a novel. Acts can be further divided into scenes.

THE BASICS OF FICTION

For as long as we've been on earth, human beings have made up and told each other stories. We do it to entertain each other, to share our views, to make sense of our lives. It's impossible to imagine a world without stories.

All fiction has three basic elements: **setting**, **characters**, and **plot**. (Your own stories have them too, even if you didn't know it.)

Setting

The **setting** is the time and place in which the story occurs. The time might be a day or a season, a year or several years; it might be past, present, or future—the summer of 1904, the year 2006, or the day before yesterday. The place might be a planet, a country, a city, or a room. It might be Saturn's fifth moon, the inside of a locked vault, the ancient city of Mesopotamia, or a bedroom strikingly similar to your own.

Characters

The **characters** are the people and animals in the story. When a story is really good, we may feel that we know the characters as well as we do our own friends or family. That's because the writer has vividly described what they look like, what they talk about, how they act, what they think and feel, and what others say about them. They seem just as real as real-life people.

Most stories have a *protagonist,* or main character. Often it's this character's *conflict,* or problem, that moves the story forward; we wonder how the conflict is going to be resolved, and keep turning pages to find out.

keep in mind

Even if the setting is not specifically mentioned, use the details of the story to see how closely you can locate its setting.

• • •

The protagonist's conflict can be with another character, with society, or with nature; the character can also have an inner conflict, wherein he or she is torn about how to act.

Plot

The **plot** is the sequence of events in a novel or story. (In other words, the plot is what happens.) All fiction begins with a *conflict:* a problem that needs to be resolved. In many stories the next series of events—called the *rising action*—intensifies the character's problem. The *climax* is the story's turning point, when the conflict comes to a head, and there is a dramatic shift in the story. Finally, in the *falling action,* the conflict may be resolved, or it may only have changed into a different one.

Theme in Fiction

You may have been told that the **theme** of a story is the author's main idea, the "message" the author was trying to put into his or her story. But most authors don't use fiction for "messages." (After all, a message can be written in a telegram or on a bumper sticker; you don't need to write a whole story to send a message.) Instead, they're trying to tell stories that are interesting and moving, and may perhaps reveal something we haven't noticed before about life.

The theme of a story or a novel is the idea the author is trying to examine in the work. For example, a theme might be heroism in wartime or the mystery of falling in love. These are very general topics, which allow for a great deal of complicated exploration by the author. Good literature is too rich and interesting to be reduced to a simple one-sentence "message."

keep in mind

Not all stories follow the traditional plot-line. Some have plots that seem to run in a circle—looping back to the same place rather than moving in a straight line toward a resolution. Others use different plot schemes; see if you can figure some out for yourself!

TALK

"A story is a way to say something that can't be said any other way, and it takes every word in the story to say what the meaning is. You tell a story because a statement would be inadequate."
—*Flannery O'Connor*

FICTION TECHNIQUES

Literature has the power to transport you to other worlds. Fiction writers use many different techniques to draw you in:

Point of view refers to who is telling us the story. In first-person point of view, the storyteller, or narrator, is a character in the story and uses *I* to tell about events. In third-person point of view, the narrator is outside the world of the story and tells the story using *he, she,* and *they.*

First person: *I served my famous spaghetti sauce at the party last night.*

> *I hope everybody liked it.*

Third person: *David served his famous spaghetti sauce at the party last night.*

> *He hoped everybody liked it.*

Foreshadowing provides clues about events to come. This helps create suspense and a sense of moving forward.

Flashback is a scene describing an event that occurred before the time of the story. A flashback is often sparked when an action or object in the present reminds a character of something in the past.

Sensory language touches the senses, allowing a reader to experience what the characters see, hear, feel, taste, and smell.

Figurative language—simile, metaphor, and personification—creates interesting and often surprising comparisons to help bring images and emotions to life.

Fiction in Action

Take a look at this story. What different techniques did the writer use to bring it to life?

Not Your Average First Day of School

It began as a pretty average first day of school. Words of greeting buzzed through the hallway. "How was your summer?... Who do you have for homeroom?" The corridors smelled of fresh paint, and the walls gleamed bright white.

Sensory Language—smell, sight

My best friend, Eric, and I were in the same homeroom. We were known as "Double Trouble" for the pranks we pulled on our teacher last year. In one moment of particular inspiration, Eric and I snuck into class early and tied clear fishing line to the window shades. Once class started, we raised and lowered the shades. Everyone thought the room was haunted.

Point of View—first person, I

Flashback—going back to something that happened last year

So this year, when our teacher, Mrs. Carp, called attendance, she said, "Oh, my. Patty Sanders and Eric Lee in the same homeroom. Could anything possibly top that?" She had no idea that the answer might just be yes.

Foreshadowing—hinting that more trouble is on the way

No one noticed at first just how strange the "new kid" was. He sat in the back, hunched over, wearing a T-shirt, overalls, high-tops, and a baseball cap. Then all of a sudden, he started swinging from the lights, with a click and a clack and whooshes of air. Mrs. Carp's voice got really high and fast, like she'd swallowed helium from a balloon. "What kind of a student would do something like this?" she shrieked.

Figurative Language—simile

But it was not a student at all. It was a chimpanzee, and it's a funny story how an ape ended up in our homeroom that day.

Writers TALK

"I think it ought to be said that a fiction writer can try anything. The possibilities are endless because the stirring of the imagination never rests, and because we can never stop trying to make feeling felt."

—*Eudora Welty*

THE BASICS OF POETRY

We read the newspaper to get information. We read fiction to enjoy a story. Why do we read poetry? A poem can create many different things for the reader—powerful emotions, musical language, vivid sights and sounds.

Poets choose words carefully, for their everyday meanings as well as the associated feelings certain words create. Poets also pay attention to the *sound* of the words, using rhyme and rhythm to add another layer of meaning.

By using language in a unique way, a poem can help you see something—an object, a feeling, a picture—in a whole new light. Take a look at the following poem. What images bloom in your mind?

The Winter Evening Settles Down
(from *Preludes*)

The winter evening settles down
With smell of steaks in passageways.
Six o'clock.
The burnt-out ends of smoky days.
And now a gusty shower wraps
The grimy scraps
Of withered leaves about your feet
And newspapers from vacant lots;
The showers beat
On broken blinds and chimney-pots,
And at the corner of the street
A lonely cab-horse steams and stamps.

And then the lighting of the lamps.
—*T. S. Eliot*

POETRY FORMS

You've probably noticed that poems look and sound different from other writing. Some poems follow established **forms**—like haiku or sonnet—that have been used for many years. Here are a few traditional forms:

A **ballad** tells a story in song or poetry. This early form was often used to write about romantic love or heroic characters.

Haiku, an old form of Japanese poetry, traditionally deals with nature. It is a three-line poem that includes seventeen syllables arranged in three lines, with a five-seven-five syllable pattern.

A **sonnet** is a fourteen-line poem that follows a particular rhyme pattern. William Shakespeare and other poets often used this form to write about love.

A **villanelle**, which has nineteen lines, follows strict rhyme and uses repetition.

> *The puppy's running*
> *through the thick, leafy forest*
> *moves branches like wind.*
> *—Joy Nō*

This **haiku** creates a whole scene in a few words. What kinds of images come to mind when you read it?

Writers
TALK

"Poetry is the spontaneous overflow of powerful emotions."
—William Wordsworth

Do Not Go Gentle Into That Good Night

Do not go gentle into that good night,
Old age should burn and rage at close of day;
Rage, rage against the dying of the light.

Though wise men at their end know dark is right,
Because their words had forked no lightning they
Do not go gentle into that good night.

Good men, the last wave by, crying how bright
Their frail deeds might have danced in a green bay,
Rage, rage against the dying of the light.

Wild men who caught and sang the sun in flight,
And learn, too late, they grieved it on its way,
Do not go gentle into that good night.

Grave men, near death, who see with blinding sight
Blind eyes could blaze like meteors and be gay,
Rage, rage against the dying of the light.

And you, my father, there on the sad height,
Curse, bless, me now with your fierce tears, I pray,
Do not go gentle into that good night.
Rage, rage against the dying of the light.

—Dylan Thomas

The poet wrote this **villanelle** to his dying father. Notice which lines are repeated. What emotions does the poem make you feel? How does the repetition help convey those emotions?

Many poems, especially contemporary ones, are written in
free verse. This means that instead of using an established
form, the poet creates a form especially for that poem. It may
have rhythm and rhyme patterns, or it may not.

This Is Just to Say

I have eaten
the plums
that were in
the icebox
and which
you were probably
saving
for breakfast

Forgive me
they were delicious
so sweet
and so cold.
—William Carlos Williams

This poem is in **free verse.** It follows its own unique structure.
Try reading it out loud. Can you read in different ways to give
it different meanings?

POETRY TECHNIQUES

Poets often play with words and sounds in order to create the fullest picture with the fewest words. Here are some techniques writers use to make the most of words:

Rhythm

Rhythm is the beat of the words in a poem. When you tap your foot to a song, you're tapping to the rhythm. (Try tapping your foot to a poem—it can be done.) Some poems have a predictable, regular rhythm, which is called **meter**.

If you write a poem about peaceful moonlight, the rhythm might be slow and soft, as if it could lull you to sleep. If you write about anger, you might use a faster beat, like footsteps stomping out of the room. Read out loud "Do Not Go Gentle into That Good Night." Try tapping out its rhythm.

Rhyme

Many poems have rhymes—that is, words ending in the same sound. When rhymes occur at regular intervals or at the end of many lines, the poem has a rhyme scheme.

Rhymes make poems interesting and fun to listen to and can help guide the reader's attention. A poet might use rhymes at the end of lines (**end rhyme**) to emphasize certain words. Look at "Do Not Go Gentle into That Good Night." What words in the poem rhyme with "night"? What words rhyme with "day"?

Poets also use rhyme in the middle of lines (**internal rhyme**). What internal rhymes can you find in this poem?

> *I trace the curtain lace with my finger,*
> *thinking that I still must dust the sill.*

Repetition

Poets often use **repetition**—of lines, words, or sounds. Repetition of particular words or lines helps them gain meaning in a poem. Look how important Dylan Thomas's two last lines have become by the end. You might even know them by heart after reading the poem just a few times. In a song (which is also a poem), repeated lines are called the **refrain**.

Repetition of the same sound at the beginning of a string of words is called **alliteration**. This line from Robert Herrick is a good example: "So smooth, so sweet, so silv'ry is thy voice." Alliteration tickles your ear, and it also helps the words stand out in your mind.

Figurative Language

Poems are filled with imagery—sights, sounds, smells, tastes, or textures created in the reader's mind. One important way to create imagery is with **figurative language**. That's when poets make creative and unusual comparisons between things.

The subway train rolled in like thunder. (simile)

His face was a wrinkled prune. (metaphor)

The sun winked goodbye and dashed behind a cloud. (personification)

Figurative language is often used to compare things that are quite different but have something in common. A subway train and thunder are very different, but both make loud rumbling noises.

Simile uses the word *like* or *as* to make the comparison (the subway is *like* thunder). **Metaphor** asks the reader to pretend that one thing actually is another (his face *is* a prune). **Personification** gives a nonhuman object human qualities (the sun winks like a person).

THE BASICS OF DRAMA

Like fiction, drama (which is another way of saying "plays") tells stories. But these stories are meant to be performed, with actors playing the characters. And rather than addressing individual readers, a play is performed before an audience. In fact, being part of an audience in a theater—when you're all experiencing the story together, feeling the same things at the same time—is one of the great thrills of drama.

Characters

Like novels and short stories, all plays have characters. There's a big difference though: in drama the characters are actually presented to us, by actors. They exist in front of our eyes, not just in our imaginations.

Script

In drama we can see what the characters do and hear what they say, but we don't have a narrator who can tell us what they are thinking and feeling. That's why the script (the written text) of a play consists only of **dialog** (what the characters say to each other) and **stage directions** (which are printed in italics, and instruct the actors about what the characters do and how they speak).

Here is a passage from a famous play by Arthur Miller, *Death of a Salesman*. The salesman, Willy Loman, is talking to his wife, Linda:

> WILLY: I'm tired to the death . . . *(He sits on the bed beside her, a little numb.)* I couldn't make it. I just couldn't make it, Linda.
> LINDA *(very carefully, delicately)*: Where were you all day? You look terrible.

Because the play is meant to be acted out, not just read on the page, the playwright wrote it using only dialog and stage directions. If this were part of a novel, it might have been written like this:

> *Willy sat next to his wife, feeling a little numb. "I couldn't make it," he said. "I just couldn't make it, Linda."*
>
> *"Where were you all day?" Linda asked carefully, not wanting to anger her husband. Then, in a delicate voice, she added "You look terrible."*

Structure

Most plays are divided into **acts**, which are something like the chapters in a novel. Although a play can have any number of acts, full-length plays traditionally had three acts; now, more often, full-length plays have only one break—for intermission.

Acts can be further divided into **scenes**. When the action shifts in time or place, the play moves into another scene. Often this is indicated by the stage lights going out briefly and then coming on again—almost like the white space in books; this shows a break between sections.

Other Elements

Most plays don't take place on a bare stage. They use **scenery**, the representation of the play's setting. A play's scenery can be as simple as a few chairs and a table, or it can be extremely detailed and elaborate. (One recent Broadway play used a real helicopter as part of the scenery!)

In most cases the actors use objects during the course of the play. These are called the **props** (short for "properties"). A prop might be an umbrella, a set of dishes, a baseball cap—any of the objects onstage.

keep in mind

Many people misspell the word playwright. *Notice it is not spelled "playwrite." The suffix* -wright *means "one who makes." Just as a* boatwright *is a maker of boats and a* wheel-wright *is a maker of wheels, a* playwright *is a maker of plays.*

• • •

Not all plays use dialog. Some plays, called pantomime, *are entirely silent—the actors tell the story through their actions, without ever speaking.*

• • •

You don't have to go to the theater to appreciate a play. Many plays are published in book form, and you can read them just as you would a novel.

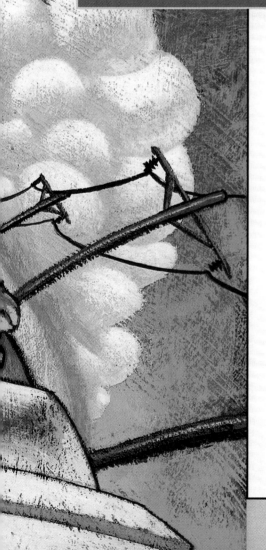

PART THREE

Speaking, Listening, and Seeing

CONTENTS

Speaking and Listening . . 72–87

Discussions 72
Oral Presentations 75
Interviews 83
Debates 85

Seeing 88–101

Reading Visual Images 88
    Symbols 89
Creative Seeing 90
    Paintings and Drawings 91
    Sculpture 94
    Photography 95
    Illustration 96
    Cartoons 97
Television 98
Advertising 100

SPEAKING, LISTENING,

You probably spend most of your time communicating with others in some way—which means you do a lot of **speaking**, **listening**, and **seeing**. In fact, you're probably an expert at these things . . . so why study them? Sharpening your communication skills is a wise move because you rely on them hundreds of times each day. Did you ever think about all the different ways you use these skills? Being in a debate is very different from chatting with your friends, for example. And looking at a painting is very different from looking at a streetsign. In this section you'll find out about how to sharpen your speaking, listening, and seeing skills in many ways.

Oral Presentations
Learn the *dos* and *don'ts* of making speeches and other oral presentations.

Interviews
Find out how to prepare for and conduct a successful interview.

Debates
Discover how arguing can get you somewhere.

AND SEEING

Reading VISUAL Images

You learn lots about the world by looking around you. You probably don't even realize how much information you take in through your eyes. In pages to come you'll find pointers that will help you get more from:

Symbols
Read the signs and symbols around you.

Paintings and Drawings
Learn about the basics of painting: *color, lines, shapes,* and *forms.*

Sculpture
Experience art in 3-D.

Photography
See how life looks through a camera lens.

Illustration
A picture can be worth 1,000 words... or more!

Cartoons
Art can be funny–and humor is often serious.

Advertisements
Do you believe everything you read? You shouldn't!

Television
Become a critic instead of a "couch potato."

GOING ONE-ON-ONE

Much of the communication you do every day is one-on-one —that is, between you and another person. As you know, it's not always easy to communicate with someone else. Sometimes you don't know exactly what you want to say, and sometimes the other person doesn't know exactly what you mean.

How you speak depends in large part on the other person— you probably speak differently to a friend or classmate than you do to a teacher or some other adult. Here are some tips that will help you communicate well no matter whom you're talking to:

When You're Speaking . . .

▶ Speak clearly and not too fast.

▶ Speak loud enough to be understood clearly.

▶ Use a vocabulary and style that your listener will understand. If you use slang, stick with words that are familiar to the other person.

▶ Make eye contact.

▶ Try to avoid sprinkling your conversation with expressions such as "um," "like," and "you know." These words don't really add anything, and they can be distracting to the listener.

When You're Listening . . .

▶ Pay attention and try not to interrupt.

▶ Show interest in what you're listening to.

▶ Look the speaker in the eye.

▶ Listen closely before drawing conclusions.

PUTTING YOUR HEADS TOGETHER

Have you ever found that you don't know what you think about something until you've heard other people discuss it? Groups can often find solutions or ideas that one or two people can't. When people "put their heads together," there's no telling what they can come up with!

Whether your group is brainstorming for a research project, discussing a book, or planning some other activity, these basic guidelines will help you in group discussions.

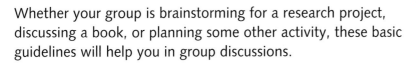

When you want . . .	Try to . . .	Try not to . . .
To agree with someone	▶ Smile and nod encouragingly. ▶ Say, "I agree" or "Good point."	▶ Waste time by making a big production out of agreeing—clapping, shouting, interrupting, and so on.
To disagree with someone	▶ Say, "Have you thought of . . . ?" or "Maybe that's true, but I think . . ."	▶ Shake your head. ▶ Roll your eyes. ▶ Make negative remarks.
To enter into discussion	▶ Listen to what people are saying. ▶ Think of ways to add to what's being said.	▶ Sigh or slump in your chair. ▶ Bring up a point that's off the subject.
To deal with rudeness	▶ Get the rude person focused on the discussion by asking, "Do you have something you want to add?"	▶ Ignore the rude behavior. ▶ Shout at the rude person.
To reach agreement	▶ Get opinions from people who aren't participating. ▶ Keep the discussion going until everyone is satisfied.	▶ Demand that the group reach a decision. ▶ Move around restlessly.

✔ *Group discussions often go more smoothly if you assign people different jobs, such as:*

- *A **leader** who organizes the discussion and keeps it moving forward.*

- *A **timekeeper** who makes sure the discussion stays on schedule.*

- *A **recorder** who writes down the main points of discussion and the group's decisions.*

- *A **reporter** who informs others of the group's decisions.*

If your group meets more than once, shift jobs so everyone gets a chance to participate.

TALK AMONGST YOURSELVES

Whether you're leading a group discussion or participating in one, it will go more smoothly if everyone follows a few basic guidelines.

When you're leading a discussion:

1. Call the group to order. State the purpose and topic of the discussion.

2. Keep the discussion on the topic. Don't let the discussion wander.

3. Encourage people to participate. Don't offer your own opinions until everyone else has had a chance to speak.

4. Create and then stick to reasonable time limitations.

5. Be polite and considerate.

When you're participating in a discussion:

1. Come prepared. Know what's going to be discussed.

2. Speak only when you're recognized by the group leader.

3. Respect other points of view. Be polite and considerate.

4. Listen carefully.

5. Speak only about the topic under discussion.

6. Restrict the amount of time you speak. Don't hog the discussion.

If you read these guidelines carefully, you'll notice three rules that apply to both leaders and participants. They're the keys to successful group discussions:

▶ *Stay on the topic.*
▶ *Observe time limitations.*
▶ *Be polite and considerate.*

BY WORD OF MOUTH

Oral presentations play a big role in every student's life. You probably have to make oral presentations all the time: oral reports, speeches, read-alouds, demonstrations, and storytelling, just to name a few kinds.

Oral presentations play a part in later life as well. Many working people—such as salespeople, teachers, engineers, actors, and politicians—make oral presentations a regular part of their jobs.

In other words, it's probably not a bad idea to know how to make effective oral presentations. On the following pages you'll find some tips for doing just that.

keep in mind

The more you re-hearse, the better your presentation will be. When you know your stuff, you won't have to keep looking at your notes as you speak.

Before Your Oral Presentation:

- Make notes of what you want to say. Write your notes in large print on cards or sheets of paper. (That way you can read them quickly and easily while you're speaking.)

- Think about how to make your presentation as interesting and appealing as possible. Try to include some humor, if it's appropriate to the topic. You might also use some visual aids such as slides or charts.

- Rehearse your presentation to see how long it will take. You don't want to run too long—or too short!

- If you're using equipment such as a slide projector or a cassette player, make sure you know how to use it. No audience enjoys watching a speaker fumble with a machine.

PSST!

Ask a friend to watch a trial run of your presentation and to give reactions and suggestions.

CHECK it OUT!

✔ *To help relax yourself, try these techniques before you begin your presentation:*

- *Take long, deep breaths and exhale slowly. Do some stretches.*

- *Jump up and down or run in place to let off nervous energy—but don't do so much that you start sweating!*

- *Visualize your presentation, step by step. Imagine it proceeding just the way you want it to.*

During Your Oral Presentation:

- Speak clearly and loud enough to be heard.

- Look at your audience as you speak. Glance at your notes when you need to, but try to maintain eye contact with the people you're speaking to.

- Be relaxed, but stand or sit straight. If you slouch, your audience will too. If you fidget, so will your audience.

- Don't distract the audience. For example, don't jingle the change in your pocket or tap your fingers on a desk while you're speaking.

- Use language that's appropriate to the group you're addressing. If you're making a formal presentation, avoid using slang. If you're speaking to an informal group, you can be more relaxed in your choice of words.

- Be enthusiastic! If you seem bored by your presentation, it's a safe bet your audience will be too.

- Don't run away after you've finished. Ask if anyone has questions. If anyone does, answer the questions politely and clearly.

PREPARING A SPEECH

The most common—and perhaps the most nerve-racking—of all oral presentations are **speeches**. Getting up in front of a crowd and telling them what you think about something is not always easy.

Some people seem to be natural-born speechmakers, but most of us need to practice. Here are a few tips to help you prepare for your speech.

Before the Speech

1. Know your audience. Who will the audience be? How large will it be? What you say and how you say it should be tuned to who's going to be listening.

2. Find out how long you're supposed to speak.

3. Decide on a topic for your speech. The topic should be narrow enough to be covered fully in the time you have.

4. Make notes. Jot down on index cards the points you want to cover.

5. If you don't feel confident that you can present a speech while reading only from notes, write out your speech on numbered pages. Type or write neatly. Don't staple the pages together.

6. Practice, practice, practice.

✔ *Before you start writing, you might want to look at a book of famous speeches. See if you can figure out some of the techniques these speechmakers used to get their points across. Can you adapt them for your own speech?*

✔ *If you have access to a video camera, you might ask someone to tape you while you run through your speech. Video is a great way to see yourself the way an audience would!*

MAKING A SPEECH

Like a written essay, a speech generally consists of three parts: the *introduction*, the *body*, and the *conclusion*.

Introduction

In the **introduction** you want to get your audience's attention. You might do this by:

▶ starting with a quotation:

As Mark Twain once said, "Man is the only animal that blushes. Or needs to."

▶ telling a brief story:

Just the other day I was walking down the street, and I saw . . .

▶ making a dramatic statement:

Did you know that the average American watches more than four hours of television every single day?

Once you have your audience's attention, state clearly what you are going to speak about.

Today I'd like to tell you how we are covering Earth with unrecycled garbage, and what you can do about it.

Body

In the **body** of the speech, state your main points, and then provide information and ideas that support each statement.

You can present your ideas more effectively by using some time-tested speech-writing techniques. For example, you might:

▶ repeat important ideas so people will remember them:
Scientists asked us to protect the ozone layer. **But we did nothing.** *Scientists asked us to reduce car exhaust.* **But we did nothing.**

- ask rhetorical questions to get people thinking about the answers:

    Why are so many kinds of fishes dying? Why can we no longer swim in our rivers?

- use emotional words that will evoke a strong reaction:

    *Our once-beautiful rivers are now **choking** with **sludge**, our landfills are **suffocating** from **toxic** waste.*

Conclusion

In the **conclusion**, repeat your main point and wrap up the speech with something that will leave a lasting impression. You can do this effectively by:

- repeating what you said at the beginning, perhaps with a slightly different twist:

    And that's why a human is the only animal that blushes. Or needs to.

- ending with a rhetorical question or an emotional request for help:

    Is this the kind of world we want our children to grow up in? Can't you spare just five minutes from your day to make sure it never comes to pass?

- using a quotation, a story, or a dramatic statement:

    Years ago, President John F. Kennedy challenged us to ask not what our country could do for us, but instead what we can do for our country. Today we must challenge ourselves by asking what we can do for our planet.

PURPOSES FOR A SPEECH

Most people make speeches for one of two **purposes**: either *to inform* or *to persuade.*

*For more on **organizing** methods, see Patterns of Information on pages 48-53.*

To Inform

If you are making a speech to **inform**, you're simply trying to give your audience some information on an important topic. Here are some tips to help you:

1. **Narrow your topic.** Choose something you can explain fully within the time limit. For instance, "Sports" is probably too broad a topic; a speech on the founding of the Special Olympics would probably work better. *You should be able to state the main idea of your presentation in one sentence.*

2. Once you've gotten your topic, choose an **organizing method**. You probably have a lot of information to present, so you'll need to figure out how to present all the details. The organizing method you choose depends on what kind of information you are presenting.

To present . . .	Organize details by . . .
A sequence of events	Time order
A comparison of two or more things or ideas	Comparison/Contrast
Why something happened	Cause/Effect
How a problem was or can be solved	Problem/Solution

3. Present your information as a series of important ideas, with **factual details** to support each idea.

4. Conclude your presentation with a **summary** of important points. You might also suggest to your audience an important point for further consideration.

To Persuade

If you are making a speech to **persuade**, you are trying to convince your audience that what you say is true—and that they should agree with you. Here are some tips to help you do that:

1. State your opinions clearly and honestly.

2. Don't assume that everyone already agrees with you. Present strong supporting facts or ideas to back up your opinions.

3. Keep your audience in mind. Don't use a vocabulary or style that they won't understand. It's often a good idea to start by making some points you're confident your audience will agree with.

4. Make a strong concluding statement. Give your audience an idea or a phrase they'll remember long after the speech is over.

more
INFO

For more on supporting details, see page 49.

• • •

For more on audience, see page 6.

Tell your listeners exactly why you think what you think.

PERSUASIVE TECHNIQUES: BE A CRITICAL LISTENER

For more on **persuasive writing**, *see page 19.*

If you've ever listened to a politician running for office or watched a TV commercial, you've already heard some **persuasive techniques.** Much of what you hear is fair and sensible. Sometimes, though, a speaker may use techniques that are dishonest or manipulative. So be a critical listener!

keep in mind

Listening critically doesn't mean you have to find fault with everything you hear. Critical listening means that you should evaluate what you hear in order to decide whether or not to believe it.

▶ **Slanted facts** present only one side of an argument. For example: *Anthony Marks is the candidate with experience. He's already been on student council for two years.* This statement doesn't mention Anthony's opponent has also been on the student council for two years.

▶ **Faulty reasoning** presents ideas that don't follow logically. For example: *My opponent, Gail Kelly, has been our student rep for the last year. And now classes are more overcrowded than ever!* Each statement might be true, but the classes are not overcrowded *because* Gail Kelly has been student rep—as the speaker is suggesting.

▶ **Bandwagon** is a technique that tries to convince you to do something because "everyone's doing it." For example: *Everyone agrees that Anthony Marks is the coolest kid in the eighth grade. Don't be left out. Vote for Anthony!* The speaker gives no evidence that "everyone" feels this way. And even if they do, that's no reason for you to believe it too.

▶ **Testimonials** use famous people to endorse products or ideas. For example, a TV commercial might show a famous basketball player enjoying a certain brand of lemonade. It suggests that if you like the basketball player, you'll like the lemonade too, even though there's no connection between the two ideas.

GOING STRAIGHT TO THE SOURCE

Whether you're researching a school report, news story, or biographical piece, interviews can be great sources of information. You might want to interview an expert in a particular field, an eyewitness to an important event, or someone who has an especially interesting job or hobby. No matter who your subject is, a good interview requires some careful planning and preparation, so be prepared. Here's how:

Before You Begin

1. Learn as much as you can about your topic. Figure out what you already know and, just as important, what else you want to learn. Think about the information you might get from the person you're interviewing.

2. Make an appointment with the person you want to interview. Explain your project, and ask politely whether the person might have some time to speak with you about it. Be ready to discuss what kinds of questions you will want to ask and how long you expect the interview to take. Be as flexible as possible about time and location.

3. Write down the questions you want to ask beforehand. Put your questions in logical order. Make your questions brief and to the point, and try to avoid asking questions that can be answered just *yes* or *no*.

4. Decide how you will record the interview. You might take written notes or use a tape recorder. If you are using a tape recorder, make sure to ask the person you're interviewing if he or she minds being taped.

more **INFO**

For an Interview writing model, *see pages 278–279.*

keep in mind

If you're using a tape recorder, make sure you know how to work it beforehand. And bring extra tapes and batteries along with you just in case!

During the Interview

1. Make sure to be on time for the interview. Introduce yourself to the person you're interviewing, and explain again the purpose and topic of the interview.

2. Speak clearly and directly.

3. Be attentive. Listen carefully to what the person says. If you're not taping the interview, write down the most important things the person says. If you are taping, write down important points or additional questions you might ask.

4. Be courteous. Don't interrupt when the person is answering your questions. If you want more information about a topic, make a note to go back to it. If necessary, you can adapt your prepared questions to respond to unexpected information the person has given you.

5. End the interview when you have reached the allotted time, and be sure to thank the person for the interview. If you plan to use direct quotes from the interview, ask the person's permission.

After the Interview

1. Review your notes. If you have taped the interview, it's often helpful to make a *transcript*—a word-for-word copy of the tape.

2. If you are using a direct quote and are unsure of the exact wording, you should check with the person before including it.

3. When you use a person's quote, it's considered polite and professional to send that person a copy of your finished work; if the work is published, send the published copy.

keep in mind

People don't always speak in perfect, complete sentences. You may need to edit quotes for grammar and punctuation. But this editing should not alter the basic content of what the person said. And you should never add things the person didn't actually say.

MAY THE BEST IDEA WIN

A **debate** is an organized, spoken argument between two sides.

Debates bring people together to explore complex and sometimes heated topics. Maybe you've heard presidential candidates debating the country's most pressing issues. Maybe your school has a debate team.

A formal debate usually involves two panels, or teams.

The debate topic is often stated as a question, such as: *Should our school have a dress code?* or *Should our town have a leash law for dogs?* One side argues *for* the argument (affirmative side) and one side argues *against* it (negative side).

Usually, both sides know the topic beforehand and come to the debating table well-prepared. Before a debate, members of each team research the topic as thoroughly as possible *and* brush up on their speaking and listening skills.

A moderator makes sure each side gets equal time to present an argument to the audience. Then there is a rebuttal. During the rebuttal each side has a chance to answer the argument of the other side. Speakers can't really prepare a rebuttal thoroughly because the teams don't know ahead of time what the other side's argument will be.

A judge, or panel of judges, or the audience decides which side has won the debate.

Be an information sponge. The more information you absorb, the more you will have to use against your opponents.

HOW TO GET A DEBATE GOING

1. *Discuss it.* With other members of your debate team, discuss the pros and cons of your debate topic.

2. *Explore it.* Gather support for your argument. Go to the library, call agencies and organizations, talk to professionals and experts on your topic. Gather facts, quotes, statistics that help your case. Find evidence that supports the opposing view too.

3. *Strategize.* Develop a game plan. With your team, hammer out the main points you'll make. Back up each point with evidence. Check your arguments for faulty logic.

4. *Anticipate.* Figure out what the other side's argument is likely to be, and how you will rebut it.

5. *Practice!* Present your case to your other teammates. Help each other present the case effectively—and within the time limit.

6. *Present it.* This is the chance for your team to present your case and supporting evidence.

7. *Think twice.* Usually, before the rebuttal, you'll have time to huddle to discuss weak points in your opponents' arguments.

8. *Rebut it.* In rebuttal the spokesperson has a given amount of time to point out weaknesses in the other team's argument and explain why his/her team's case is stronger.

9. *Settle it.* The judge or audience decides which team presented a stronger case.

A debate provides a chance to discuss the pros and cons of an issue calmly and in depth. A debate is a valuable alternative to an argument that is often based largely on emotion.

Although it will rarely settle a question once and for all, debating is a great way to sharpen your speaking, listening, and critical-thinking strategies. Here are some tips to help you debate effectively:

Before the Debate

1. Be prepared. Learn as much about your topic as possible. Try to predict what your opponents' arguments will be and how you will answer them.

2. Prepare note cards you can use during the debate. You can jot down a brief outline of your argument, points, facts, and examples you may want to use.

During the Debate

1. Stick to the debate topic. Your task is to speak for or against a given issue.

2. Remember that your performance will be judged not just on what you say but also on how well you present it. Try to appear calm, confident, and knowledgeable (even if you're scared witless!).

3. Present your argument as persuasively as possible. Be as clear, focused, and logical as you can be.

4. Listen attentively to your opponents' statements. Jot down points you want to rebut. Listen for weak points or incomplete information, which you can address during your rebuttal.

5. Listen for unfair methods of persuasion, like slanted arguments or bandwagons. You can rebut them with a logical analysis.

more **INFO**

For more on **persuasive techniques,** *see page 82.*

You can do a very good job arguing a point you disagree with—in fact, that's a great way to make sure you see both sides of an issue.

READING VISUAL IMAGES

Does your shirt match your pants? Should you cross the street now? Which kind of licorice costs less? We get most of our information about the world through what we *see*. You might not think about it often, but much of your day is spent **reading visual images**. Here are just a few examples of how you gather information with your eyes:

For entertainment and information you can look at television, videos, movies, computer screens, and street signs. Of course, books, magazines, newspapers, and other reading material are rich sources of information and entertainment, too. You can also look at visual art, such as painting, sculpture, and photography.

It may sound funny, but like everything else, seeing takes practice. In the following pages you'll find out about ways to understand and appreciate many of the things you look at.

PSST!

You get lots of information from looking at people's faces. Did your mother find that joke funny? Is your teacher mad at you? You can often tell by looking at facial expressions.

YOUR VISUAL CLUES

Countless times each day, we rely on **symbols**, or signs, to give us information. A symbol, quite simply, is something that stands for something else. For instance, an **H** on a faucet stands for "hot water."

Symbols can convey important information, sometimes more quickly than words can. Think of the picture of a skull and crossbones on a bottle of poisonous household cleaner. That does a more effective job of scaring you away than a complicated explanation of how and why the poison is bad for you. Effective symbols are vivid and easy to figure out.

When you look at a symbol, think about how well it communicates its message. Can you tell right away what it's telling you?

Here are some common symbols to look at. How well do you think they work?

Some symbols are designed to give information in places where people may speak different languages or may not be able to read.

Many symbols tell us about rules we need to follow.

Highway signs have to be large and simple because you see them for just a few seconds as you pass by.

Some symbols convey ideas, perhaps better than words might be able to. This Olympic symbol is meant to show a sense of unity among nations.

LOOKING AT ART

All day long you look around you to gather information about the world. Looking at art requires a slightly different "gear." Art is about seeing and thinking in a creative way. Art, like literature, gives you an opportunity to reflect, to imagine, and to explore ideas and feelings in a personal way.

Art can convey powerful feelings, beautiful images, and complicated stories. Art can link us to tradition *and* can introduce us to new, mysterious, and controversial topics. But have you ever looked at a famous painting and wondered: *What's the big deal?*

Looking at art can be challenging—in fact, it's often meant to be. One of the biggest challenges is this: art asks questions that we must try to answer in our own individual ways. The same sculpture or print may hold different messages or meanings for you than it does for others. Artists often prefer not to talk about the messages in their art, because they want you to find your own meaning in it. So how are you supposed to figure out what it means?

In the coming pages you'll find tips for how to look at and experience different types of visual art.

BEFORE YOUR EYES

Have you ever seen a **painting** or **drawing** you really liked without knowing just why you liked it? Maybe it was a picture of the ocean, and you like the ocean. Or it had lots of red in it, and you love red. Or maybe it had to do with the layout of the painting or drawing.

Learning about the basics of painting and drawing—*colors, lines, shapes,* and *depth*—will help you begin to understand why you respond the way you do to different pieces of visual art. These four elements together add up to a drawing's or painting's **style**:

Colors are used to depict things realistically and also to create emotion with paint. Colors have the power to make you respond strongly, either positively or negatively. (Imagine how reluctant you'd be to bite into a bright blue peanut butter sandwich!) Colors can be used to create beauty and harmony, conflict or gloom. The red, yellow, and orange families are called "hot" colors—they can suggest emotions like passion and excitement. Blues, purples, and greens are known as "cool" colors—they suggest calmness and serenity, the cooler emotions.

PSST!

You already know that someone who *paints* is a *painter*. But did you know that someone who *draws* is called a *draftsperson*?

PAINTINGS AND DRAWINGS

Lines are used to create images in all kinds of ways. Straight lines suggest order. Wavy or curved lines can suggest motion, like the path of a tossed football, or softness, such as the folds of the long dress in the painting to the right by Auguste Renoir. Jagged lines can suggest something powerful and even frightening—like a lightning bolt or a monster's teeth. Thin lines can seem very delicate, like tiny feathers on a bird. Thick lines suggest boldness. Lines can actually pull your eye across a painting in a particular direction.

Shapes can create a sense of balance and order or of tension and chaos. Most shapes suggest basic geometric figures like circles, triangles, or rectangles, but there are countless possibilities for free-form shapes. Painters often use shape very subtly in their work. For instance, can you find the ovals Renoir used in the painting to the right? (Hint: Look at the shapes of faces, hats, overhead lights.) What other shapes do you see?

Depth is created with size, light, and shading. Even though most paintings are flat, they usually give you a sense of depth. Notice how small the people at the top of Renoir's paintings are. He wanted you to think they are far back in the crowd. Painters and draftspeople also use light and shading to create an impression of three dimensions.

Many painters also draw, and vice versa. When planning a painting, many painters do some sketching first—sort of like a first draft of a paper.

Artists living in different places and times have very different influences. The styles and subject matter of their teachers' work, the landscape around them, the quality of daylight, and other influences all show up in their work. Here are three

pieces to look at, by three artists whose work differs quite a bit. Which do you like best? Can you explain why?

What do you think of this painting? It's by an Impressionist painter from France named Auguste Renoir.

Now look at this classic print, "The Great Wave" by Katsushika Hokusai, an artist from Japan. How are color, line, shape, and depth used here, compared to how they are used in the other two pieces?

Not all art depicts something "real." When you look at abstract paintings like this one by the Russian painter Wassily Kandinsky, don't worry about trying to "figure it out." Many abstract artists claim their work doesn't mean anything. But even a painting of splotches of color or geometric shapes can trigger a response from you.

What do you think of this abstract painting? Do you like the way it uses color, line, shape, and depth?

ART TAKES SHAPE

Sculpture is three-dimensional art. The most traditional form of sculpture is the statue, but any art that exists in three dimensions is sculpture. A sculpture can create an effect with size, shape, and texture, as well as with the same elements as a painting—color, line, shape, and depth.

As with painting, there are many different styles of sculpture. A sculpture can be very realistic, like the one by Edgar Degas on the left. Or it can be abstract, like the piece by the artist Christo at the bottom of the page.

Sculpture can be made from all kinds of materials: clay, stone, wood, metal, or even fabric (that's what the piece below by Christo is)!

What is your response to these sculptures? How are they different? How do textures, lines, and colors create an effect?

Notice how real this girl looks. Her skirt is made of fabric instead of metal. When Edgar Degas first showed this piece in 1874, viewers were scandalized by how ordinary-looking the girl is. Up until then, ballerinas had been portrayed as perfect, almost imaginary figures.

With the help of hundreds of local people, the Bulgarian artist Christo wrapped metallic silver fabric around the Reichstag, a huge, empty government building in Germany, creating a temporary sculpture in the middle of Berlin. The piece required 300 tons of scaffolding, and cost $7 million to make. When it was taken down, all materials were recycled.

TAKE A PICTURE...

Lots of artists use **photography** as an art form. Because they portray the world so vividly, photographs have the power to convey strong moods and to trigger strong responses. When you look at an art photograph, think about its subject, its style, and its layout, just as you would with a painting.

Although most photographs portray the world realistically, taking a good picture is not as easy as you might think. A good photographer carefully chooses the subject, the angle of the shot, and its layout.

What do you think of these two photographs? How does each use color, line, and shape?

Think about what this piece might mean. Then consider its title, Art is . . ., *and think again—what might the artist, Lorraine O'Grady, be trying to say? Could she be making a statement about art in general? What is the mood of this piece?*

This photograph shows a fire from an artist's point of view. Notice the color scheme. Why do you think the artist, Joel Sternfeld, decided to include the pumpkins in his picture? Would a picture accompanying a news story of this fire include the pumpkins?

95

WORTH A THOUSAND WORDS

Just like writing, pictures can convey information. An **illustration** is a drawing or painting that is meant to accompany a piece of writing.

Although all illustration is more or less realistic in style, a good illustrator thinks carefully about the subject when planning an illustration. For a funny story the artist might choose a humorous style. To illustrate a recipe, a more straightforward type of drawing would work better.

As you probably remember, most books for young children are illustrated. But there are many other uses for illustrations. A map accompanying a news article, a drawing of a car's dashboard in an owner's manual, the pictures of George Washington on a dollar bill—these are all illustrations.

When you look at an illustration, think about how well it goes with the text it is illustrating.

Here are two illustrations to look at. The first was drawn to go with a humorous story. The second illustrates a piece of historical nonfiction about a Native American boy. How do the styles differ? How does each illustration match the kind of text it accompanies?

BUT SERIOUSLY, FOLKS...

Cartoons and comic strips are also illustrations. Most cartoonists use humor to get their points across. You've probably seen cartoons and comic strips in most newspapers. Maybe you've read comic books or seen animated cartoons on television. Many cartoons contain political or social messages.

Look at the cartoons below. Can you find any message in each one? How do the illustrators manage to get their points across?

"Now here's my co-anchor, Nancy, with a conflicting account of that very same story."

The characters Lucy and Snoopy in the comic strip above are grappling with a common human problem—how to live in a violent world. The co-anchors in the cartoon at the left are in another common situation—a clash of opinions. The cartoonists have found humor in these problems . . . and you can too!

WATCH IT...BUT WATCH OUT

Most Americans watch several hours of **television** every day—but would probably admit that much of that time is wasted. You don't have to leave the house to watch television, and it doesn't require much thought or energy. It's very easy to be a "couch potato" when you're bored or even when you want to avoid something you have to do—like your homework.

When you watch television, it's usually to be entertained or to get information. No matter what you're watching, it pays to be a critical viewer. As you develop a critical eye, you will be able to make more informed decisions about what you choose to watch.

PSST!

Some people say watching TV turns off your mind and can even be sort of addicting. How difficult would it be for you not to watch TV for a week?

When you watch sitcoms or other entertaining shows:

1. Does the show grab my attention right away and make me want to watch it all the way through? Are the jokes funny? Is the plot believable?

2. How effective is the acting? Does it seem realistic, or am I constantly reminded that it's fake?

3. If there are special effects, do they add to the show, or are they distracting?

4. What else is good—or not so good—about the show?

keep in mind

When the show is over, ask yourself: Was it worth my time to watch this?

When you watch the news:

1. Are both sides of an issue presented, or just one? Does the story answer each of the 5 Ws and H questions: *who? what? when? where? why? how?*

2. What sources of information are used? Are they reliable?

3. Do the "on the scene" film clips seem to give a balanced idea of the event? Or do they give a distorted impression of what actually happened?

When you watch a documentary or educational special:

1. Before you watch, make a list of questions you want answered. As you watch, ask yourself: *What am I learning from the documentary?*

2. Is it entertaining, as well as being informative?

3. After you see it, think about what you've viewed and the ideas and facts you've learned. Look at your original list of questions. Were they answered to your satisfaction?

Most of these tips can apply to movies too.

DO YOU "BUY" IT?

We're all surrounded by **advertisements**. They're on television, in store windows, in magazines, on billboards, and even on many people's clothing. Some ads are beautiful, some are helpful, some are amusing, some are downright annoying . . . but they all exist for one purpose. The purpose of an advertisement is to sell you something.

You can make better, more informed decisions about what to buy if you learn to analyze what ads are saying and think carefully about how much of them you can believe.

Ads do not tell the whole story about the products they promote. For instance, ads rarely mention prices. Many ads are based on fantasy of one sort or another. For example, many suggest that some unimportant product will change your life. So they may not be realistic even when they *do* tell you the price of a product.

When you look at an ad, try to get inside the advertisers' heads. Think about what information has been left out . . . and why. Ask yourself questions like this:

- ▶ What claims are made? Can I believe them? What does the ad promise about the benefits of the product? Are the promises realistic?

- ▶ How does this ad appeal to my intellect and to my emotions? What kind of emotional response does the ad aim for?

- ▶ Photographs and illustrations are often used in advertising because they can create an idealized impression without actually saying anything untrue. What does the image promise me? How realistically does the image relate to the product being advertised?

Television commercials are advertisements too.

Seeing

Here are a couple of advertisements. Read between the lines. What impressions do these ads try to create about the products? Do the claims they make seem realistic?

What does this ad promise you? It promises that Fruity Power Bites tastes like fruit. Why not just eat a piece of fruit? (What does "the power of fruit taste" even mean?) How could anyone know whether this will be your favorite cereal before you've even tried it? Does the ad claim that the cereal is good for you? No. It just says Fruity Power Bites cereal is sweet and crunchy—it's probably loaded with sugar.

This ad promises that a Baseball Watch will make you "the center of attention" and "the envy of your friends." That's a pretty incredible claim, isn't it? Have you ever seen someone become popular because of a watch? Wouldn't a baseball fan want to pick a favorite team to be on his or her watch? If your favorite team's colors are blue and orange, do you want a green watch? How well does this watch even keep time? We don't know—there's no mention of that!

PART FOUR

Study Skills

CONTENTS

Using the Library 105–122
Study Strategies 123–131
Using Computers 123
Taking Research Notes 126
Outlining 128
Study Strategies 129
Test-Taking Strategies . .132–133

STUDY SKILLS

Get it *together*

Learning involves getting information and then putting it to use in some way. Some of the information you get is from your teachers, school books, and classmates . . . but sometimes you need to search for it yourself. Finding the information you need takes skill.

Figuring out how to put information to good use is often up to you too. There's not a "secret" to studying, but there *are* some tips that will help. In this section, you'll learn about:

Using the Library
Learn your way around the world of knowledge at your local library. Find out how to do research. Explore the Dewey Decimal System, library catalogs, the reference room, and more!

Study Strategies
Find out how you learn best—and develop a game plan accordingly. Learn about using computers, taking research notes, outlining, and more.

Test-taking Strategies
With these test-taking techniques, you can eliminate test anxiety forever.

BE A CARD-CARRYING MEMBER

Imagine a place where you could go, browse to your heart's content, pick out as many items as you want, take them home with you, use them as much as you like, and bring them back a few weeks later—without paying a cent. This place really exists: it's called a **public library**. Your free library card is all you need to get access to an almost unlimited variety of books and other resources.

Research Game Plan

When you look for materials on a given topic, you're doing **research**. Because the library is so packed with information, you may feel overwhelmed by the experience of researching one fact you might need in a whole building or roomful of books, tapes, magazines, encyclopedias, and more. If you don't have a game plan, it can be like finding the proverbial needle in a haystack. Here's how to find what you need:

What part of the library should you go to first? ⟶ The card or computer catalog. Write down titles and call numbers for materials you need.

Then what? ⟶ Using call numbers to guide you, go to the section(s) where the materials are kept.

Then what? ⟶ Be selective. Which material is the most useful? Current? To the point? Complete? Now's the time to assess whether you need to adjust your topic.

Don't forget ... ⟶ to browse through books on nearby shelves—you may find something quite useful.

CHECK it OUT!

✔ Before you go *to the library is the time to get directed. Think about what you want to look for. Plan ahead, and then stick to your plan.*

✔ *Of course, no library has every book in the world. You might need to adjust your research topic slightly so you can use available materials. Be flexible enough about your topic that you can use what's there.*

HOW A LIBRARY IS ORGANIZED

Since libraries are packed to the rafters with books and other materials, they need to be expertly organized.

Most libraries arrange materials into five major sections, as shown on the map below.

The **Nonfiction** section includes books of factual information about real people, places, and events. Nonfiction books are classified by one of two systems. Most libraries use the *Dewey Decimal System*. (In some libraries biographies are organized separately, arranged alphabetically by the subjects' last names.) Some libraries—mostly at colleges and universities—use another system, called the *Library of Congress System*.

The **Fiction** section includes works of literature, such as novels, short stories, plays, and poems. Books in the Fiction section are arranged *alphabetically* by the authors' last names. But they too can be given a number based on the Dewey Decimal System.

CHECK it OUT!

✔ *Why's it called the Dewey Decimal System? It was invented by a man named John Dewey, and uses decimals (mixed numbers like this: 1.2342) to distinguish between subjects.*

✔ *Most libraries are organized according to the Dewey Decimal System, so you'll have an easy time with libraries all your life if you get familiar with it now.*

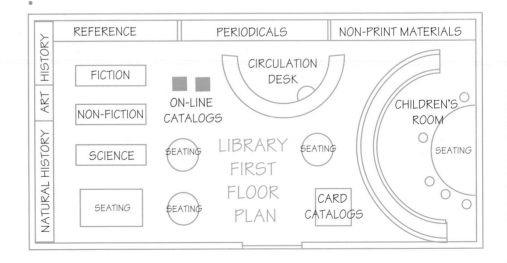

The Dewey Decimal System

In the **Dewey Decimal System** books are given numbers (known as *call numbers*) between 000 and 999. Books are arranged on the shelves according to these numbers. The number of each book is indicated on the spine, or binding, of the book below the title.

Here are the major categories for the Dewey Decimal System:

000 General Works
100 Philosophy
200 Religion
300 Social Sciences
400 Language
500 Science
600 Technology
700 Fine Arts
800 Literature
900 History and Geography

Reference resources are available in the library only—you can't take these books out of the reference section. The Reference section of the library contains general reference books, such as dictionaries, encyclopedias, atlases, and almanacs.

The **Periodicals** section contains newspapers, magazines, and other publications that are printed periodically—daily, weekly, monthly, and so on.

The **Audiovisual Resources** section may be the fastest growing part of the library, due to rapid changes in technology. This section includes all the resources that are *not* printed books, such as audiovisual aids and computer software. For example, a library might offer collections of records, videos, CDs, and/or audiotaped books. Many also provide computers and printers for your use.

Many libraries also have other special areas. In the **Young Adult** section, for instance, you will find materials geared to readers your age. Be sure to investigate this section, if your library has one. But don't dismiss books from other sections. That fact you're researching could be somewhere in **Reference**—or even in the **Children's Room.**

THE LIBRARY'S CATALOGS

Now that you know the sections of the library, how can you find out the names of the books and other resources available in each section? Your next move is to look through the library's catalogs.

The Card Catalog

The traditional resource is the **card catalog**—a system of filing book information on a set of cards in drawers. Each drawer is labeled with an alphabetized range of letters. The cards inside each drawer are arranged alphabetically, according to the information on the top line of each card.

Card catalogs generally have three cards for each **nonfiction** book: an **author card,** a **title card,** and a **subject card.** Each card has a **call number** in the upper left-hand corner. The call number is a code for how the book is classified and, thus, where to find the book in the library.

There are generally two cards for **fiction** books: an **author card** and a **title card.**

Suppose you want to research and write a report about mythological dragons in England during the Dark Ages. If you look up *dragons* in the card catalog, you might find these cards:

CHECK
it
OUT!

✔️ *Sometimes you'll see the words* See also *on the computer screen. This is called a cross-reference. It directs you to related key words or titles that you may want to look for.*

Subject Card
DRAGONS
398.2 Johnsgard, Paul A.
JOH   Dragons and unicorns: a natural
history/Paul and Karin Johnsgard.
        New York: St. Martin's Press, 1982
        p. cm.
1. Dragons. 2. Unicorns.
   II. Title

Author Card
  398.2 Johnsgard, Paul A.
JOH   Dragons and unicorns: a natural
  history/Paul and Karin Johnsgard.
  New York: St. Martin's Press, 1982
        p. cm.
1. Dragons. 2. Unicorns.
   II. Title

Title Card
  398.2 Dragons and unicorns
JOH   Johnsgard, Paul A.
        Dragons and unicorns: a natural
history/Paul and Karin Johnsgard.
New York: St. Martin's Press, 1982
        p. cm.
1. Dragons. 2. Unicorns.
   II. Title

The Computer Catalog

Many libraries have replaced their card catalogs with **computer catalogs.** To search for materials by computer, you type in **key words,** which the computer uses in its search. If you type in *dragon,* for example, the computer will call up all books that the library has with *dragon* in the title. If you type in an author's name, such as *Johnsgard,* the computer will call up all of that author's books. Most computer catalogs can even tell you which books are available and which are currently out on loan, lost, or being repaired.

The Key to Using Key Words

You may need to try different combinations of key words. If you type in only *England,* for example, you will probably get more titles than you can use. You can narrow down your search by adding more key words.

Each key word you add will narrow the search. For example, if you type in *England* and *Dark Ages,* you will get titles about England only during this period in history.

(Record 1 of 7)

Author: Johnsgard, Paul A.

Title: Dragons and unicorns: a natural history

Publisher: St. Martin's Press, New York, 1982.

Subjects: Dragons and Unicorns

Call Number	Volume	Material	Location	Status
398.2/JOH		Book	Cambridge	Available

Press [ENTER] to display books in other locations.

Press cursor to view previous title or next title.

PARTS OF A BOOK

A book isn't just a mass of unarranged information—each one is designed to help you find what you're looking for. Knowing how books are organized will help you get the most out of your research.

Judge a Book By Its Cover!

Ask friends if they've read the book. If so, did they like it?

Have you read other books by this author? Has a friend?

The title page tells you the book's title, author(s), and, if applicable, its illustrator(s). It also gives the name and location of the publisher.

Dragons and Other Creatures
by Julie St. Georges

Copyright © 1997 by Legendary Press, Inc All rights reserved

Illustrated by Carmen Lord

Legendary Press
BOSTON

The copyright page tells you when the book was published. Is the information still current?

Look at the table of contents. Does the book seem to cover a lot of subjects? Or cover one in great detail?

The **title page** gives the title of the book, its author(s) and, if applicable, its illustrator(s). It also gives the name of the publisher and where the book was published.

The **copyright page** gives a copyright notice and a date. The date on this page will tell you how current the information in the book is.

Copyright © 1995 by Legendary Press, Inc. All rights reserved. No part of this book may be reproduced or transmitted in any form or by any means, electronic or mechanical, including photocopy, recording, or by any information storage and retrieval system, without permission in writing from the Publisher.

Printed in the United States of America.

The **table of contents** is a handy outline of the topics covered in the book showing how they are organized.

The **index** lists the information that the book offers about specific topics.

TABLE OF CONTENTS
Foreword
Myths and Legends...............3
Dragons......................10
Unicorns.....................22
Elves and Leprechauns.........31
Gryphons....................37

INDEX
Elves, 31-32, 35
English legends
  King Arthur, 5-6, 14
  Sir Lancelot, 6, 14
  St. George, 15-16
Europa, 9
Evensong, 33
Excalibur See King Arthur

A **glossary** lists definitions of technical terms used in the text.

A **bibliography** lists references to books and other materials used by the author in writing the subject matter of the book.

THE REFERENCE ROOM: YOUR INFO HEADQUARTERS

You may not know everything . . . but when you learn your way around your library's **reference room**, there's no telling what you might find.

Whether you're exploring the life of the historical figure Pocahontas or doing a report on the country Lithuania, be sure to check out your library's reference sources. They come in many varieties. Some give general information about a topic; others go into more depth. Some, like an article from last week's newspaper, give you a current look at your subject; others, like encyclopedia entries, give you more comprehensive information.

The better you know your options in the reference room, the more information you can uncover. The following pages will help you find your way around **encyclopedias, periodicals** (magazines and newspapers), **atlases, visual aids,** and other reference sources. You will also find **dictionaries** and **thesauri** in the reference room.

Different kinds of reference materials can work well together. An encyclopedia article gives you an overview, while a magazine article gives you a more current look. Studying a map might lead you to wonder about a particular place, so . . . back to the encyclopedia. It's like a treasure hunt. With so much information out there, where do you begin?

more
INFO

For more on using the **dictionary** *and* **thesaurus**, *see pages 234–236.*

Thesauri **means more than one thesaurus... but it's also correct to say** *thesauruses.*

✔The encyclopedia's Index will tell you the volume and the page to turn to for the entry on your topic. It will also point you to **cross-references**—other encyclopedia articles related to your topic. For example, if you look up Pocahontas, you might find this cross-reference: See Jamestown Settlement.

✔Most encyclopedias list cross-references at the end of an article. Others indicate them with capital letters or italics within the text of an article.

ENCYCLOPEDIAS: INFO FROM A TO Z

As you may already know, an **encyclopedia** is a collection of factual articles containing the most important points about a wide range of subjects. When you are researching a report, looking in the encyclopedia is a good first step, because it gives you a brief, general overview of the subject.

Most encyclopedias contain several books, called *volumes.* On the spine of each book you will find the volume number and one or more **guide letters,** the first letters of the subjects covered in that volume. The entries are arranged alphabetically within each volume. Many large encyclopedias also include an **index** in a separate volume.

The most efficient way to use an encyclopedia is to focus on the main word of your subject—such as *Pocahontas.* On the pages of the encyclopedia, the main word, or **entry word,** for each article is identified in bold print so you can find it quickly. To make your search even easier, you will see **guide words** in bold print at the top of each page, indicating the first and last topics on that page. For instance, you might find the article on Pocahontas between the guide words **Pluto** and the **Pocono Mountains.**

A Look Inside:

Po–Podgorica ← Guide words

Po, the longest river in Italy, about 405 miles (640 km) long. It flows from the Alps through the Po Valley, one of Italy's most important industrial and agricultural regions, to the Adriatic Sea.

Po, chemical symbol of the element POLONIUM.

Entry word → **Pocahontas,** c. 1595-1617, a Native American woman, daughter of Chief POWHATAN. She visited the English colonists at the JAMESTOWN Settlement in Virginia and is said to have saved the life of Captain John Smith. In 1614 she married a colonist named John Rolfe, with whom she went to England in 1616 and was treated as a princess. She fell ill before returning to America and died in 1617.

Podgorica: *see* TITOGRAD, Yugoslavia

↑
Cross-reference

In this encyclopedia, words in all CAPITAL LETTERS indicate the titles of other related articles.

✔ *Many libraries now have periodicals indexed on computers. These indexes, such as the Magazine Index, provide information at the touch of a button! You can search by author, subject, or title by typing in key words. The Index then gives you a listing of all related articles appearing in periodicals.*

PERIODICALS: WHAT'S NEW

Once you get the basics from the encyclopedia, you can go on to explore more current information sources. For that, you might want to turn to **periodicals**—newspapers, magazines, journals, and other publications that are published more frequently than books.

To help you find what you are looking for, the library provides **periodical indexes.** Organized alphabetically by author's name and by subject, they list all articles that have appeared in a wide range of publications. The most widely available index is the *Readers' Guide to Periodical Literature,* which appears in book form every year, with updates every month.

The noun *periodical* **is related to the adjective** *periodic,* **which means occurring at regular intervals. A newspaper or magazine is published at regular intervals— daily, weekly, or monthly.**

Suppose you wanted to find recent articles about Pocahontas. If you looked in the *Readers' Guide* for 1995, you'd find information about an article that might interest you:

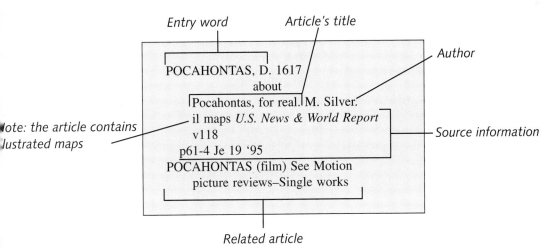

Entry word   *Article's title*

Author

POCAHONTAS, D. 1617
      about
Pocahontas, for real. M. Silver.
il maps *U.S. News & World Report*
   v118
   p61-4 Je 19 '95
POCAHONTAS (film) See Motion
    picture reviews–Single works

Note: the article contains illustrated maps

Source information

Related article

You can usually find major newspapers, such as the *New York Times,* in the library, but most newspapers are not indexed as comprehensively as magazines are. However, some computer services and newspaper indexes can help you find newspaper articles on specific subjects. Ask your librarian about access to these services.

Periodicals are often stored on *microfilm* and *microfiche.* **Ask your librarian about these.**

ATLASES: WHERE IT'S AT

In reading about Pocahontas, you will come across references to the Jamestown Settlement, and you might begin wondering just where it was located. The next stop in your quest for information would be an **atlas**. An atlas is a reference book that contains a collection of maps. There are many different kinds of maps.

A **political map** shows state and national boundaries, as well as cities and towns.

A **historical map** shows what an area may have looked like at a particular time in history.

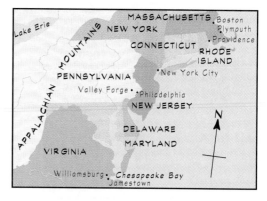

A **road map** shows roads and highways to help drivers get from one place to another.

Other kinds of maps show special information, such as elevation, climate, products produced in a certain region, or population.

THE ELEMENTS OF A MAP

Once you know how to read them, maps can provide a wealth of information—from the crops a particular country grows to the roads between towns. Here's a list of features to help you decode and understand maps:

Map Scale   The **map scale** shows how distances on a map are related to actual distances. It helps you determine actual distances. If the map scale is 1 inch = 100 miles, for instance, and the coast of Virginia is 1 inch on the map, then the coast of Virginia is actually 100 miles long.

Legend   The **legend,** usually a box in the corner of the map, lists the meanings of the symbols shown on the map. Depending on the type of map, the symbols might refer to kinds of roads, sizes of cities and towns, major crops or industry, campgrounds, weather or any number of things.

Grid and Index   Many maps are arranged on a **grid.** A grid is a set of numbers, letters, and crisscrossed lines that help you locate places on the map. You will notice letters on the sides of the map and numbers across the top and bottom. To find a location, first look it up on the map's **Index** to find the letter-number combination. Jamestown, for example, is located in D-1. Find the box where that letter and that number intersect on the map, and you will find Jamestown.

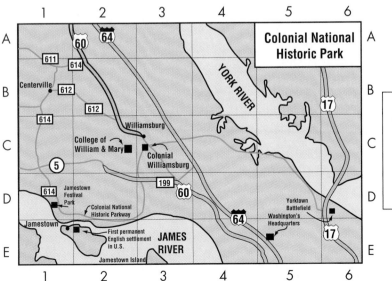

INDEX

College of William and Mary C-2

Colonial Williamsburg C-3

Jamestown Festival Park D-1

Jamestown settlement E-2

Washington's Headquarters E-5

Yorktown Battlefield D-6

LEGEND

• City or town

■ Point of Interest

64 Interstate highway

60 Federal highway

5 State highway

614 County or Local road

119

ALMANACS: THIS YEAR'S NEWS

Encyclopedias are useful for finding information about events in the past or about subjects that do not change from year to year. What if you want to find out about something that happened within the last year—say, who won the most recent election for the U.S. Senate in Virginia?

A valuable resource for recent information is an **almanac**. Almanacs are published every year. They contain current information about a wide variety of subjects. Most almanacs have a complete index in the front of the book and a shorter one, an abbreviated index, in the back. Like other indexes you have been learning about, the almanac's index is a good first stop in locating the information you need.

Sample–Abbreviated Index

INDEX
Election Day, 480, 488
Elections:
    Congress, 132-134
    Election results, 1996, 133-135
    Election results (1788-1994), 539-542
    Presidential, 132, 540
    Women's success rates, 140
Electoral College, 524-528
Electrical equipment, sales, 204
Electricity:
    Economic statistics, 453
    Hydroelectric plants, 468
    Inventions and discoveries, 650
    Nuclear power plants, 470

Sample–Complete Index

ELECTIONS: THE SENATE
The senior senator is listed first. The dates indicate period of service. The political party is shown in parentheses.

Texas	
1985-1997	
1995-2001	Phil Gramm (R)
Utah	Kay Bailey Hutchison (R)
1977-2001	
1993-1999	Orrin G. Hatch (R)
Vermont	Robert Bennett (R)
1975-1999	
1989-2001	Patrick J. Leahy (D)
Virginia	James M. Jeffords (R)
1979-1997	
1989-2001	John H. Warner (R)
	Charles Robb (D)

VISUAL AIDS: SEEING IS BELIEVING

Have you ever heard the saying *A picture is worth a thousand words?* **Visual aids** such as *tables*, *charts*, and *graphs* can sometimes convey information more vividly than words alone can.

Suppose you're writing a report about how many people use computers. Here are examples of some visual aids you might find:

Tables and charts organize information into lists or boxes, for easy reading. Tables tend to have labels and numbers. Charts may also include text and pictures.

There are several types of **graphs** that present numerical amounts of something in different ways. A **bar graph,** for example, uses "bars" to indicate amounts. With a bar graph, you can compare the amounts easily.

Computers per 1,000 People

United States	265
Australia	175
Canada	162
Norway	153
Denmark	145
New Zealand	138

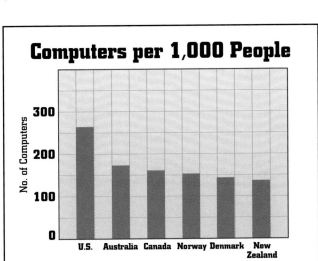

Computers per 1,000 People

No. of Computers

| U.S. | Australia | Canada | Norway | Denmark | New Zealand |

Be sure to read titles and labels carefully, so you don't misinterpret the information shown.

A **circle graph** or pie graph, uses a circle to represent 100 percent of whatever's shown. Each section of the circle, or slice of the "pie," represents a part of the whole. In a circle graph, you can compare amounts easily by looking at how big each section is.

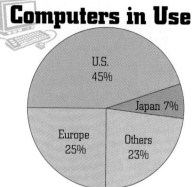

Computers in Use

U.S. 45%

Japan 7%

Europe 25%

Others 23%

Computers per 1,000 people

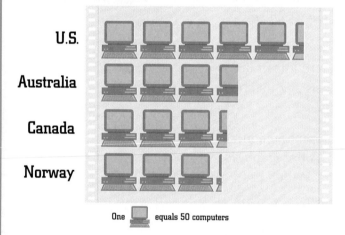

U.S.

Australia

Canada

Norway

One ▭ equals 50 computers

Pictographs are similar to bar graphs, but they use pictures or symbols (computers, in this graph) instead of bars to represent amounts. Like bar graphs, pictographs allow you to quickly compare different amounts.

Line graphs are best suited to showing trends over a period of time. On a line graph, one side edge, or axis, indicates units of time, and another edge indicates the amount being measured. Points are then drawn, or "plotted," to show where these two factors meet. The line that connects the points shows you whether the trend is going upward or downward. In this graph, for instance, the line is heading upward—showing you in a glance that the numbers of computers sold in the United States are increasing.

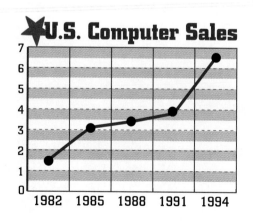

★U.S. Computer Sales

7
6
5
4
3
2
1
0

1982 1985 1988 1991 1994

COMPUTER RESOURCES: GET WISE—GET WIRED

More and more resources are now available on **computer**. For instance, you can conduct research on a computer—either at home or the library—by connecting to **on-line services** or the **Internet.** You can use these services to tap into volumes of materials. Here are just a few examples of what you can find on the Internet:

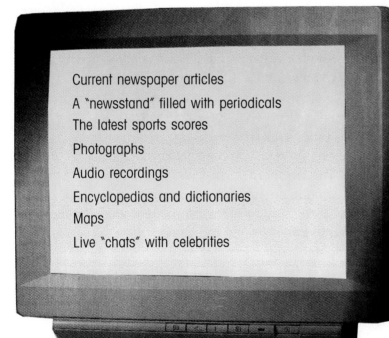

Current newspaper articles
A "newsstand" filled with periodicals
The latest sports scores
Photographs
Audio recordings
Encyclopedias and dictionaries
Maps
Live "chats" with celebrities

Other nonprint materials you might want to investigate:

✔ **Audiotapes** *are cassettes you can listen to (you might have music on audiotapes at home). You can practice a foreign language or hear a dramatic poetry reading on tape. Many libraries also have "Books on Tape."*

✔ *Your library may also have movies, nature shows, and/or "how-to" videos, which show you how to do things . . . from painting with watercolors to fixing a car engine.*

Many computers today have **CD-ROM drives.** A CD is a "compact disk" that can hold an enormous amount of written information, as well as pictures and sound. With a CD-ROM drive, you can access everything on the CD. On CD-ROM you can find encyclopedias, indexes, atlases, and many other kinds of information.

ROM stands for "Read-Only Memory."

PLUG IN, POWER UP

If you have never used a computer, you may think it's going to be difficult, but fear not—it's not so bad. A computer is a tool—you tell it what to do.

There are many different kinds of computers, but they all have things in common. Every computer and every software program comes with a manual of instructions. People around you can also be a valuable source of information—if you get stuck, talk to someone familiar with the kind of computer and software you're using.

You've already learned about on-line searches and CD-ROM resources. Another way computers can help you is with **word processing**. You can type the report on the computer, proofread and edit it on screen, and print it out on a printer.

Computer Terms

A computer has several components which are called **hardware.** The **keyboard** is what you use to type in words and give the computer commands. The **monitor** is the TV-like screen that allows you to see what you're doing. The **mouse** enables you to move around the screen and "click" commands to the computer. Your computer may also be hooked up to a **printer,** which prints what you type, and a **modem,** which connects your computer to a telephone line.

Here are some computer terms:

> ▶ **backup** a copy of a set of data or a document made to protect the original.

> ▶ **byte** a single character *(see below)*. The size of a computer disk, memory, or a document can be expressed in *bytes*, *kilobytes*, *megabytes*, and *gigabytes*.

▶ **character** a single letter, numeral, or space. Any key stroke on the keyboard produces a character.

▶ **command** an order you give the computer, such as OPEN or SAVE.

▶ **cursor** a blinking line, square, or arrow on the screen that shows where the next character will appear.

▶ **disk** a magnetic object for storing information. A **hard disk** is a permanent part of your computer. A **floppy disk** is a portable version used to save and store documents. You can store the equivalent of many notebook pages of information on a disk.

▶ **document** written text stored on or printed from a computer, such as a report.

▶ **font** a set of type characters, or typeface, of a certain design. For example, this page is set in *Helvetica.*

▶ **format** format means style. A disk must be formatted, or made to fit the style of the computer, before it can be used. Most computers can format disks for themselves. *Format* can also refer to the layout of a printed page.

▶ **function** something that the computer does on command, such as PRINT or SAVE.

▶ **memory** the part where information is stored.

▶ **menu** a list of functions that you can choose from.

▶ **software** programs that run on a computer. A word-processing program is an example of software.

Computer Commands

Cut-and-Paste: *take out a portion of highlighted text and put it somewhere else*

Delete: *take out or "erase" one or more characters*

Find: *search for a certain word in a document or for a document in the computer*

Open: *open a document*

Print: *print a document or what you see on the screen*

Quit: *exit a program*

Save: *store the document on a disk for later use*

Tab: *indent a line of text, as in the beginning of a paragraph*

KEEPING IT STRAIGHT

Okay, so you've found good information sources in the library. Now you'll need to keep track of all the information you collect. **Taking research notes** will help you to remember it. Of course, your notes will also come in handy when you write a report or study for a test. You may not be surprised to hear there's an art to taking research notes.

Note-Taking Tips

1. **Label your notes** with a subject heading at the top of your page or notecard.

> John Steinbeck (1902–68)
> most famous novels:
>   Of Mice and Men
>   The Grapes of Wrath (Pulitzer Prize, 1939)

If you're working on a research report, also write down the title, author, editor (if any), publisher, city of publication, publication date, and page numbers of each source. You'll need this information if you plan to include a *bibliography* in your report.

Index cards are especially handy for note-taking. You can write one fact on each card. Later, you can rearrange the cards in the order that works best.

title	American Literature: The Makers and the Making, Vol. II
editors	Brooks, Cleanth Lewis, R.B. Warren, Robert Penn
location	New York
publisher	St. Martin's Press
date	1973

2. You may want to make a separate **bibliography card** for each source. Then, when you prepare your bibliography, you can arrange the cards alphabetically and list each source.

3. **Paraphrase and summarize your notes.** Rewrite information from sources in your own words. If the subject is broad, summarize the information by including only the main ideas and most important details.

4. **Record quotes** *exactly.* If you find a sentence or passage in your reading that would work perfectly in your report, write it down *exactly* as it appears in the source. Include all punctuation, unusual spellings, and so on. Be *sure* to include the name of the person who said it, and where the information is taken from (including the page number). Put quotation marks around the entire quote.

5. **Abbreviate.** To save time write in groups of words instead of in complete sentences. Use abbreviations and symbols wherever it makes sense. Some people invent their own forms of shorthand to save time and work.

6. **Organize your notes** by subject or theme. This is particularly easy if you use notecards because you can shuffle the cards into any sequence you want.

keep in mind

Unless you are including a direct quotation from a book or other source, always take notes in your own words. *Using other writers' works without giving them credit is* plagiarism. *It's illegal!*

John Steinbeck The Grapes of Wrath, plot

John Steinbeck quote

John Steinbeck family

John Steinbeck
birthplace:

John Steinbeck review

John Steinbeck (1902–68)
most famous novels:
 Of Mice and Men
 The Grapes of Wrath (Pulitzer Prize, 1939)

✔ *In a formal outline, you must have at least two items at each level—you can't have a I without a II, an A without a B, and so on.*

✔ *A formal outline is best when you have to show it to someone else, such as a teacher or classmate. For your own use, feel free to use a more informal outline.*

IT'S AS EASY AS I, II, III

A good way to start planning your report is to make an **outline**. In a formal outline, you list all your main topics with **Roman numerals (I, II, III)**. Subtopics are indented and listed with capital letters. Then, supporting details are indented further and listed with **Arabic numerals (1, 2, 3)**. Finally, details that support those details are indented even further and listed with small letters.

Let's say you want to do a report on the author John Steinbeck. You might set up your outline like this:

The Life and Work of John Steinbeck

I. Biographical Information ← *Main topic*
   A. Early Years ← *Subtopic*
      1. Born in California in 1902 ← *Supporting*
      2. Attended Stanford University *details*
      3. Worked at menial jobs
   B. Middle Life
      1. Achieved success with <u>Tortilla Flat</u> ← *Supporting*
      2. Won Pulitzer Prize for <u>The Grapes of Wrath</u> *details*
   C. Later Years
      1. Traveled in United States and Mexico
      2. Won Nobel Prize for Literature
      3. Died in New York in 1968

II. Literary Work
   A. Major Novels
      1. <u>Of Mice and Men</u>
      2. <u>The Grapes of Wrath</u>
      3. <u>East of Eden</u>
   B. Literary Themes
      1. Focus on simple rural people
        a) relationship to land
        b) struggle for justice
      2. Biblical titles and themes

Outlines can be very helpful for nonfiction writing. However, when you're doing creative writing, an outline can block your creative flow.

TAKE TIME TO MANAGE YOUR TIME

Now you've read about all kinds of great information resources: the library, reference sources, computers. You've read about how to take notes and how to make an outline. But those resources won't help you much unless you know some good **study strategies** too.

Some of these strategies will work for you, and some might not. Use the ones you feel comfortable with.

Keep an Assignment Notebook

Have you ever woken up one morning and realized that you had forgotten to do a homework assignment due that day? We've all had that sinking feeling.

You can keep track of your homework assignments and projects with an *assignment notebook.* (It's good to use a small book, so that you can easily carry it around with you.)

keep in mind

It's a good idea to leave a few extra days at the end, in case you run into unexpected delays.

• • •

Make sure to check off each step as you complete it. This reminder will show you what you've already done and what's still left to do . . . and it's very satisfying!

- Write down each homework assignment as soon as you get it. You might forget something important if you don't!
- Include all the important information: what class the assignment is for, the due date, the pages to be read, the length of written assignments, and so on.
- Before you close your notebook, picture yourself doing the assignment. What books and other resources will you need to complete it?
- Before leaving school, go over the day's assignments. Make sure to take home all the materials you'll need.
- Hand in report.

129

Make a Checklist

A **checklist** can come in handy for planning long-term projects. Sometimes there are just too many details to keep them all in your mind at once!

In making your checklist, think about the goal you want to accomplish. Figure out what steps you'll need to accomplish that goal, and how long each one will take.

In your assignment notebook, write down the steps to be taken and the dates to complete each one. List your steps in the order in which you'll do them. For example, if your goal is to finish a research report, your checklist might look like this:

Research report due June 2

Step	Date
Do basic research on topic.	May 1–9 ✔
Get books from library.	May 11 ✔
Prepare working outline.	May 12–15 ✔
Go back and do additional research as necessary.	May 16–21
Write first draft.	May 22
Ask Peter and Maribel for comments on draft.	May 24–27
Revise draft.	May 28
Put together bibliography.	May 29
Type final draft.	June 2
Hand in report.	

Use a Reading Method

One of the best of all study strategies is knowing how to **read effectively:** knowing what information is important and how to take notes about it.

You can use a number of methods to read effectively. One is the SQ3R method, which you read about earlier.

Another method is called **PROTO. PROTO** is an acronym for five basic steps:

1. **Preview**. Preview the material by scanning the title and major headings. This step will give you a good overview of what you'll be reading.

2. **Read**. Read the entire text. Identify the most important points in each section. If there's something you don't understand, look at the headings again and reread that section.

3. **Organize**. After you've read the material once, decide how you want to organize it in your notes. For example, you might organize historical information in chronological order. Scientific information might be organized by classification or by cause and effect.

4. **Take Notes**. Record the important points of each section, organizing your notes according to the scheme you chose in the previous step.

5. **Overview**. Read through your notes again to form an overall summary of what you've read. Make sure you've included all the important points.

more **INFO**

For more on the SQ-3R method *see page 44.*

CURE YOUR TEST ANXIETY!

Have you ever sat down to take a test and gotten a case of "test anxiety"—sweaty palms, a fluttery stomach, and a brain that feels like it's been frozen in a block of ice? Don't be ashamed to admit it! Everyone has.

Mainly, test anxiety stems from a lack of self-confidence. The best way to build your self-confidence, of course, is to know the material very well. Even if you know the material, however, you'll probably do even better if you use some basic test-taking strategies. Here are a few of the most important ones:

▶ **Preview the test.** Take a quick look at the entire test. See what it covers and how long it is.

▶ **Plan your time.** Your teacher will tell you how much time you have to finish the test. After you've finished previewing the test, you'll know how many questions there are. Decide how much time to spend on each section; keep track of the time as you work.

▶ **Follow directions.** Listen carefully to any directions read aloud and read the directions at the beginning of each section of the test. Don't start on a section until you're sure of what you're supposed to do.

▶ **Read questions carefully.** Key words—such as *when, where, why, different from, same as, before, and after*—will help you figure out exactly what the question is asking.

▶ **Don't get hung up on a question.** Almost every test has some hard questions. If you can't think of an answer, skip it and return to it later.

▶ **Check your work.** When you've finished answering all the questions, use whatever time you have left to go back and check your work.

▶ **Learn from your mistakes.** After the test has been graded, look carefully at the questions you have answered incorrectly. Figure out why you got each one wrong and then study the material again . . . so that next time you'll get the answers right!

PART FIVE

Grammar, Mechanics, and Usage

CONTENTS

Grammar 136–197

Sentences 138
Nouns 148
Pronouns 154
Verbs 162
Adjectives & Adverbs 178
Prepositions, Conjunctions & Interjections . .188
Clauses & Verbals 194

Capitalization 198–201

Punctuation 202–210

Periods 202
Question Marks & Exclamation Points 203
Commas 204
Apostrophes & Quotation Marks 207
Italics, Underlining & Colons 208
Semicolons & Hyphens 209
Dashes & Parentheses 210

Answer Key .212–219

The answer to the questions:
Why should you care about grammar and usage? (And what are mechanics, anyhow?)

Writing is a little like building a house—it can be hard work, but when you're done, you've created something that didn't exist before. If you want to write—and writing can be one of the most exciting activities you'll ever do—then you need to know what the rules are. This part of your handbook gives you the tools you need to do the job right.

Sure, improving your grammar and usage may not be the most fun you'll ever have. It's nuts-and-bolts work—the basics. Writing is the same as any other craft: to do it well, you need to master the basics. If you want to play the piano, you have to practice the scales. If you want to act, you have to memorize your lines. If you want to play a game, you need to learn how the pieces work and what the rules are. It's the same with writing.

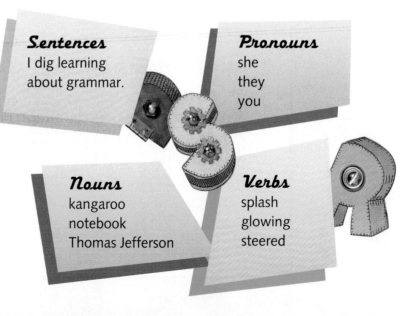

Sentences
I dig learning about grammar.

Pronouns
she
they
you

Nouns
kangaroo
notebook
Thomas Jefferson

Verbs
splash
glowing
steered

. . . Oh, and you can get a definition for **Mechanics** (and for **Grammar** and **Usage** too) in the margin to the right.

Learning about grammar, usage, capitalization, and punctuation gives you tools you'll need to use to write effectively. Think of this part of the book as an instruction manual—so that you can start putting those tools to work! You'll learn about these things and more:

CHECK
it
OUT!

✔ **What exactly is grammar?** *Rules about how language is arranged.*

✔ **What are mechanics:** Mechanics *refers to the way parts of language work together. Think of it as similar to how the mechanisms in a car engine work together.*

✔ **What's usage?** *The way people use words when they talk and when they write.*

Prepositions
from
until
under

Adjectives/Adverbs
glamorous
mighty
cheaply

Capitalization
earth/Earth
bob/Bob
the kinks/The Kinks

Conjunctions
and
but
yet

Interjections
Whoa!
C'mon!
No way!

Clauses/Verbals
running around
like crazy

Punctuation
! ? : ; " ( ) —

Perry wants a cracker.
May I have a cracker?
I'm starving!
Get me a cracker, please.

SENTENCES

A sentence is a group of words that expresses a complete thought.

Sentences are probably the most useful and important units of communication we have. Most everything you say is in sentence form. Every sentence is a group of words, but not every group of words is a sentence.

A complete sentence has:

▶ a *subject*—the person, place, or thing the sentence is about.

▶ a *predicate*—which tells what action the subject does.

Here's a complete, simple sentence:

Lucy *brought home a parrot.*

    subject   predicate

As you know, plenty of sentences are more complicated than this. Luckily, because you have been speaking and reading for years, you're probably a sentence expert already. Now it's just a matter of learning the names and reasons for what you do in sentences. You'll see how to form more elaborate sentences later on.

Types of Sentences

Since sentences cover so much ground, you won't be surprised to hear that there are different types of sentences. Each type does a certain job, and has a certain form.

A **declarative** sentence makes a statement and ends with a period.

> *Lucy's parrot squawks when she's on the phone.*

An **interrogative** sentence asks a question and ends with a question mark.

> *Has Lucy tried to train her parrot?*

An **exclamatory** sentence expresses strong feeling and ends with an exclamation mark.

> *That bird is just too loud!*

An **imperative** sentence gives a command or makes a request and ends with a period.

> *Try to see the humor in it.*

For more on punctuating sentences, see pages 202–203.

 **RACTICE** Rewrite each sentence, adding correct end punctuation. Label each sentence *declarative, interrogative, exclamatory,* or *imperative.*

1. Lucy thinks her parrot gets jealous when she's on the phone
2. Have you ever heard of a problem like this
3. Putting a cover over his cage is supposed to calm Perry down
4. Try putting a sheet over his cage
5. I think Perry is a beautiful parrot
6. His tail feathers are a pretty color
7. Have you spoken to any parrot experts about this problem
8. What a strange situation this is
9. Do Lucy's roommates complain about Perry
10. Find out whether other pet birds behave this way

139

SUBJECTS AND PREDICATES

You already know that every sentence has a subject and a predicate. The **subject** names what or whom a sentence is about. The **predicate** is the part of the sentence that tells what action the subject does, is, or is like.

<u>The first mechanical clock</u> **was invented in China.**
          subject   predicate

Here are examples of predicates that tell what action the subject does, is, or is like:

The Chinese **invented paper and block printing.**
            (tells what the subject did)

The ancient Chinese **were primarily farmers.**
            (tells what the subject was)

The ancient Chinese **were scientifically advanced.**
            (tells what the subject was like)

In an interrogative sentence (a sentence that is a question), the subject usually comes right in the middle of the predicate. The predicate is usually divided by the subject.

subject
Do *you* **know any other Chinese inventions?**
                predicate

**RACTICE** Rewrite each sentence. Draw one line under the subject and two lines under the predicate.

1. Many early scientific inventions came from China.
2. I-Hsing designed a water clock.
3. Chang Heng invented an earthquake-measuring machine.
4. The manufacture of silk dates back to early China.
5. One of China's most important contributions was the compass.
6. Was the abacus introduced during the Sung dynasty?
7. The Chinese discovered herbal medicine.
8. Another important Chinese invention was the horse harness.
9. During the Shang dynasty people used cowrie shells for money.
10. When was the first printed book produced in China?

Simple Subjects
and Simple Predicates

The **simple subject** of a sentence is the main word or words in the complete subject. It names what or whom the sentence is about.

subject

Many European **explorers** *came to North America in the 1700s.*

simple
subject

The **simple predicate** of a sentence is the main word or words in the complete predicate. It tells what action the subject does or what the subject is or is like.

predicate

The Europeans **brought** *horses to North America.*

simple
predicate

CHECK it OUT!

✔ *You can't always see the subject in imperative sentences.*

subject

[You] Shut the door, please.

The simple subject you is often not stated. It's understood that the word you is to be included.

P RACTICE
Rewrite each sentence. Draw one line under the *simple subject* and two lines under the *simple predicate*.

1. Native Americans did not have horses until the late 1600s.
2. Spanish explorers introduced sheep and horses to the Southwest.
3. Tell us why many Navajo raised large flocks of sheep.
4. Sheep provided food, wool, and many other helpful products.
5. Some of the Plains peoples of Texas had horses in the 1690s.
6. Did the Navajo adopt horses from the Spanish?
7. The Blackfoot Nation used horses for carrying supplies.
8. Describe how the Comanche raised horses on the Great Plains.
9. When did the Lakota begin hunting on horseback?
10. By 1790, horses had spread throughout North America.

keep in mind

Some compound sentences may need a comma before the conjunction to keep the meaning clear.

For more on commas, see pages 204–206.

Compound Subjects and Compound Predicates

A **compound subject** is two or more simple subjects with the same predicate.

simple subjects
Alison *and* **Maya** *gave a presentation about the Mongol Empire.*
compound subject

A **compound predicate** is two or more simple predicates with the same subject.

simple predicates
Genghis Khan **united** *and* **ruled** *the many Mongol tribes.*
compound predicate

Compound subjects and compound predicates may be joined by conjunctions such as: *and, but, or, either . . . or, neither . . . nor, both . . . and,* and *not only . . . but also.*

compound subject
Both *Alison* **and** *Maya worked on a map of the Mongol Empire.*

**PRACTICE** Rewrite each sentence. Draw one line under the *complete subject* and two lines under the *complete predicate*. **Then write** whether the sentence has a *compound subject* **or** *compound predicate*.

1. The Mongol Empire was the largest land empire in history.
2. China and Iran were part of the empire.
3. Mongol tribes lived in tents and moved from place to place.
4. The tribes feuded and fought for many centuries.
5. Genghis Khan and Kublai Khan were both fierce leaders.

Phrases

A **phrase** is any group of words in a sentence that:

- ▶ acts as a single unit.
- ▶ has a subject or a predicate, but not both.

You can add meaning and interest to a simple sentence by using a phrase. Since a phrase doesn't have both a subject and a predicate, a phrase can't work alone as a sentence.

To identify a phrase in a sentence, find the simple sentence. Then see if there is an attached group of words acting as a single unit, with either a subject or predicate in it—that's a phrase.

      simple sentence   phrase added

Rhonda brought home a pineapple **in a gigantic bag.**

Clauses

A **clause** is also a group of words. Clauses have both a subject and a predicate.

When a clause can form a complete sentence on its own, it's called an **independent clause.**

    independent clause   independent clause

Medieval feasts were elaborate affairs, *and* **many guests attended.**

Dependent clauses can't stand alone. Dependent clauses begin with words like *although* or *because,* which link them to independent clauses. They can come either before or after an independent clause.

                  dependent clause

The princess sneaked her puppy into the castle, **although it was forbidden.**

For more on kinds of **phrases,** *see pages 196–197.*

• • •

For more on **clauses,** *see page 194.*

PRACTICE Rewrite each sentence. Underline all phrases and circle all clauses. Label each clause *independent* or *dependent.*

1. Holding her puppy Sir Lancelot, Princess Lillian ran into the castle.
2. Princess Lillian named him after a famous knight because she loves history.
3. The puppy is not allowed into the castle, but Lillian sneaks him in.
4. Allergic to dogs, Queen Penelope gets angry at Lillian.
5. Lillian tries to keep Lancelot in her room so he won't bother the queen.

Compound Sentences

As you know, a simple sentence contains a subject and a predicate. Sometimes a sentence has two or more subjects and two or more predicates. This is called a **compound sentence.**

subject   predicate   subject   predicate
A lord *presided over his castle,* but **the cook** *ruled the kitchen.*

independent clause   independent clause

As you can see, a compound sentence joins two or more independent clauses. The clauses are usually joined by a conjunction, such as *and, but,* or *or.*

> *A lord presided over his castle,* **but** *the cook ruled the kitchen.*

Two independent clauses can also be joined by a semicolon.

> *A lord presided over his castle*; *the cook ruled the kitchen.*

**RACTICE** Rewrite each sentence. Add a comma or semicolon if needed. Label the sentence *simple* or *compound.*

1. The main meal is served mid-morning, but it could last for two or three hours.
2. Meat dishes were popular they included venison, pheasant, and partridge.
3. People ate with their fingers or the points of their knives.
4. People sometimes used spoons to eat soup but forks were not introduced until much later.
5. The lord, his family, and their guests sat at a separate table.
6. Meals consisted of several courses each course included a variety of dishes.
7. Young boys from noble families carried the meals to the table.
8. Food was served on thick slices of bread called trenchers.
9. Servants threw out the leftover trenchers and beggars outside the castle felt lucky to get them.
10. The pieces of bread were soaked with juices from the meat this soggy food was later called Yorkshire pudding.

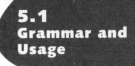

Complex Sentences

A sentence made up of an independent clause and one or more dependent clauses is called a **complex sentence**.

When he was 17 years old, *Marco Polo left Venice.*
　　　　dependent clause　　　　　　independent clause

Dependent clauses are introduced by words that describe how the meaning of the dependent clause relates to the meaning of the independent clause. These words are called **subordinating conjunctions**.

COMMON SUBORDINATING CONJUNCTIONS			
after	though	although	unless
as	until	because	when
before	whenever	if	where
since	whereas	than	wherever

A comma usually comes after a dependent clause at the beginning of a sentence. When the dependent clause comes at the end of a sentence, you sometimes don't need a comma.

dependent clause at beginning—with comma
When he reached China, *he stayed for almost 20 years.*
subordinating
conjunction

dependent clause at end—no comma
He stayed in the city we now call Beijing **because that's where the action was**.
　　　　　　　　　　　subordinating
　　　　　　　　　　　conjunction

PRACTICE

Rewrite each sentence. Draw one line under each dependent clause and two lines under each subordinating conjunction.

1. Before Marco Polo traveled to China, Europeans knew little about eastern Asia.
2. While he was living in Beijing, he worked with Kublai Khan, the emperor of China.
3. Marco Polo wrote a book about the Far East when he returned to Venice in 1295.
4. Very few Europeans had been to China, so Polo's book gave Europe its first detailed view of China and its neighbors.
5. After Marco Polo returned, trade increased between Europe and China, especially the trade in spices and silk.

Sentence Problems: Fragments and Run-ons

A **sentence fragment** is a group of words that is only part of a sentence. A complete sentence has both a subject and a predicate. A fragment doesn't have both, so does not express a complete thought. You can correct a fragment by adding the missing part.

Walked on the moon.
(fragment: missing a subject)

The astronaut Neil Armstrong
(fragment: missing a predicate)

The astronaut Neil Armstrong walked on the moon.
(complete sentence)

Run-on sentences are trying to do too much. A run-on is actually two or more sentences disguised as one. Often, the problem is missing punctuation, or a comma where a period should be. Just as you can't keep talking without taking a breath, you can't keep writing a sentence without adding a period.

> *The first person in space was a Russian cosmonaut named Yuri Gagarin, the first American in space was Alan Shepard.*

You can correct a run-on sentence by dividing it into two sentences, or adding a conjunction—a word like *and* or *but*. (If you add a conjunction, you might need to rewrite the sentence somewhat to make it flow.) Or you might try adding a subordinating conjunction like *though* or *unless.* If it's a compound sentence, you can also choose to fix it by adding a semicolon.

Look at this run-on sentence:

The first person in space was a Russian cosmonaut, Yuri Gagarin the first American in space was Alan Shepard.

You could fix this run-on by dividing it into two:

The first person in space was a Russian cosmonaut, Yuri Gagarin. The first American in space was Alan Shepard.

Adding a conjunction:

*The first person in space was a Russian cosmonaut, Yuri Gagarin, **but** the first American in space was Alan Shepard.*

Adding a subordinating conjunction:

*The first person in space was a Russian cosmonaut, Yuri Gagarin, **whereas** the first American in space was Alan Shepard.*

Adding a semicolon:

The first person in space was a Russian cosmonaut, Yuri Gagarin; the first American in space was Alan Shepard.

more
INFO

For more on **conjunctions,** *see* page 192.

• • •

For more on **semicolons,** *see* page 209.

PRACTICE Rewrite each example, and label each as a *complete sentence, fragment,* or *run-on.* Rewrite each fragment as a complete sentence. Revise each run-on to make correct sentences.

1. Astronaut John Glenn orbited the earth in 1962, he went around the earth three times, but he returned safely.

2. The Gemini Space Program began in 1965.

3. Virgil Grissom and John Young in the first Gemini spacecraft.

4. There were fifteen Gemini spacecraft, they were used to prepare for a trip to the moon.

5. In 1968 astronauts made the first manned space flight around the moon.

NOUNS

A noun is a word that names a person, place, or thing.

From aardvarks to xylophones to zippers, from freedom to the Gulf Stream to Bart Simpson, the words for everyone and everywhere and everything in the world are **nouns**—so you won't be surprised to hear that there are many kinds of nouns. For starters, all nouns are either **common nouns** or **proper nouns**.

Common nouns name people, places, or things in general.

> *dancer, mountains, rock band*

Proper nouns name particular people, places, and things.

> *Fred Astaire, Blue Ridge Mountains, Pearl Jam*

The word *name* is a common noun, but your own name is a proper noun. Like your name, proper nouns always begin with capital letters.

Name: **Sylvia Kim Epps**

common noun

proper noun

Those are the basics. You'll find out about other ways to group nouns in coming pages.

CONCRETE/ABSTRACT NOUNS

Common nouns are either *concrete or abstract.*

A **concrete noun** names something that can be seen or touched.

> The **boy** dashed across the **field** on a **horse**.

> When my **grandmother** gets sick, she lives on **vitamin pills, orange juice, tea,** and **toast.**

> Your **dog** chased my **skateboard** down the longest **hill** in **town.**

An **abstract noun** names something that cannot be seen or touched, such as an idea or a feeling.

> **Friendship** requires **trust** and **affection.**

> The philosopher said that **citizenship** is the highest **good.**

> Your **beauty** is enhanced by your **intelligence** and **sense of humor.**

✔ *Some concrete nouns name things that can't literally be seen or touched—elf or unicorn, for instance. But since* elf *and* unicorn *are things you could imagine seeing, they are still considered concrete nouns.*

✔ Concrete *itself is a concrete noun.*

PRACTICE

On a separate piece of paper, write down the nouns in each sentence. Circle each proper noun and underline each common noun. Then label each common noun *concrete* or *abstract.*

1. Tony and Kim led a group of students up Mount Greylock.
2. The mountain is one of the tallest in New England.
3. Before the expedition, the climbers learned how to pack their backpacks.
4. The trip was a challenge for Gail, because her boots were new.
5. At the top, Tony and Kim felt full of freedom and excitement, but Gail felt only fatigue.

SINGULAR/PLURAL NOUNS

A **singular noun** names one person, place, or thing: *singer, jungle, box, fear.*

A **plural noun** names more than one person, place, or thing: *singers, jungles, boxes, fears.*

Most plural nouns end in s, but there are plenty of exceptions. Here's a chart that will help you with plural nouns:

Singular Nouns	To Form Plural	Examples
Most singular nouns	add **s**	*singer, jungle, box, fear* *singers, jungles, boxes, fears*
Nouns ending with **s, ss, x, z, zz, ch, sh**	add **es**	*loss, box, dish* *losses, boxes, dishes*
Nouns ending with **consonant and y**	change **y** to **i** and add **es**	*lady, buddy, hobby* *ladies, buddies, hobbies*
Nouns ending with **vowel and y**	add **s**	*ray, monkey, alloy* *rays, monkeys, alloys*
Nouns ending with **f, ff,** or **fe**	most add **s**; some change **f** to **v** and add **es**	*chief, skiff, elf, wife* *chiefs, skiffs, elves, wives*
Nouns ending with **vowel and o**	add **s**	*studio, video, duo* *studios, videos, duos*
Nouns ending with **consonant and o**	most add **es**; some add **s**	*hero, potato, solo* *heroes, potatoes, solos*
Some irregular nouns	change spelling	*woman, mouse, ox* *women, mice, oxen*
A few irregular nouns	keep the same spelling	*sheep, trout, moose* *sheep, trout, moose*

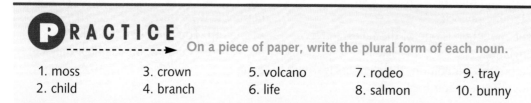

PRACTICE
------------> On a piece of paper, write the plural form of each noun.

1. moss
2. child
3. crown
4. branch
5. volcano
6. life
7. rodeo
8. salmon
9. tray
10. bunny

POSSESSIVE NOUNS

To show who has, or possesses, something, you use **possessive nouns**. Possessive nouns can be **singular** or **plural**.

To create the possessive form of a **singular** noun, you usually add an **apostrophe** and an **s** to the end of the word:
> **catcher's** *mitt*, **Stephen's** *key chain*, **Mexico's** *rivers*

To create plural **possessive** nouns, add an **s** and an **apostrophe**:
> **states'** *rights*, **swans'** *beaks*, **Beatles'** *songs*

. . . except when the plural noun doesn't end in **s**. Then put the **apostrophe** before the **s**, like in the singular form:
> **oxen's** *yokes*, **children's** *clothing*

When two or more people, places, or things possess something together, add the ending after the last one named:
> **Mom and Dad's** *car;* **Geri, Suki, and Will's** *friend*

To create the possessive form of a proper noun, add an **apostrophe** and an **s** to the end of the word. This is true even when a proper noun ends with **s***:*
> **Imiri's** *backpack*, **Jess's** *book*

. . . except for some proper nouns ending with a vowel and **s**. Then just add an **apostrophe**:
> **Hercules'** *adventures*, **Herodotus'** *writings*

 **PRACTICE** Rewrite each sentence creating the possessive form of the noun or nouns from parentheses.

1. (Tasha) dream is to be a pirate.
2. She read about (Blackbeard) booty.
3. (New Mexico) mountains contain hidden stashes of gold, Tasha says.
4. According to legend, the (bandits) treasure has never been found.
5. In (Mom and Dad) opinion, she's wasting her time.

For more on verb forms, *see page 175.*

COLLECTIVE NOUNS

A **collective noun** names two or more people or things that you refer to as a group.

> team, flock, class, herd, audience, crowd, family, committee, swarm, orchestra, club

When a collective noun acts as a single unit, use a singular verb form with it:

> Our **team loves** *the coach.*
> The **flock nests** *in mangrove trees.*

But collective nouns can be tricky. Sometimes a collective noun is meant to refer to the individual members of a group. Then its meaning is plural, and you use a plural verb form:

> The **herd run** *in different directions.*
> The **orchestra play** *their separate instruments.*

keep in mind

Pairs of nouns can work as compound adjectives too. Like compound nouns, compound adjectives function as one word: **middle-school** *students,* **ten-inning** *game. Like all adjectives, they work to identify or describe.*

COMPOUND NOUNS

A **compound noun** is a group of two or more words that work together as a noun. Some compound nouns are written as separate words, some are hyphenated, and some are written as one word.

separate words	*diving board, water hose, combat boots*
hyphenated	*hand-me-downs, ex-Marine, yo-yo*
one word	*skateboard, notebooks, ultrasound*

 PRACTICE On a separate piece of paper, rewrite the compound nouns in each sentence.

1. Georgia keeps her snake in a fishtank.
2. Michelle hit a home run over the fence.
3. Billy hung his tie-dyes on the clothesline.
4. I sold raffle tickets to friends on my block.
5. My brother-in-law works at the lighthouse.

APPOSITIVES

A noun or pronoun that identifies or gives information about another noun in the sentence is called an **appositive.** An appositive most often follows the noun it identifies.

> *The guy I have a crush on,* **Shane,** *sat next to me at the bus stop.*

> *Sitting next to me at the bus stop was the guy I had a crush on,* **Shane.**

An appositive can have more than one word. Then it's called an **appositive phrase.**

> *Beethoven,* **a brilliant composer,** *went deaf toward the end of his life.*

Most appositives are set off from the rest of the sentence with commas. However, if the sentence would not mean the same thing without the appositive, do not use commas.

> *My favorite singer,* **Neil Young,** *was in a band called Crazy Horse.*

(The meaning of the sentence would be the same without the name *Neil Young*. It's clear what you're talking about—your favorite singer.)

> *The singer* **Neil Young** *was in the band Crazy Horse.*

(Without the name *Neil Young,* it's not clear who you're talking about—it could be any singer.)

keep in mind

Unless it comes at the end of a sentence, never set off an appositive with only one comma. Put a comma both before and after an appositive.

PRACTICE Rewrite each sentence on a separate piece of paper. Underline each appositive or appositive phrase. Insert commas where needed. Then draw an arrow from the appositive or appositive phrase to the noun it modifies.

1. New Mexico the "Land of Enchantment" has many lovely tourist attractions.
2. Santa Fe my favorite city is its capital.
3. A collection of southwestern art is housed in the Palace of Governors, a museum there.
4. The Palace of Governors the oldest government building in the United States was built in 1610.
5. My best friend Manuel wants to go there next summer.

PRONOUNS

A pronoun is a word that takes the place of a noun or a group of words acting as a noun.

Imagine that you're telling someone about a basketball game you and a friend watched on TV. Would you tell the story like this?

> "Gloria came over to see the game because Gloria is a big fan of Patrick Ewing. Patrick Ewing really inspired Patrick Ewing's teammates that day; the teammates played the best game of the teammates' careers."

Definitely not! You would probably tell it something like this:

> "Gloria came over to see the game because she is a big fan of Patrick Ewing. He really inspired his teammates that day; they played the best game of their careers."

As you can see, you often use words to stand in for nouns; these words are called **pronouns**. The words that the pronouns stand in for are called **antecedents**. In the previous example, the words *she, he, his, they,* and *their* are pronouns, because they stand in for other words.

There are several different types of pronouns. You use them according to the type of word you want them to stand in for.

PERSONAL PRONOUNS

Personal pronouns stand in for people or things. They're the most commonly used pronouns.

When the personal pronoun is the *subject* of the sentence, it's called the **subject pronoun**:

> Carlos volunteers at the library.
> **He** volunteers at the library.

> The library is in Brooklyn.
> **It** is in Brooklyn.

SUBJECT PRONOUNS	
Singular	*Plural*
I	we
you	you
he, she, it	they

When the personal pronoun is the *object* of a verb, it's called an **object pronoun**:

> Carlos gave the book to Jerry.
> Carlos gave the book to **him**.

> The librarian helped Jerry and Inez pick out books.
> The librarian helped **them** pick out books.

OBJECT PRONOUNS	
Singular	*Plural*
me	us
you	you
him, her, it	them

P RACTICE

Rewrite each sentence, replacing the underlined word or words with a personal pronoun. Label the pronoun *subject* or *object*.

1. <u>Mrs. Szafir</u> is the school librarian.
2. People visit <u>the library</u> all the time.
3. <u>The students</u> know how to use the card catalog.
4. Mrs. Szafir showed <u>Inez</u> where to find the audiotapes.
5. <u>Jacob</u> asked if the library had any books about soccer.
6. The librarian showed Jacob where to find <u>books about soccer</u>.
7. <u>My friends and I</u> go to the library every week.
8. Mrs. Szafir always helps <u>my friends and me</u>.
9. <u>The Library of Congress</u> is the largest library in the world.
10. I told <u>Stephanie</u> that I will work there someday.

PRONOUN-ANTECEDENT AGREEMENT

keep in mind

Make sure it's clear what your pronouns are referring to. Sometimes it may be necessary to retain the original noun or even to rewrite the sentence. For instance, in the sentence "Helen told Eve that she was a very nice person," does "she" refer to Helen or to Eve? To clear it up, you might rewrite it: "Helen told Eve that she, Eve, was a very nice person" or " 'You're a very nice person,' Helen told Eve."

As you've seen, a pronoun is a word that takes the place of a noun or a group of words acting as a noun. The word or group of words that the pronoun replaces is called the **antecedent**.

Because the pronoun is taking the place of the antecedent, it should have the same features as the antecedent. The pronoun should agree with its antecedent in **person** (first, second, or third person), **number** (singular or plural), and **gender** (masculine, feminine, or neuter). Plural pronouns are always neuter.

Martin Luther King, Jr. *believed in nonviolence, and* **he** *never wavered from that belief.*

(third person, singular, masculine)

Did **the students** *receive* **their** *test results today?*

(third person, plural)

PRACTICE

Rewrite each pair of sentences, filling in the correct pronoun. For each pronoun, circle the antecedent and draw an arrow from the pronoun to its antecedent.

1. Ashanti collects autographs. ___ has over 250 of ___.
2. Ashanti treasures his autographs. ___ keeps ___ in a box.
3. Some autographs are rare. ___ are worth a lot of money.
4. Ashanti likes sports autographs the best. ___ especially likes to collect basketball players' signatures.
5. His sister collects coins. ___ thinks autographs are silly.
6. Ashanti and I disagree with her. ___ both think his hobby is great.
7. Tara wanted Shaquille O'Neal's autograph. ___ wrote ___ to ask for ___.
8. Norah keeps track of both Norah collections. ___ likes to compare ___.
9. Norah and I are old friends. ___ spend a lot of time together.
10. Mr. Crome looked at Tara's collection yesterday. ___ offered ___ one-hundred dollars for ___.

POSSESSIVE PRONOUNS

A **possessive pronoun** shows who or what has or owns something else. Some possessive pronouns come before a noun.

> **My** *dog likes to bark when I play my records.*
> *The cat stared at* **its** *reflection in the water.*

Other possessive pronouns stand alone; they do not have to come before a noun.

> *That basketball is* **mine.**
> *I've never seen that jacket before; it must be* **yours.**

keep in mind

Possessive pronouns **never** *have apostrophes. Don't confuse possessive pronouns such as* **its, your,** *or* **their** *with the contractions* **it's, you're,** *and* **they're.**

POSSESSIVE PRONOUNS

Used Before Nouns		Stand Alone	
Singular	*Plural*	*Singular*	*Plural*
my	our	mine	ours
your	your	yours	yours
his, her, its	their	his, her, its	theirs

For more on contractions, see page 207.

PRACTICE Rewrite each sentence, replacing the underlined words with a possessive pronoun.

1. <u>Sharryn's</u> brother Michael plays in a rock group.
2. "Wildfire" is <u>the group's</u> name.
3. The bass guitar is <u>Michael's</u>.
4. The drum set, though, is <u>Sharryn and Michael's</u>.
5. I really like <u>the song's</u> melody.

157

REFLEXIVE AND INTENSIVE PRONOUNS

✔A pronoun ending in -self *should never stand alone; it must have an antecedent in the same sentence. It is not correct to say, for example, "Grace and myself went to the movies." Instead, you would use the subject pronoun I.*

A **reflexive pronoun** directs the action of the verb back to the sentence's subject. It always ends in *-self* or *-selves.*

> My sister figured out how to fix the bike **herself.**
> I gave **myself** credit for not getting angry at him.

An **intensive pronoun** looks just like a reflexive pronoun, but it has a different use. As its name would suggest, an intensive pronoun adds emphasis to a noun or a pronoun.

> I **myself** would never go see that movie.
> Justice **itself** is the political movement's goal.

REFLEXIVE AND INTENSIVE PRONOUNS

Singular	Plural
myself	ourselves
yourself	yourselves
himself, herself, itself	themselves

A reflexive pronoun adds new information to a sentence. An intensive pronoun merely emphasizes its antecedent; it can be removed without changing the meaning of the sentence. For example, in the sentence "She **herself** admitted I was correct," you can remove the intensive pronoun **herself** without changing the meaning of the sentence.

PRACTICE
Rewrite each sentence. Underline and label each pronoun *reflexive* **or** *intensive.*

1. The pilot herself checked the plane's engines before we left the airport.
2. The flight attendants caught themselves as the plane dropped and recovered.
3. The plane steadied itself and continued uneventfully.
4. One passenger checked himself for splashed coffee.
5. The president of the airline himself apologized to us for the rough flight.

INDEFINITE PRONOUNS

Most pronouns have specific antecedents; they refer to particular people, places, or things. **Indefinite pronouns**, though, do not refer to someone or something specific. Indefinite pronouns can be either singular or plural.

INDEFINITE PRONOUNS				
Singular	another	everybody	neither	one
	anybody	everyone	nobody	somebody
	anyone	everything	no one	someone
	each	much	nothing	something
	either			
Plural	both	few	many	others
	several			
Singular or Plural	all	some	most	none
	any			

Use a singular verb with a singular indefinite pronoun; use a plural verb with a plural indefinite pronoun.

> **Everyone likes** *that band's music.* (singular)
> **Many are** *excited about the concert.* (plural)

Some indefinite pronouns can take either a singular or a plural verb, depending on whether the phrase that follows the pronoun is singular or plural:

> **Most** *of the game* **is** *still to be played.* (singular)
> **Most** *of the players* **are** *still on the bench.* (plural)

keep in mind

In the past, masculine pronouns were used to refer to both males and females as a group. This is no longer acceptable. Instead, use both a male and female pronoun, or rewrite the sentence into the plural. For instance, instead of writing "Everyone had *his own locker," you might write, "Everyone* had *his or her own locker," or "All* had *their own lockers."*

PRACTICE

Rewrite each sentence, choosing the correct verb form from the parentheses. Draw a line under the indefinite pronoun.

1. Nearly everyone at school (is, are) dressed strangely.
2. Somebody (has, have) declared today "Back to the '70s" Day.
3. Many (put, puts) on bellbottom pants.
4. One of my friends (wear, wears) a fringed leather vest.
5. Several (look, looks) like the cast of an old TV show.

INTERROGATIVE AND DEMONSTRATIVE PRONOUNS

Interrogative Pronouns

A sentence that asks a question and ends with a question mark is called an interrogative sentence. An **interrogative pronoun** (*who, whom, which, whose, what*) introduces an interrogative sentence.

Use *who* as the subject of the sentence:
> **Who** *is reading that book?*

Use *whom* as the object of the verb, or the object of a preposition:
> **Whom** *did you call? With* **whom** *did you go to the game?*

Use *which* and *what* to refer to things:
> **Which** *knapsack is the biggest one?* **What** *is inside it?*

Use *whose* to indicate possession:
> **Whose** *is this ball-point pen?*

Who's on first?

Demonstrative Pronouns

Demonstrative pronouns (*this, these, that, those*) point out specific people, places, or things. *This* and *these* point out something close; *that* and *those* point out something at a distance.

> **This** *is a delicious piece of pie.*
> **These** *are my sneakers.*
> **That** *is where we'll be by tonight.*
> **Those** *are the worst paintings I've ever seen.*

If the word *this, that, these,* or *those* comes directly before a noun rather than in place of a noun, it is functioning as an *adjective* (which modifies a noun) rather than as a pronoun.

> **These** *sneakers are mine.* (demonstrative adjective)
> **These** *are my sneakers.* (demonstrative pronoun)

keep in mind

Don't tack the words here *or* there *onto a demonstrative pronoun.* This *and* that *are all you need—not* this here *or* that there.
 Wrong: *I love* **this** *here pie.*
 Right: *I love* **this** *pie.*

PRACTICE Rewrite each sentence choosing the correct pronoun from the parentheses.

1. (Whose, Who) will be the leader of the discussion group?
2. (That, Those) is the table where we'll sit.
3. (Which, What) of the three topics will we discuss?
4. (Whose, Whom) is this notebook?
5. Are (this, those) the notes from last week's meeting?
6. With (who, whom) did you go on vacation?
7. Was (this, these) your idea?
8. Is (this, these) the best map to follow?
9. (That, Those) looks like the most detailed one.
10. Of these two roads, (which, what) do you think is quicker?

VERBS

A verb is a word that expresses action or a state of being.

Every sentence has a **verb**. Verbs make sentences spring into action. Imagine what happens on a movie set after the director calls, "Lights, camera, action!"

> The sky **is** dark, the villain **rides** into town, the horse **whinnies**, the sheriff **flashes** his badge, the villagers **are playing** cards.

All the bold-faced words above, which describe action, are verbs. Any time you want to express happening or being, you use a verb.

There are two basic types of verbs—**action verbs** and **linking verbs.**

ACTION VERBS

An **action verb** is a word that expresses just that —action. Anyone or anything can perform the action. An action might be physical, emotional, or mental.

> The paper airplane **soared** over the fence. (physical)
> The car **screeched** to a halt. (physical)
> David **loves** his mother. (emotional)
> They **realize** they are lost. (mental)

LINKING VERBS

A **linking verb** expresses a state of being. A linking verb connects, or links, the subject of the sentence to another word or phrase that identifies or describes that subject.

> *The soup* **is** *gazpacho.*   (Identifies)
> *The soup* **is** *delicious.*   (Describes)

COMMON LINKING VERBS

is	become	look
am	remain	sound
was	feel	taste
were	seem	appear
be	stay	smell
been	grow	

Some verbs may be used as either action or linking verbs, depending on whether the verb is expressing action or a state of being.

Action: *Josie* **smells** *the flowers.*
    (The verb is expressing an action.)

Linking: *The flower* **smells** *wonderful.*
    (The verb is expressing a state of being.)

PRACTICE On a separate piece of paper, write the verb in each sentence. Label each as an *action verb* or a *linking verb*.

1. Zen masters developed the Japanese tea ceremony.
2. The ceremony is rich in tradition.
3. The tea master acts as the host.
4. Each guest sips the tea exactly three times.
5. The tea tastes strong and slightly bitter.
6. It looks green and almost transparent.
7. Each guest wipes the rim of the tea bowl.
8. The tea master mixes the tea with a special whisk.
9. The first guest receives the bowl.
10. The tea ceremony seems quite slow and formal.

USING LINKING VERBS: PREDICATE NOUNS AND PREDICATE ADJECTIVES

Linking verbs live up to their name by *linking* the subject of a sentence with a noun or adjective in the rest of the sentence (the predicate).

When the verb links the subject to a noun, that noun is called a **predicate noun**. A predicate noun identifies the subject.

When the verb links the subject to an adjective, the adjective is called a **predicate adjective**. A predicate adjective describes the subject.

Predicate nouns:
> *J.R.R. Tolkien was* **a writer.**
> *The tree appeared to be* **a cypress.**

Predicate adjectives:
> *J.R.R. Tolkien was* **talented.**
> *The tree grew* **tall.**

PRACTICE ----▶ Rewrite each sentence on a separate piece of paper, and circle each linking verb. Draw a line under the predicate noun or predicate adjective and label it *PN* or *PA*.

1. J.R.R. Tolkien's real name is John Ronald Reuel Tolkien.
2. He was a professor of English language and literature.
3. Tolkien appeared dignified to his students.
4. He became famous all over the world for his novels.
5. His first novel was *The Hobbit*.
6. *The Hobbit* is a fantasy novel.
7. Bilbo Baggins is the main character of the story.
8. At first the plot of *The Hobbit* seems complicated.
9. Bilbo's companions are thirteen dwarfs.
10. The dwarfs' search for treasure appears fruitless.

TRANSITIVE AND INTRANSITIVE VERBS

An action verb that has a direct object is called a **transitive verb.** The verb is transferring its action onto someone or something else.

> *I **stubbed** my toe.*

An action verb that has no direct object is called an **intransitive verb**. With an intransitive verb, the action is complete without needing a direct object.

> *Delores **spoke**.*

Many verbs can be used as either transitive or intransitive verbs.

Transitive: *Dad **drove** Shelly to the airport.* (*Shelly* is the direct object; the verb *drove* is transitive.)

Intransitive: *Dad **drove** slowly.* (No direct object, so the verb *drove* is intransitive.)

PRACTICE Rewrite each sentence on a piece of paper, and circle the action verbs. Label the verb *T* if it's *transitive* or *I* if it's *intransitive*. If the verb is transitive, underline the sentence's direct object.

1. Shelly took a long flight to Arizona.
2. She visited the Grand Canyon with a group of hikers.
3. Everyone in the group walked quickly.
4. One hiker saw a rattlesnake near the trail.
5. Shelly froze instantly.

DIRECT/INDIRECT OBJECTS

A sentence might contain only a subject and a verb. If the sentence has an action verb, however, it may direct its action onto something else or someone else. The word that receives the action is called a **direct object**. It answers the questions *whom?* or *what?*

> **No direct object**: *We ate.*
> **Direct object**:   *We ate **pie**. (Ate what? Pie.)*

You've learned that a direct object receives the action of a verb. Some sentences also have another kind of object: an **indirect object**. An indirect object is a noun or pronoun that tells *to whom* or *to what* the verb's action is done.

> **Direct object:**
> *Pedro threw **the baseball**. (Threw what? The baseball.)*

> **Indirect object:**
> *Pedro threw **me** the baseball. (To whom? To me.)*

Direct/Indirect Objects

- A sentence that contains an indirect object always contains a direct object.
- You can often rewrite the sentence by using the preposition **to** or **for** before the indirect object without changing the meaning.

  We gave **the Gluckmans** apricot jam.
  We gave apricot jam **to the Gluckmans**.

PRACTICE

On a separate piece of paper, list the object or objects in each sentence. Label each *DO* for a *direct object* or *IO* for an *indirect object*.

1. Aunt Margaret promised me a quilt.
2. She gave Lee one with sailboats on it.
3. Quilts provide us warmth and beauty.
4. She made Mom and Dad a quilt too.
5. I picked an abstract design for my quilt.

ACTIVE/PASSIVE VERBS

Do your action verbs live up to their names? Action verbs can be written in **active voice**, when the subject *performs* the action—or in **passive voice**, when the subject *receives* the action.

> **Active voice:**
> **Alonzo** *slam-dunked the ball.*
>
> **Passive voice:**
> **The ball** *was slam-dunked by Alonzo.*

In the active voice, the subject—*Alonzo*—is performing the action, so we get a quick picture of the verb's excitement. In the passive voice, however, the subject—*ball*—is receiving the action. Imagine going to a game and not focusing on the players; that's what this sentence does.

Strive for active voice whenever possible; it makes your writing more lively. When it comes to action verbs, 'tis better to give than receive.

✔ *If you write in the passive voice: "The chores must be done before the party," it is unclear* **who** *must do the chores. That becomes clear when you write, "Samantha and Derek must do the chores before the party."*

 On a separate piece of paper, indicate whether each sentence is *active* or *passive*. **If the sentence is passive, rewrite it by changing the voice to active.**

1. Benjamin Banneker was taught to read, write, and count by his grandmother.
2. Part of his childhood was spent at a Quaker school.
3. A wooden clock was made by Banneker at the age of 21.
4. Banneker borrowed math and science books whenever he could.
5. In later years, a plan for world peace was written by Banneker.
6. Politicians referred to it one hundred years later.
7. Banneker was asked by George Washington to help plan the new city of Washington, D.C.
8. The first design was created by Pierre de L'Enfant.
9. It was not liked by President Washington.
10. The final design was completed by Banneker.

HELPING VERBS

Just as its name implies, a **helping verb** works together with another verb, the **main verb**, to express the action of the sentence. Together the two create a **verb phrase**.

helping main
  verb   verb
We **can walk** to the lake.
verb phrase

helping main
  verb   verb
You **may see** a deer.
verb phrase

Helping verbs are often forms of the verb *be*, such as: *am, is, was, were, be, being,* or *been*.

OTHER COMMON HELPING VERBS			
do	shall	can	will
may	might	must	

The verbs *be, do,* and *have* can be either main verbs or helping verbs.

Main Verb:
Is *that you?* (*Is* is the main verb.)

Helping Verb:
Jed **is walking**. (*Is* is the helping verb; *walking* is the main verb.)

Principal Parts of Verbs

Every main verb can appear in four ways; these ways are called **principal parts**. You will be able to form all tenses of regular verbs if you know the four principal parts and can use them with helping verbs.

The principal parts of verbs are shown in the chart below:

FOUR PRINCIPLE PARTS OF VERBS			
Present	**Present Participle**	**Past**	**Past Participle**
Verb used alone	*Verb + ing;* main verb used with helping verb *be*	*Verb + d* or *ed;* verb used alone	*Verb + d* or *ed;* main verb used with helping verb *have*
walk	**(is) walking**	**walked**	**(has) walked**

keep in mind

Have often sounds like *of* when you speak. Don't get this confused when you write:
Right: *He will* **have** *left.*
Wrong: *He will* **of** *left.*

P **RACTICE** Rewrite each sentence. Underline the *main verb* once and the *helping verb* twice.

1. Paula has said that the Everglades is a 4,000-square-mile region of marshlands.
2. The Everglades National Park was established in 1947.
3. Can you believe all the varieties of plants and wildlife?
4. A century of draining and clearing has threatened the Everglades.
5. Ecologists are working in the marshlands.
6. Scientists have studied the water cycle for many years.
7. How much rain does the area receive each year?
8. Temperatures have rarely dipped below freezing.
9. The abundance of insects can support a wide variety of wildlife.
10. Paula and I may apply for jobs at the park.

VERB TENSES

Right: Vince **walked** to the store. On the way, he **dropped** his money.
   (All verbs are past tense.)

Right: Vince **walks** to the store. On the way, he **drops** his money.
   (All verbs are present tense.)

Wrong: Vince **walked** to the store. On the way, he **drops** his money.
   (Walked is past tense while drops is present, though there's no time shift.)

Verbs indicate not just what happens, but when it happens. To express when the action occurs—whether something *happened* yesterday, *is happening* today, or *will happen* tomorrow—you use different **verb tenses**.

English has six verb tenses: three **simple tenses** and three **perfect tenses**. Simple tenses, the more common ones, are **past**, **present**, and **future**.

▶ Use the **past tense** to express an action that already happened. For many verbs, add *-ed* to form the past tense.
   *Alex **tuned** his guitar yesterday.*

▶ Use the **present tense** to express an action that is happening now or happens repeatedly.
   *He **practices** in the garage all the time.*

▶ Use the **future tense** to express an action that will happen in the future. The helping verbs **will** or **shall** indicate future tense.
   *Alex **will play** in a band when he gets to high school.*

 **PRACTICE** Rewrite each sentence on another piece of paper, selecting the correct tense of each verb in the parentheses. Label each *present, past,* or *future* tense.

1. Last week Alex _____ his guitar in a talent show. (play)
2. He _____ all the time about being a famous musician. (dream)
3. Next summer Alex _____ to a music camp. (go)
4. His sister _____ the same camp two years ago. (attend)
5. Now Alex _____ to form a band with some classmates. (hope)
6. When I was younger, I _____ a guitar with a cigar box. (create)
7. For the strings I _____ rubber bands. (use)
8. My brother _____ us to the concert yesterday. (invite)
9. He _____ tickets for all of us tomorrow. (buy)
10. Maybe I _____ my cigar-box guitar. (take)

PRESENT-PROGRESSIVE AND PAST-PROGRESSIVE VERBS

When the action you want to express with a verb is either continuing in the present or was continuing in the past, you need to use a different form of the verb—the **progressive form**. The **present progressive** expresses an action that keeps going in the present (now, today, this year).

> *The students* **are organizing** *a beach cleanup this week.*
> (The organizing is an ongoing action.)

The **past progressive** expresses an action that was ongoing in the past (earlier this morning, yesterday, last year).

> **Past** *Keith* **was enlisting** *students all month.*
> (The enlisting was ongoing when it took place all month.)

To form the progressive, use the helping verb *be* along with the present participle (remember: the present participle ends in *-ing*). It is the helping verb that indicates the tense—whether the action *is* happening in the present or *was* happening in the past. Take a look at the chart below:

Verb	**Present Progressive**	**Past Progressive**
walk	She **is walking** They **are walking** I **am walking**	She **was walking** They **were walking** I **was walking**

PRACTICE

Rewrite each sentence, forming the correct tense of the verb in parentheses.

1. Mrs. Diaz _____ her students about pollution. (instruct—present progressive)
2. The students _____ the subject. (study—present progressive)
3. We _____ about local litter problems. (talk—past progressive)
4. Some students _____ a recycling drive. (start—present progressive)
5. Mike and Terry _____ a bottle drive. (plan—past progressive)

PERFECT TENSES

While progressive tenses indicate action that is ongoing, **perfect tenses** indicate a different kind of action. The **present perfect tense** of a verb names an action that has recently happened, that happened at an indefinite time in the past, or that started in the past and is still happening. To form the present perfect, use the present tense of *have* (*has* or *have*) with the past participle of the main verb.

> *Charles* **has created** *stories for years.*
> *He* **has printed** *one of his favorites for the class.*

The **past perfect tense** names an action that happened *before* another past action or event. To form the past perfect, use *had* with the past participle.

> *Lois* **had circled** *the track three times before we finished once.*
> *Jack* **had promised** *to win, but Kelly beat him.*

The **future perfect tense** indicates an action that will be completed in the future *before* some other future event. To form the future perfect, use *will have* or *shall have* with the past participle.

> *We* **will have typed** *our reports before we turn them in.*
> *The class* **will have reviewed** *our first draft by Tuesday.*

PRACTICE
Rewrite each sentence, forming the correct tense of the verb in parentheses.

1. Marie _____ her social studies paper. (edit—present perfect)
2. I _____ my rough draft. (finish—past perfect)
3. We _____ our papers by Tuesday. (discuss—future perfect)
4. Susan _____ from her vacation before the reports are due. (return—future perfect)
5. She _____ on her report before she left. (work—past perfect)

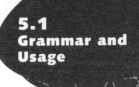

Irregular Verbs

For regular verbs, form the past tense and the past participle by adding *–ed* or *–d* to the base form of the verb.

Irregular verbs, however, do not follow this rule. Here are some common irregular verbs:

IRREGULAR VERBS		
Verb	*Past Tense*	*Past Participle*
be	was, were	(have, has, had) been
do	did	(have, has, had) done
have	had	(have, has, had) had
come	came	(have, has, had) come
run	ran	(have, has, had) run
drink	drank	(have, has, had) drunk
sing	sang	(have, has, had) sung
spring	sprang	(have, has, had) sprung
swim	swam	(have, has, had) swum
swing	swung	(have, has, had) swung
bring	brought	(have, has, had) brought
buy	bought	(have, has, had) bought
catch	caught	(have, has, had) caught
teach	taught	(have, has, had) taught
think	thought	(have, has, had) thought
feel	felt	(have, has, had) felt
hold	held	(have, has, had) held
leave	left	(have, has, had) left
lend	lent	(have, has, had) lent
make	made	(have, has, had) made
say	said	(have, has, had) said
sit	sat	(have, has, had) sat

PRACTICE

Rewrite each sentence, using the past or past participle form of the verb in parentheses.

1. Last month Hannah (buy) a book about Homer Price. **past**
2. In the story, Homer (make) a donut machine. **past**
3. The customers (buy) only a few donuts before the machine broke down. **past participle**
4. Hannah told me she (feel) inspired to invent something. **past participle**
5. She (catch) "inventor's fever." **past participle**

IRREGULAR VERBS

Verb	Past Tense	Past Participle
build	built	(have, has, had) built
burst	burst	(have, has, had) burst
set	set	(have, has, had) set
blow	blew	(have, has, had) blown
grow	grew	(have, has, had) grown
know	knew	(have, has, had) known
throw	threw	(have, has, had) thrown
fly	flew	(have, has, had) flown
break	broke	(have, has, had) broken
draw	drew	(have, has, had) drawn
drive	drove	(have, has, had) driven
get	got	(have, has, had) gotten
write	wrote	(have, has, had) written
eat	ate	(have, has, had) eaten
choose	chose	(have, has, had) chosen
freeze	froze	(have, has, had) frozen
speak	spoke	(have, has, had) spoken
dive	dove (dived)	(have, has, had) dived
give	gave	(have, has, had) given
go	went	(have, has, had) gone
ride	rode	(have, has, had) ridden
begin	began	(have, has, had) begun
see	saw	(have, has, had) seen
take	took	(have, has, had) taken
tear	tore	(have, has, had) torn
wear	wore	(have, has, had) worn

PRACTICE
Rewrite each sentence, using the past or past participle form of the verb in parentheses.

1. We (get) some plans for a deck. *past*
2. Tom (build) decks before. *past participle*
3. He (set) his tools down on the ground just as it began to rain. *past participle*
4. Jason and I (begin) stacking the lumber. *past*
5. Before we started, Tom (speak) to us about job safety. *past*
6. He (take) his cap off and put on a hard-hat. *past*
7. Selena (choose) a piece of wood for the first post. *past*
8. Maggie (break) the seal on the box of nails as soon as we bought them. *past participle*
9. I (know) Maggie for a long time. *past participle*
10. She (wear) her denim overalls for the deck project. *past*

SINGULAR AND PLURAL VERBS

Just as verbs change to indicate time, they also change depending on the number of people or things performing the action. If *one* person or thing is performing the action, the verb is **singular**. If *more than one* person or thing is performing the action, the verb is **plural**.

Here are singular and plural forms of the verb *to walk*. All regular verbs follow this pattern:

Verb	Singular	Plural
to walk	I **walk** you (one person) **walk** he, she, it **walks**	we **walk** you (more than one) **walk** they **walk**

The box below shows the singular and plural forms of the irregular verb *to be*. As with past and present participles, singular and plural forms of irregular verbs follow a variety of patterns:

Verb	Singular	Plural
to be	I **am** you (one person) **are** he, she, it **is**	we **are** you (more than one) **are** they **are**

CHECK it OUT!

✔ *Be careful with sentences in which a phrase follows the subject. Make sure the verb agrees with the subject rather than the phrase.*

The **pot** with stripes and squares **is** old.
(The subject, pot, is singular.)

One of the sites **looks** promising.
(The subject, one, is singular.)

P RACTICE Rewrite each sentence, choosing the verb that agrees with the subject.

1. The workers carefully (digs, dig) in the desert.
2. Dr. Shirazi (think, thinks) we will find some valuable treasures.
3. Every member of the three teams (know, knows) we will find something today.
4. Excitement suddenly (fill, fills) the air.
5. Stone steps (lie, lies) under the sand.
6. The stairway (lead, leads) to a buried tomb.
7. Each of the workers (clean, cleans) sand off a step.
8. The broken pieces of the pot (rest, rests) on the floor.
9. One of the pieces (scratch, scratches) Kit's finger.
10. The old clay (is, are) still sharp.

Subject-Verb Agreement

How do you decide whether a verb should be singular or plural? First, identify the subject and decide whether it names one person or thing (singular) or more than one (plural). Then use the appropriate form of the singular or plural verb. This is known as **subject-verb agreement**.

Singular	Plural
An archaeologist **joins** *the group.*	*Archaeologists* **join** *the group.*
Kit **is** *an archaeologist.*	*They* **are** *archaeologists.*
I **study** *ancient artifacts.*	*We* **study** *ancient artifacts.*

Here are some tips on subject-verb agreement:

▶ In a verb phrase, the helping verb should agree with the subject. The main verb stays the same.

Singular	Plural
Kit **was sent** *to the cave.*	*They* **were sent** *to the cave.*

▶ Sometimes a helping verb comes before the subject, especially when you're asking a question. Locate the subject, then make sure the helping verb agrees.

Singular	Plural
Does *this artifact* **look** *old?*	**Do** *these artifacts* **look** *old?*
(The subject, *artifact,* is singular, so the helping verb *does* is singular.)	(The subject, *artifacts,* is plural, so the helping verb *do* is plural.)

▶ For sentences beginning with *There is/are* or *Here is/are,* locate the subject by asking "There is *what?*" or "Here is *what?*" Then make sure the verb agrees.

Singular	Plural
Here **is** *a broken clay* **pot.**	*There* **are** *several* **shards.**
(The subject *pot* is singular; the verb *is* is singular.)	(The subject *shards* is plural; the verb *are* is plural.)

▶ A collective noun can take a singular or plural verb. When the noun refers to a group acting as a unit, the verb should be singular. When the noun refers to group members acting individually, the verb should be plural.

Singular
The team **takes** *a break.*

Plural
The team **eat** *their lunches.*

▶ In a sentence with a compound subject, subjects joined by *and* take a plural verb. When the subjects are joined by *or* or *nor,* the verb should agree with the subject nearer the verb.

Singular
Kit *or* **Dr. Shirazi brings** *the shovel.*

Plural
Kit *and* **Dr. Shirazi work** *together.*

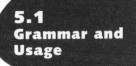

For more on collective nouns, see page 152.

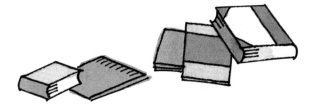

 RACTICE Rewrite each sentence, choosing the verb that agrees with the subject.

1. There (is, are) something interesting about this site.
2. To an archaeologist, a broken pot (represents, represent) a treasure.
3. Here (is, are) some more paint pots!
4. (Do, Does) ancient artifacts interest you?
5. Heat and sandstorms (slow, slows) the archaeologists.
6. They (have, has) been working with Dr. Shirazi since noon.
7. The crew (spread, spreads) out in many directions.
8. Dr. Shirazi and I (inspect, inspects) the site carefully.
9. The workers and the foreman (show, shows) up the next day.
10. The foreman and the workers (show, shows) up the next day.

ADJECTIVES AND ADVERBS

When you describe a person, place, thing, or action, you use words that tell what it's like. You might mention size, shape, color, number, or other qualities. The words you use to describe and identify are called **adjectives** and **adverbs.** They're also known as **modifiers**, because they modify, or change, your knowledge about someone or something.

An adjective is a word that identifies or describes a noun or pronoun.

Two busy astronomers watched the **dark** sky.
It was a **starry** night.
Look at those **tiny blue** lights.

An adverb is a word that modifies (tells more about) a verb, an adjective, or another adverb.

I touched the garden snake **gingerly**. (modifies a verb)
Its skin was **surprisingly** *dry.* (modifies an adjective)
The snake moved **very** *quickly.* (modifies an adverb)

An **adverb** usually answers one of these questions: *how?*
when? where? or *to what extent?*

I waited **excitedly** *for the snake to reappear.* (how?)
Now I **often** *look for snakes in my yard.* (when?)
It slithered **nearby**. (where?)
It was **amazingly** *cute.* (to what extent?)

KINDS OF ADVERBS

How?	When?	Where?	To What Extent?
slowly	today	there	very
quietly	after	backward	quite
suddenly	later	everywhere	extremely

Many adverbs are formed by adding *−ly* to an adjective.

Adjective	+ -ly	= Adverb
slow		*slowly*
bright		*brightly*
miraculous		*miraculously*

P RACTICE
Rewrite each adverb. Then write the word it modifies. Label the modified word as a *verb*, an *adjective*, or an *adverb*.

1. Our class visited a wildlife center yesterday.
2. The experience was extremely interesting.
3. A guide spoke quite extensively about bird-watching.
4. Afterward we went for a two-mile nature walk.
5. We headed northward through the woods.

It was a **good** story. (adjective)
It was written **well**. (adverb)
Did you feel **well** yesterday? (adjective)

✔ *Don't confuse* **feel bad** *and* **feel badly**. **I feel bad** *means* I feel rotten, *or* I'm sorry. **I feel badly** *means* "my sense of touch is impaired."

I felt **bad** when you said that.
I felt **badly** because I was wearing thick gloves.

Be sure not to confuse adjectives and adverbs. For example:

Real, **bad**, and **good** are adjectives.
Really, **badly**, and **well** are adverbs.

The story was a **real** *cliffhanger.* (adjective)
The story was **really** *a cliffhanger.* (adverb)

Yussef was a **good** *runner.* (adjective)
He ran **well** *in every race.* (adverb)

You'll find out about more adjectives and adverbs, and the different jobs they do, in coming pages.

PRACTICE

On a separate piece of paper, rewrite each sentence, using the correct word from the parentheses.

1. Mira writes (frequent, frequently) letters to her friends in India.
2. She (clear, clearly) describes details about life in America.
3. Bharati, who misses Mira very much, (careful, carefully) saves the letters.
4. Mira sends tapes of (current, currently) music to Bharati.
5. Bharati is (real, really) interested in American pop and hip-hop bands.

MORE ON ADJECTIVES

Usually, adjectives go before the noun they describe or identify.

> My **black plastic** *sandals fit perfectly.*
> My **wonderful** *sister gave them to me.*
> My **long denim** *dress is from her too.*

But sometimes adjectives come after a noun.

> My *sandals,* **black** *and* **plastic***, fit perfectly.*
> My *sister,* **wonderful** *as always, gave them to me.*
> My *dress,* **denim** *and* **long***, is from her, too.*

Adjectives can even follow a noun *and* a linking verb.

> My *sandals are* **black plastic** *and fit perfectly.*
> My *sister is* **wonderful** *for giving them to me.*
> I *feel* **glamorous** *when I wear them.*

Adjectives can describe any noun in a sentence. An adjective in the predicate that describes or identifies the *subject* of a sentence is called a **predicate adjective**.

> *That beachball is* **red**.
> predicate
> adjective

> *I feel* **great**.
> predicate
> adjective

CHECK it OUT!

✔ *Some verb forms can also be used as adjectives.*

The **experienced** astronomer knows where to look.
Dr. Albert is **fascinating**.

✔ *Nouns can also function as adjectives.*

He discovered a **dwarf** star.

 **P RACTICE** On a separate piece of paper, write down these sentences. Circle the adjectives in each sentence, and underline the word each modifies. Label predicate adjectives with a *PA*.

1. Stacey felt excited about Thelma's six-teenth birthday.
2. She asked Thelma to pick out a good restaurant.
3. The Chinese restaurant looked new and smelled wonderful.
4. Both girls felt hungry.
5. They ate two delicious eggrolls.
6. Thelma had spicy noodles.
7. She had to drink a tall glass of ice water, too.
8. The main course was stir-fried broccoli and crispy tofu.
9. Both girls ordered sherbet coolers for dessert.
10. The meal was inexpensive and tasty.

Comparing with Adjectives

Sometimes you use adjectives to compare two or more things.

When you compare two persons or things, use the **comparative** form of an adjective. For many adjectives, you can form the comparative by adding *–er*.

> *Aunt Marie is* **tall**, *but Aunt Joan is* **taller**.

When you want to compare more than two persons or things, you use the **superlative** form of an adjective. For many adjectives, you can form the superlative by adding *–est*.

> *Vincent's hair is* **red**, *and Paki's hair is* **redder**, *but Deborah's hair is the* **reddest** *I have ever seen.*

Adjective	Comparative	Superlative
high	higher	highest
nice	nicer	nicest
great	greater	greatest

For some adjectives, you add the word *less* or *more* to form the comparative, and you add the word *least* or *most* to form the superlative.

Adjective	Comparative	Superlative
famous	more famous	most famous
exciting	more exciting	most exciting
difficult	more difficult	most difficult

Some adjectives are irregular. Their comparative and superlative forms are not formed by adding *–er* or *–est*.

Adjective	Comparative	Superlative
good, well	better	best
bad	worse	worst
many, much	more	most

Here are some tips to help you use adjectives to compare.

- For most one-syllable adjectives, add *–er* or *–est*.
  high, high**er**, high**est**

- For many two-syllable adjectives, add *–er* or *–est*, or use the words *more* and *most* or *less* and *least*.
  lovely, loveli**er**, loveli**est**
  honest, **more** honest, **most** honest

- For adjectives with three or more sylla-bles, use the words *more* and *most* or *less* and *least*.
  successful, **more** successful,
  most successful

PRACTICE Rewrite each sentence, using the correct form of the adjective in parentheses.

1. The snowy owl is the ___ of all owls. (striking)
2. The grass in the meadow is ___ than the grass in the woods. (green)
3. Saturday's hike was the ___ hike of the season. (good)
4. The mosquitoes are ___ today than yesterday. (bad)
5. Red-shouldered hawks have ___ feathers than short-tailed hawks. (colorful)
6. In folk tales, foxes are ___ than other creatures. (intelligent)
7. Br'er Fox is the ___ fox of all. (popular)
8. A spotted rabbit is ___ than a white one. (unusual)
9. A hare has ___ ears than a rabbit. (long)
10. Voles are actually ___ than moles. (common)

Definite and Indefinite Articles

A, *an*, and *the* are special adjectives called **articles**.

A and *an* are called **indefinite articles** because they refer to any of a group of people, places, things, or ideas. You say, "I want **an** apple," when you don't have a particular apple in mind.

Whether a noun is plural or singular, its definite article isn't affected

The road
The roads

• • •

. . . but indefinite articles are affected.
a joke
some jokes

Use *a* before a word beginning with a consonant sound; use *an* before a word beginning with a vowel sound.

a *book*	**an** *atlas*
a *car*	**an** *automobile*
a *fish*	**an** *eel*

The is called a **definite article** because it identifies a particular person, place, or thing. Use the definite article when you have a particular item or person in mind. When you say, "I want the apple," you're referring to a specific apple.

the *tablecloth*
the *apartment*
the *window*

P RACTICE Rewrite each word with a definite or indefinite article, as indicated.

1. sandwich *(definite)*
2. otter *(indefinite)*
3. tetherball *(definite)*
4. unicorns *(definite)*
5. elevator *(indefinite)*

Proper Adjectives

A proper noun can also work as an adjective. This type of adjective is called a **proper adjective**. They always begin with a capital letter.

Most proper adjectives are formed from the names of places.

> **Mexican** *culture*
> **Danish** *flag*
> **Norwegian** *salmon*

Sometimes they're formed from peoples' names.

> **Victorian** *era*
> **Orwellian** *thinking*
> **Socratic** *method*

Some proper adjectives are just like proper nouns.

> **Adidas** *sneakers*
> **Georgia** *peach*
> **Superchunk** *song*

For more on proper nouns, see page 148.

 **RACTICE** Rewrite each phrase using a proper adjective to describe the common noun. Form the proper adjective from the proper noun. Change *a* to *an* if necessary.

1. a stallion from Arabia
2. the people of China
3. an exhibit in Poland

4. a city in South Africa
5. the coast of Brazil

MORE ON ADVERBS

Comparative and Superlative Adverbs

The **comparative** form of an adverb compares two actions or qualities. The **superlative** form of an adverb compares more than two actions.

> *Lizards move **faster** than turtles.*
> *Reptiles move **more slowly** in cold weather than in hot.*
> *Among large reptiles, crocodiles move **most quickly**.*

Here are some tips to help you form comparatives and superlatives.

▶ For most one-syllable adverbs and some two-syllable adverbs, add *−er* or *−est*.

  fast, fast**er**, fast**est**   early, earl**ier**, earl**iest**

▶ For most adverbs with two syllables and all adverbs with more than two syllables, use *more/most* or *less/least*.

  sharply, **more** sharply, **most** sharply
  impressively, **more** impressively, **most** impressively

▶ Do not use *−er* with *more* or *less*; do not use *−est* with *most* or *least*.

Some adverbs have irregular comparative and superlative forms. Here are some common irregular adverbs:

ADVERB	COMPARATIVE	SUPERLATIVE
badly	worse	worst
well	better	best
far (distance)	farther	farthest
far (degree)	further	furthest
little	less	least

Avoiding Double Negatives

Some adverbs, like *no* and *not*, are called **negatives** because they negate the meaning of a sentence.

Positive form: *We do have corn.*

Negative form: *We do **not** have corn.*

Negative form: *We have **no** corn.*

Here are some more examples:

Common negatives				
no	nobody	none	no one	never
nothing	nowhere	hardly	scarcely	barely

Two negatives cancel each other out, so use only one negative in a sentence. Using two negative words is a mistake called a **double negative**.

Wrong: *There **wasn't nothing** we could do.*

Right: *There **wasn't anything** we could do.*
            or

Right: *There **was nothing** we could do.*

**RACTICE** For 1-5, rewrite each sentence using the correct form of the adverb in parentheses. For 6-10, rewrite each sentence to eliminate double negatives. (You may find more than one correct solution.)

1. The reptile show lasted ____ than the bird show. (long)
2. Of all the spectators, Lennie watched ____. (closely)
3. The lizards behaved ____ than the snakes. (well)
4. The flying dragon performed ____ of all. (spectacularly)
5. Sarah's iguana blinks ____ than mine. (slow)
6. Yoko doesn't need no more shoes.
7. I can't hardly count how many she has now.
8. She can't scarcely fit them in her closet.
9. I can't remember never meeting someone with a shoe collection like hers.
10. They have all been given to her; she doesn't have none that she bought.

PREPOSITIONS

A preposition is a word or group of words that shows the relationship between a noun or pronoun and some other word in the sentence.

Imagine you're playing a game of catch with a friend. One of you throws the ball high and wide, in the direction of a parked delivery truck. Now you have to try and find the ball. It could be *behind* the truck, *on* the truck, *against* the truck, *near* the truck, *in front of* the truck, or even (if you're unlucky and you've broken a window) *inside* the truck.

All of the italicized words above show the relationship between the ball and the truck. These words are called **prepositions**.

Here's a list of some common prepositions. Notice that some of the prepositions are compound—that is, they consist of more than one word.

COMMON PREPOSITIONS				
about	below	inside	through	due to
above	beneath	into	to	except for
across	beside	like	under	in addition to
after	between	near	until	in back of
against	by	of	up	in front of
among	down	off	with	in regard to
around	during	on	within	in spite of
as	except	outside	without	instead of
at	for	over	according to	next to
before	from	past	along with	on account of
behind	in	since	because of	prior to

PREPOSITIONAL PHRASES

As you've seen, the preposition relates a noun or pronoun to another word in the sentence:

preposition

*The politician spoke **to** the voters.*

preposition

*It looks like the new zoo will be built **in** the park.*

preposition

*That movie was great **in spite of** some of the performances.*

If you look at the first few words that follow the preposition, you'll find a noun or pronoun. This noun or pronoun is called the **object of the preposition**. The group of words that begins with the preposition and ends with the noun or pronoun is called the **prepositional phrase**.

*The game was canceled **on account of rain.***
*Everyone **in the crowd** was very disappointed.*
*They wanted the game to continue **in spite of it.***

✔ Use **between** when you are talking about two things, and **among** when you are talking about three or more. "The chess game was a struggle **between** two equally matched players." "Karen chose **among** the many elective classes the school offered."

✔ **Beside** means next to; **besides** means in addition to. "**Besides** Charlie, no one would sit **beside** me in homeroom."

 **RACTICE** On a separate piece of paper, rewrite each sentence. Underline the prepositional phrase in each sentence. Then, circle the object of the preposition.

1. One tale of Cinderella dates back to ancient China.
2. In the Chinese version, the heroine is named Yeh-hsien.
3. She wishes on magic fish bones.
4. At the ball Yeh-hsien drops a golden slipper.
5. A merchant finds the slipper and fits it on Yeh-hsien's foot.

For more on **object pronouns,** *see page 155.*

Using Prepositional Phrases

Many times, the object of the preposition is a pronoun. When the object of the preposition is a pronoun, you should use an **object pronoun.** Here are some examples:

> *I'm sick of waiting for* **them.**
> *The mayor spoke to* **us** *about her ideas for the future.*
> *Because of* **him,** *the project is on time.*

Sometimes a preposition has an object that consists of two or more nouns or pronouns; this is called a **compound object.** (The words in a compound object are joined by a conjunction such as *and.*) Always use object pronouns in a compound object.

> *Just between* **you and me,** *I'm not crazy about Karen's sculpture.*

> *The man tried to talk to* **my parents and me** *as we passed by.*

> *He didn't meet anyone at the party except for* **you and her.**

keep in mind

Don't use reflexive pronouns as the object of a preposition.

Wrong: No one finished the assignment except for Patty and myself.

Right: No one finished the assignment except for Patty and me.

PRACTICE Rewrite each sentence, using the correct pronoun in parentheses.

1. Did you order that book for Claudia and (I, me)?

2. He had to walk around (you, yourself) to get to the door.

3. Kiko glanced at (us, we) as she left.

4. I don't recognize anyone except for (he, him) and (she, her).

5. The line ends here, so you'll have to stand behind (me, myself).

Prepositional Phrases as Adjectives and Adverbs

As you've already seen, adjectives describe nouns and pro-nouns. When a prepositional phrase describes a noun or a pronoun, it is called an **adjective phrase**.

> *Stars* **of baseball** *earn huge salaries.*
> *(The phrase* of baseball *modifies the noun* stars.*)*

> *Some* **in the crowd** *don't like this.*
> *(The phrase* in the crowd *modifies the pronoun* some.*)*

Always place an adjective phrase as close as possible to the noun or pronoun it modifies. Otherwise you may end up con-veying a meaning you didn't intend.

Right: *Musicians* **with catchy songs** *have a lot of fans.*
Wrong: *Musicians have a lot of fans* **with catchy songs.**
(This makes it sound as though the *fans* have catchy songs!)

As you have also seen, adverbs often modify verbs. When a prepositional phrase modifies a verb, it is called an **adverb phrase**. An adverb phrase helps describe *where, when, why,* or *how* an action takes place.

> *The circus came* **to town.** (Where?)
> *The circus people began setting up* **after midnight.** (When?)
> *We wanted to see the show* **for the trapeze artists.** (Why?)
> *Unfortunately, they didn't perform* **with great agility** *that day.* (How?)

PRACTICE

Rewrite each sentence on a separate page. Then, underline each preposition phrase and label it either *adjective* or *adverb*.

1. When the movie ended, many people ran for the exits.
2. Martin edited his work after he finished.
3. Tamara loves hot dogs with lots of mustard.
4. Members of the media asked the President questions.
5. Below the surface, sharks lay in wait.

CONJUNCTIONS

Conjunctions are words that join parts of a sentence.

COORDINATING CONJUNCTIONS

and	so
but	yet
for	where
or	while

CORRELATIVE CONJUNCTIONS

both...and
either...or
just as...so
neither...nor
not only...but also
whether...or

SUBORDINATING CONJUNCTIONS

after	since
although	than
as	unless
because	until
before	when
if	whenever

Conjunctions are the connectors of language. They connect words, groups of words, or even simple sentences. There are three different kinds of conjunctions.

A **coordinating conjunction** connects words or groups of words used in the same way; it can link a subject and another subject, a verb and another verb, or two simple sentences.

> *Joan* **and** *Maureen are friends.*
> *Maureen moved to Nashville,* **so** *now they talk less frequently.*

Correlative conjunctions are pairs of words used to connect parts of a sentence.

> **Neither** *Rose* **nor** *Mickey understand that book.*
> *Some of its pages* **not only** *confuse* **but also** *mislead.*

Subordinating conjunctions connect two clauses, making one dependent on the other.

> *I don't believe in UFOs,* **since** *I have never seen one.*
> **Unless** *one is finally captured, I will continue to disbelieve.*

PRACTICE Rewrite each sentence. Circle each conjunction and label it *coordinating conjunction, correlative conjunction,* **or** *subordinating conjunction.*

1. Just as the Brothers Grimm became famous in Germany, so did Louisa May Alcott find fame in America.
2. After working as a seamstress, servant, and schoolteacher, Louisa May Alcott became a famous writer.
3. Although she is best known for *Little Women,* Alcott wrote almost three hundred other works.
4. Because of its vividness and deep feeling, Alcott's *Little Women* is loved by millions.
5. Her father Bronson Alcott was well-educated, but he and his family were poor.

INTERJECTIONS

Interjections are exclamations that express strong feelings.

Everyday life is full of powerful emotions such as pleasure, pain, surprise, disgust, and fright. We often use **interjections** to express these emotions vividly. You probably hear dozens in the course of a single day.

If the interjection expresses a really strong feeling, use an exclamation point after it. Then capitalize the word that follows:

Ouch! *That really stings!*
Wow! *That was the best roller coaster I've ever been on!*
Aha! *I always knew you liked her.*

If the feeling expressed is not that strong, you can just use a comma after the interjection. Don't capitalize the word that follows:

Uh-oh, *the bus is late today.*
Okay, *that's enough for now.*
Hey, *I think I've already seen this movie.*

COMMON INTERJECTIONS
Aha!
And how!
C'mon!
Hey!
No way!
Oh!
Okay!
Oops!
Ouch!
Shhh!
Ugh!
Whew!
Wow!

PRACTICE
Rewrite each sentence. Underline the interjection and add any needed punctuation.

1. Ouch I dropped my suitcase on my toe!
2. Oh no The strap on my knapsack broke.
3. Okay let's board the bus.
4. Shhh I'm trying to get some sleep.
5. Hooray This section is over now!

CLAUSES

A clause is a group of words that
has a subject and a predicate.

As you've seen, there are several different kinds of clauses;
this section will tell you about them.

Think back to the earlier section on sentences, where you first
read about clauses. You'll remember that there are two main
kinds of clauses: independent and dependent clauses. Even
though it's only part of a sentence, an independent clause expresses a complete thought and can stand alone as a
sentence.

independent clause | independent clause

Do you want to go to the beach, *or* **do you want to stay at
home?**

independent clause | independent clause

It's too cloudy to go to the beach; let's go to the movies.

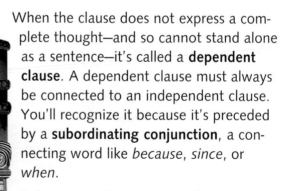

When the clause does not express a complete thought—and so cannot stand alone
as a sentence—it's called a **dependent
clause**. A dependent clause must always
be connected to an independent clause.
You'll recognize it because it's preceded
by a **subordinating conjunction**, a connecting word like *because*, *since*, or
when.

Before noon *the movie is half-price.*

I always pay for the movies, **unless I'm
with my parents**.

There are three different kinds of dependent clauses: **adjective clauses**, **adverb
clauses**, and **noun clauses**.

You'll recall that adjectives describe or identify nouns. An **adjective clause** describes or identifies a noun or a pronoun in an independent clause. Most of the time you can spot an adjective clause because it begins with a relative pronoun (*who, whom, whose, which, that*); it can also begin with *where* and *when*.

> *This director,* **whose influence is felt around the world,** *is now working on another film.*

Just as an adverb usually modifies (tells more about) a verb, an **adverb clause** usually modifies the verb in an independent clause. Like an adverb, an adverb clause tells *how, when, where,* or *why* an action occurs. Most of the time, an adverb clause begins with a subordinating conjunction (see the box on this page).

> **After the lights came up,** *Mom was still in tears.*

Some dependent clauses act as nouns; these are called **noun clauses**. They act just as you would expect a noun to act—as a subject, a direct object, or a predicate noun.

> **Whoever you are,** *I wish you'd leave me alone.*

Some words that introduce noun clauses are: *how, that, why, what, whatever, when, where, which, whichever, who, whom, whoever, whomever, whose.*

SUBORDINATING CONJUNCTIONS

after	though
although	unless
as	until
because	when
before	whenever
if	where
since	whereas
than	wherever

more **INFO**

For an intro to clauses, see pages 143.

P RACTICE Rewrite each sentence. Draw a line under each dependent clause. Label it *adjective clause, adverb clause,* **or** *noun clause.*

1. When they reached North America, the earliest inhabitants hunted or gathered.
2. What life was like for these early travelers is largely unknown.
3. The land bridge, which connected Asia and North America, was covered with water when glaciers melted.
4. I read that Asia and America were once a single large land mass.
5. Early hunters used stone-tipped spears for hunting because they had no metals.

VERBALS AND VERBAL PHRASES

Verbs can act as adjectives, adverbs, or nouns. In these cases, they're called verbals.

The **blooming** *daffodils made her happy.* (adjective)
She hoped **to pick** *some.* (adverb)
Gardening *was her specialty.* (noun)

If a verbal consists of more than one word and has a modifier or an object, it's called a **verbal phrase**. There are three kinds of verbals and verbal phrases: participles and participial phrases, gerunds and gerund phrases, and infinitives and infinitive phrases.

As you'll recall, the present participle of a verb is formed by adding *-ing* to the base form of the verb; the past participle is usually formed by adding *-ed.* Participles are often used as adjectives:

The **hushed** *spectators awaited the start of the tournament.*
The **waiting** *knights grew impatient.*

A **participial phrase** includes a participle, plus a group of words that helps complete the participle's meaning. Usually, the phrase begins with the participle and acts as an adjective.

Sporting their colors, *the knights rode into the ring.*
(The participial phrase modifies the noun *knights.*)

Awed by the spectacle, *the crowd watched in amazement.*
(The participial phrase modifies the noun *crowd.*)

A **gerund** is a verb form that can be used as a noun. It's formed in exactly the same way as the present participle—by adding *-ing* to the base form of the verb.

> **Jousting** *was a popular sport in the Middle Ages.*

A **gerund phrase** consists of a gerund and a group of words that completes the phrase's meaning. The entire phrase acts as a noun.

> **Riding a horse in full armor** *was no easy task.*

Like a gerund, an **infinitive** is a verb form that can be used as a noun. An infinitive is formed by adding the word *to* to the base form of the verb. Usually an infinitive functions as a noun, but sometimes it can be used as an adverb.

> **To attack** *was the essential strategy used in jousting.* (noun)
> *Every contestant hoped* **to win.** (adverb)

An **infinitive phrase** includes an infinitive and a group of words that completes the phrase's meaning. Like an infinitive, an infinitive phrase is most often used as a noun.

> **To knock another knight off his horse** *was the goal.*

CHECK *it* OUT!

✔ *A participial phrase at the beginning of a sentence is* **always** *followed by a comma.*

✔ *Always put the participial phrase as close as possible to the noun it modifies or you may end up saying something you don't mean!*

Wrong: *Neighing loudly, we watched the horses run into the barn.*

Right: *We watched the horses, neighing loudly, run into the barn.*

PRACTICE

Write each sentence. Underline each verbal or verb phrase and label it as a *participle*, *gerund*, or *infinitive*.

1. A glittering audience gathered.
2. Kings, bishops, and courtiers all came to watch.
3. Lords and ladies enjoyed showing off their finery.
4. Pawing the ground, the horses waited.
5. To ensure fair play was the umpires' job.
6. Fighting in a dishonorable manner brought disgrace to the knights.
7. Because knights were often called into battle, the tournaments were a way of practicing.
8. The highest honor was to win the king's praise.
9. Knights also wanted to impress the young ladies.
10. Challenging a knight to a joust was heroic.

CAPITALIZATION

You might not think **capitalization** is that important, but consider this: Without capitalization, how could you tell the difference between a Rolling Stone (a member of an incredibly famous and successful rock band) and a rolling stone (which merely gathers no moss)? Or between Reading (a city in Pennsylvania) and reading (what you're doing right now)?

Capitalization helps make your meaning clear to your reader, because it shows that you're naming something *specific.* In the next few pages, you'll learn about capitalization—what to capitalize and what not to.

First Words

Capitalize the first word in a sentence.

> **M**y favorite poet is Walt Whitman.

Capitalize the first word of a direct quotation.

> She asked, "**W**ho are you?"

When a direct quotation is interrupted, do *not* begin the second part of the quotation with a capital letter—unless the second part begins a new sentence.

> "My name," he replied, "**i**s a secret."
> My name is Mark," he replied. "**T**hat's no secret."

Capitalize the words in the greeting of a letter. Capitalize only the *first* word of the closing.

> **D**ear **M**rs. **T**yler: **D**ear **L**iz,   **S**incerely yours, **Y**ours truly,

In many poems the first word of every line is capitalized.

> **I** celebrate myself;
> **A**nd what I assume you shall assume;
> **F**or every atom belonging to me, as good belongs to you...
>   —Walt Whitman, from "Song of Myself"

The Pronoun "I"

Always capitalize the pronoun *I*, no matter where it appears in the sentence.

> **I** don't know what **I**'m doing half the time, but **I** pretend **I** do.

People

Capitalize the names and initials of specific people and animals.

> **S**alman **R**ushdie, **J**ane **D**ark, **K**ermit the **F**rog

Capitalize titles used with names, including titles that are abbreviated.

> **P**resident **J**ohn **F**. **K**ennedy, **D**r. **S**pock, **G**eneral **E**isenhower, **J**ustice **O**'**C**onnor, **M**rs. **J**ones

Capitalize family titles when they're used as names.

> *Where are you going, **D**ad?*
> *I'm going to visit **U**ncle **C**arl.*

Do *not* capitalize family titles when they come after a possessive noun or pronoun or an article.

> *My **s**ister teaches at the university.*
> *I've always wanted a **b**rother.*

Times and Dates

Capitalize days and months.

> **T**uesday, **A**pril

Don't capitalize the seasons, though.

> *We're going camping this **s**ummer.*

Capitalize special events and holidays.

> **W**orld **S**eries, **M**emorial **D**ay, **S**enior **P**rom

PRACTICE

Rewrite each sentence using correct capitalization.

1. every november our family gathers to celebrate thanksgiving.
2. last year we all went to grandpa abe's house.
3. he once sent a fan letter to the great ballplayer babe ruth.
4. ruth wrote back, signing his letter, "your pal, babe."
5. "i heard these stories all the time," dad said, "when i was a boy."

Geography

Capitalize the names of specific places, including:

- cities, states, countries, and continents.

  Paris, **K**ansas, **I**ndia, **A**sia

- bodies of water, mountains, other geographical features.

  Lake **V**ictoria, **G**rand Canyon, **M**ount **F**uji

- sections of the country and compass points when they refer to specific regions.

  Atlantic **S**eaboard, the **M**idwest

- named streets and highways.

  Juniper **L**ane, **R**oute 66, **P**acific **C**oast **Highway**

- specific buildings, bridges, and monuments.

  Sears **T**ower, **B**rooklyn **B**ridge, **W**ashington **M**onument

- heavenly bodies, such as planets, stars, and constellations.

  Venus, **M**ars, **H**alley's **C**omet, the **M**ilky **W**ay, **O**rion

NOTE: Capitalize *Earth* when it refers to the planet but not when it is preceded by *the*.

  orbiting Earth but *landing on the earth*

Nationalities

Capitalize the names of ethnic groups, nationalities, and languages.

  Chinese **A**mericans, **M**exicans, **D**utch

Capitalize the proper adjectives that are formed from the names of ethnic groups and nationalities.

  Japanese *lantern*, **S**wiss *cheese*

PRACTICE

Rewrite each sentence using correct capitalization.

1. Near the canadian border you may hear people speaking french.
2. marco porcino lives on baltic street in brooklyn, new york.
3. He celebrates his italian heritage by visiting new york's historic sites.
4. marco's grandfather sailed across the atlantic ocean from italy.
5. ellis island is located in upper new york bay.

Titles

Capitalize important words in the title of a written work, a song, a movie, or a television show.

> *Life on the Mississippi*
> "Stopping by Woods on a Snowy Evening"
> "Let It Be"
> *The Return of the Jedi*

Historical Events

Capitalize the names of historical events, periods of time, and documents.

> French Revolution, World War I, the Renaissance,
> the Bill of Rights, the Declaration of Independence

Brand Names, Organizations

Capitalize brand names and the names of specific clubs, businesses, organizations, institutions, and political parties.

> Kleenex, Rotary Club, United Savings Bank, Democrats

 **P**RACTICE ------------▶ Rewrite each sentence using correct capitalization.

1. The citizens of massachusetts are famous for being staunch democrats.
2. The revolutionary war began in lexington and concord.
3. A museum in hartford, connecticut, contains the desk on which abraham lincoln signed the emancipation proclamation.
4. The american national anthem is "the star-spangled banner."
5. francis scott key wrote it during the war of 1812.
6. My favorite song is "somewhere over the rainbow."
7. It is from the movie *the wizard of oz*.
8. The movie came out in 1939, during the great depression.
9. The japanese attacked pearl harbor in 1941, which began america's involvement in world war II.
10. The united states war department grew during world war II.

PUNCTUATION

Punctuation marks show where sentences end and where pauses occur— and a whole lot more. Like capitalization, punctuation helps you communicate your meaning to readers. Think about the phrase *That's the way to do it.* With a period at the end, it's a simple explanation: "That's the way to do it." Replace the period with a question mark, though, and you express confusion: "That's the way to do it?" And with an exclamation point at the end, it becomes a statement of praise: "That's the way to do it!" This section will give you some guidelines for using punctuation marks.

PERIODS

Use a period at the end of a statement or a mild command.

The school band is marching in the parade on Sunday.
Remember to be on time for the bus that morning.

Use a period after an indirect question or a polite request.

He asked if he could bring his sister to the picnic.
Please send me information about your summer program.

Use a period after a person's initials.

J.D. Salinger, E.B. White, K.T. Merz

Use a period after most abbreviations that show that letters have been left out, such as:

- titles of people.
  Mr.   Mrs.   Ms.   Dr.   Rev.   Prof.
- geographic locations.
  Rd.   St.   Ave.   Pl.   U.S.A.   N. Dak.
- time references.
  A.M.   P.M.   B.C.   A.D.   Mon.   Jan.

QUESTION MARKS

Use a question mark at the end of a direct question or an incomplete question.

> *Has the bus left yet***?** (direct question)
> *When***?** *Why now***?** *In which direction***?**
> (incomplete questions)

Use a question mark after a statement intended as a question.

> *The bus has already left***?**

EXCLAMATION POINTS

Use an exclamation point at the end of an exclamatory statement or a strong command.

> *That's the most ridiculous thing I've ever heard!*
> (exclamatory statement)
> *Get away from that stove right now!* (strong command)

Use an exclamation point after an interjection expressing strong emotion.

> *Wow***!** *This chocolate cake is incredible!*
> *Whew***!** *That was a close call!*

keep in mind

Do not use periods with **acronyms***, words made up of the first letters of a series of words:*

> AFDC (**A**id to **F**amilies with **D**ependent **C**hildren)
> NATO (**N**orth **A**tlantic **T**reaty **O**rganization)

For more on **interjections***, see page 193.*

PRACTICE

----------➤ Rewrite each sentence with correct punctuation.

1. There are eight teams in our soccer league
2. Tell me which team we will play next week
3. Who is the captain of your soccer team
4. How I love to play soccer
5. Are you going to watch the game
6. Kelly P Jones is the best player on our team
7. Wow What an amazing goal she scored
8. We have won every game so far this season
9. I can't wait until the playoffs begin on Nov 9
10. Do you think we will win?

COMMAS

Commas indicate a pause or separation between parts of a sentence. One good way to help figure out the correct placement of commas is to say a sentence aloud; often, a comma goes wherever you naturally pause in the sentence. Here, though, are some more specific guidelines:

Separating Items

Use commas to separate three or more items in a series.

> *My favorite foods are burritos, spaghetti, and blueberry pancakes.*

Use a comma to separate some adjectives that come before a noun. As a rule of thumb, you should use a comma if it makes sense to put the word *and* between the adjectives; if it doesn't make sense, don't use a comma.

> *Boston is a small, pleasant city.*
> *I own a small red car.*

Use a comma to separate clauses in a compound sentence. Put the comma before the conjunction.

> *Playing this music is difficult, but we've had a lot of practice.*
> *We have a concert next Thursday, and we're working like crazy for it.*

Introducing a Sentence

Use a comma after an introductory word, phrase, or clause.

> *Well, I've got to be going.* (word)
> *Come to think of it, I guess I can stay for a while.* (phrase)
> *Since I missed the bus, I'll take a taxi.* (clause)

Use a comma after a participial phrase at the beginning of a sentence.

> *Carrying our bags, we checked into the hotel.*

keep in mind

Don't use a comma when only two items are separated by a conjunction. "I traveled to Boston and New York."

• • •

A comma isn't necessary if the clauses to be separated are very short. "Terry played and I listened."

Appositives and Clauses

Use commas to set off appositives from the rest of the sentence. However, do *not* use commas if the sentence's meaning would change significantly without the appositive.

> *Roseanne,* **the famous actress,** *sang "The Star-Spangled Banner."*
> **The actress** *Roseanne sang "The Star-Spangled Banner."*

Use a comma to set off an adjective or adverb clause from the rest of the sentence. However, do *not* use a comma if the clause is necessary to the basic idea of the sentence.

> *Paul Bunyan,* **who supposedly created the Grand Canyon,** *is a legendary figure in American tall tales.*
> *He traveled with a blue ox* **that helped him accomplish some amazing feats.**

Direct Address

Use commas to set off a noun of direct address (when you are speaking to someone directly).

> *Hal,* *your brother seems very interesting.*
> *I'm disappointed in you,* *Quincy.*

Interrupters

Use commas to set off an **interrupter**—a word or phrase that breaks up the main thought of a sentence.

> *Coal miners,* *by the way,* *have very dangerous jobs.*
> *Their rate of lung disease,* *for example,* *is extremely high.*

Direct Quotations

Use a comma between a speaker and a direct quotation (the speaker's exact words). When the quotation is at the beginning of the sentence, the comma goes before the final quotation marks; this is true even if the quotation contains more than one complete sentence.

> *Ms. Werthan said,* *"I'm sorry. I lost track of time."*

In a divided quotation use commas to set off the interrupting words, such as *he said* and *she said.*

> *"That's all right,"* *said Rachel,* *"it's no big deal."*

more
INFO

For more on appositives, see page 153.

**SOME COMMON
INTERRUPTERS**

actually
after all
by the way
for example
however
in fact
in my opinion
incidentally
nevertheless
on the other hand
therefore

Places, Dates, and Titles

Use a comma before and after the name of a state or country when it comes after the name of a city.

> *The Rose Bowl is held in Pasadena, California, once a year.*

Use a comma between the day and the year, and after the year.

> *I was born on March 26, 1983, in Athens, Ohio.*

Use commas to set off a title or degree following a name.

> *John DeSantis, Jr., served as chaperone.*
> *Dr. Owens, D.V.M., tended to the cows.*

In Letters

Use a comma after the opening of a friendly letter and after all letter closings.

> *Dear Dad,   Dear Jacob,   Yours truly,   Sincerely,*

keep in mind

You don't need a comma before a zip code: Northhampton, MA 01060

PRACTICE
Rewrite each sentence using correct punctuation.

1. Did you know that Texas was the thirty-second state

2. On our way to San Antonio we visited Dallas Austin and Fort Worth

3. On November 22 1963 President John F Kennedy was assassinated in Dallas

4. In Fort Worth Texas we toured the Amon Carter Museum of Western Art

5. Austin is the capital of Texas and it is a major educational center

APOSTROPHES

Use an apostrophe and the letter *s* to form possessive nouns.

> *driver***'s** *license, "A Hard Day***'s** *Night"*

Use apostrophes to replace the missing letters in contractions.

> *she***'**ll *(she will), you***'**re *(you are), won***'**t *(will not), it***'**s *(it is)*

QUOTATION MARKS

Use quotation marks to set off a direct quotation (a person's exact words).

> *"The show is over," he said.*
> *I replied, "And not a minute too soon."*

When one quotation is inside another, set it off with single quotation marks.

> *"Curtis said, 'And not a minute too soon,'" Joe told me.*

Always place periods and commas inside quotation marks.

> *"I never use microwave ovens***,***" Isaac said, "even when I'm pressed for time***.***"*

Place question marks and exclamation points inside quotation marks if they are part of the quotation.

> *"You're nuts***!***" Martha cried. "What's the matter with microwave ovens***?***"*

If they are not part of the quotation, do *not* place question marks and exclamation points inside quotation marks.

> *Did Isaac say, "I never use microwave ovens"***?*** *It's as if he were saying, "I'm trying to waste time"***!***

Use quotation marks to set off the titles of short works, such as short stories, essays, poems, book chapters, articles, songs, or TV episodes.

> *"The Tell-Tale Heart" (short story)*
> *"A Supermarket in California" (poem)*

more
INFO

For more on **possessive nouns**, *see page 151.*

keep in mind

You do not *need quotation marks to set off an indirect quotation:* Joe said the show was over.

ITALICS/UNDERLINING

Underline or italicize the titles of long works, such as novels, plays, movies, and TV series, as well as newspapers and magazines, and records and CDs. Underline or italicize the names of ships, trains, and spacecraft.

> <u>For Whom the Bell Tolls</u> or *For Whom the Bell Tolls* (novel)
> <u>Death of a Salesman</u> or *Death of a Salesman* (play)
> <u>Gone With the Wind</u> or *Gone With the Wind* (movie)
> <u>Newsweek</u> or *Newsweek* (magazine)
> <u>Seinfeld</u> or *Seinfeld* (TV series)
> <u>Titanic</u> or *Titanic* (ship)

Underline or italicize foreign words.

> *Gracias* means "thank you" in Spanish.
> <u>Gracias</u> means "thank you" in Spanish.

COLONS

Use a colon to introduce a list of items.

> *Bring three things*: *your résumé, a photo, and a reference.*

Use a colon to introduce a long quotation.

> *As Abraham Lincoln once said*: *"As I would not be a slave, so I would not be a master. This expresses my idea of democracy. Whatever differs from this, to the extent of the difference, is no democracy."*

Use a colon after the opening of a business letter.

> *Dear Dr. Walker*: *Dear Sir or Madam*:

Use a colon between numbers showing the hour and minute.

> *12:00*   *9:30 A.M.*   *6:42 P.M.*

SEMICOLONS

Use a semicolon to join parts of a compound sentence when a conjunction like *or*, *but*, or *and* is not used.

> *A television variety show is being cast*; *auditions start today.*

Use a semicolon to join independent clauses that are subdivided by commas, even if a conjunction is used.

> *Somersaulting acrobats, barking dogs, and clowns filled the waiting room*; *but the office door remained shut.*

Use semicolons to join parts of a series that contain commas within them.

> *The touring company will be stopping in Des Moines, Iowa*; *Kansas City, Missouri*; *and Nashville, Tennessee.*

HYPHENS

Use a hyphen in compound numbers from twenty-one through ninety-nine, fractions used as modifiers, some compound nouns, and with some prefixes.

> *sixty-eight (compound number)*
> *two-thirds majority (fraction as modifier)*
> *brother-in-law (compound noun)*
> *ex-champion (prefix)*

Use a hyphen in compound adjectives that precede nouns.

> *the seventy-year-old woman*
> *the middle-school student*

✔ *You don't need a hyphen in compound adjectives that don't come before nouns or that contain an adverb ending in -ly.*

> I'm seventy years old.

> That was a carefully prepared report.

DASHES

Use a dash to set off words that interrupt a main idea.

Bernie Feldman—he's my agent—says I'm going to be a big star.

Use a dash to show that a thought has been interrupted.

The man lying on the floor said, "The killer was—" and then he fell back and died.

Use a dash to sum up what has come before.

Van Gogh never sold a painting, hated almost everybody, cut off his ear, ate paint—he was really a tortured artist.

PARENTHESES

Use parentheses to set off material that is not part of the main statement but is still important to include.

Our family's cat (who we have just named Pigeon) is nearly full grown.

When a complete sentence is in parentheses, put the period *inside* the parentheses. Otherwise, the period goes *outside* the parentheses.

I was thinking I'd like to name the cat "Seamus." (My brother objected to that, though.)
It turns out he has a very different idea for a name (just as I had suspected).

PRACTICE Rewrite each sentence using correct punctuation.

1. The director asked Have you ever seen The Gong Show on television
2. Mona's résumé lists the following talents singing acting dancing
3. The auditions are open anybody may try out
4. The waiting room was three quarters full by 830
5. At least forty five people stood outside the door
6. Do you know any songs from the movie Grease Mr Chaffee asked
7. I cant quite hear lets see can you sing a little louder he suggested
8. Mona couldnt remember the lyrics so she asked for help
9. An assistant provided cue cards cardboard signs with words printed on them
10. Youve done a fine job said the director
11. Lena asked Have you seen the movie Dr Zhivago
12. Kelly says she has seen it twenty five times but I dont believe her
13. My great grandmother lived in Germanys capital city Berlin
14. Did you know that Monicas father is Russian American
15. Peer Gynt a play set in Norway was written by Ibsen
16. Major cities in Scandinavia include the following Stockholm Oslo and Copenhagen
17. No we arrived in Helsinki at 940 yesterday morning
18. Every Finnish house seems to have a sauna a small room with dry heat and a woodstove
19. I cant find the map said Norma Jean
20. When did you have it last asked Jasmine

ANSWER KEY—GRAMMAR, MECHANICS, AND USAGE

SENTENCES
Types of Sentences
1. Lucy thinks her parrot gets jealous when she's on the phone. (declarative)
2. Have you ever heard of a problem like this? (interrogative)
3. Putting a cover over his cage is supposed to calm Perry down. (declarative)
4. Try putting a sheet over his cage. (imperative)
5. I think Perry is a beautiful parrot. (declarative)
6. His tail feathers are a pretty color. (declarative)
7. Have you spoken to any parrot experts about this problem? (interrogative)
8. What a strange situation this is! (exclamatory)
9. Do Lucy's roommates complain about Perry? (interrogative)
10. Find out whether other pet birds behave this way. (imperative)

Subjects and Predicates
1. <u>Many early scientific inventions</u> came from China.
2. <u>I-Hsing</u> designed a water clock.
3. <u>Chang Heng</u> invented an earthquake-measuring machine.
4. <u>The manufacture of silk</u> dates back to early China.
5. <u>One of China's most important contributions</u> was the compass.
6. Was <u>the abacus</u> introduced during the Sung dynasty?
7. <u>The Chinese</u> discovered herbal medicines.
8. <u>Another important Chinese invention</u> was the horse harness.
9. <u>During the Shang dynasty people</u> used cowrie shells for money.
10. When was <u>the first printed book</u> produced in China?

Simple Subject and Simple Predicate
1. <u>Native Americans</u> <u>did</u> not <u>have</u> horses until the late 1600s.
2. Spanish <u>explorers</u> <u>introduced</u> sheep and horses to the Southwest.
3. [You] <u>Tell</u> us why many Navajo raised large flocks of sheep.
4. <u>Sheep</u> <u>provided</u> food, wool, and many other helpful products.
5. Some of the Plains <u>peoples</u> of Texas <u>had</u> horses in the 1690s.
6. <u>Did</u> the <u>Navajo</u> <u>adopt</u> horses from the Spanish?
7. The <u>Blackfoot Nation</u> <u>used</u> horses for carrying supplies.
8. [You] <u>Describe</u> how the Comanche raised horses on the Great Plains.
9. When <u>did</u> the <u>Lakota</u> <u>begin hunting</u> on horseback?
10. By 1790, <u>horses</u> <u>had spread</u> throughout North America.

Compound Subject and Compound Predicate
1. <u>The Mongol Empire</u> <u>was the largest land empire in history</u>. (neither)
2. <u>China and Iran</u> <u>were part of the empire</u>. (compound subject)
3. <u>Mongol tribes</u> <u>lived in tents and moved from place to place</u>. (compound predicate)
4. <u>The tribes</u> <u>feuded and fought for many centuries</u>. (compound predicate)
5. <u>Genghis Khan and Kublai Khan</u> <u>were both fierce leaders</u>. (compound subject)

Phrases and Clauses
1. <u>Holding her puppy Sir Lancelot</u>, **Princess Lillian ran <u>into the castle</u>.** (independent)
2. **Princess Lillian named him <u>after a famous knight</u> because she loves history.** (independent, dependent)
3. **The puppy is not allowed <u>into the castle</u>, but Lillian sneaks him in.** (independent, independent)
4. <u>Allergic to dogs</u>, **Queen Penelope gets angry at Lillian.** (independent)
5. **Lillian tries <u>to keep Lancelot in her room</u> so he won't bother the queen.** (independent, dependent)

212

Compound Sentences

1. The main meal was served mid-morning, but it could last for two or three hours. (compound)
2. Meat dishes were popular; they included venison, pheasant, and partridge. (compound)
3. People ate with their fingers or the points of their knives. (simple)
4. People sometimes used spoons to eat soup, but forks were not introduced until much later. (compound)
5. The lord, his family, and their guests sat at a separate table. (simple)
6. Meals consisted of several courses; each course included a variety of dishes. (compound)
7. Young boys from noble families carried the meals to the table. (simple)
8. Food was served on thick slices of bread called trenchers. (simple)
9. Servants threw out the leftover trenchers, and beggars outside the castle felt lucky to get them. (compound)
10. The pieces of bread were soaked with juices from the meat; this soggy food was later called Yorkshire pudding. (compound)

Complex Sentences

1. Before Marco Polo traveled to China, Europeans knew little about eastern Asia.
2. While he was living in Beijing, he worked with Kublai Khan, the emperor of China.
3. Marco Polo wrote a book about the Far East when he returned to Venice in 1295.
4. Very few Europeans had been to China, so Polo's book gave Europe its first detailed view of China and its neighbors.
5. After Marco Polo returned, trade increased between Europe and China, especially the trade in spices and silk.

Correcting Fragments and Run-on Sentences

1. (run-on) Astronaut John Glenn orbited the earth in 1962. He went around the earth three times, but he returned safely.
2. The Gemini Space Program began in 1965. (complete sentence)
3. (fragment) Virgil Grissom and John Young rode in the first Gemini spacecraft.
4. (run-on) There were fifteen Gemini spacecraft; they were used to prepare for a trip to the moon.
5. In 1968 astronauts made the first manned space flight around the moon. (complete sentence)

NOUNS
Kinds of Nouns

1. **Tony** and **Kim** led a group (concrete) of students (concrete) up **Mount Greylock**.
2. The mountain (concrete) is one of the tallest in **New England**.
3. Before the expedition (concrete), the climbers (concrete) learned how to pack their backpacks (concrete).
4. The trip was a challenge (abstract) for **Gail**, because her boots (concrete) were new.
5. At the top (concrete), **Tony** and **Kim** felt full of freedom (abstract) and excitement (abstract), but **Gail** felt only fatigue (abstract).

Singular and Plural Nouns

1. mosses
2. children
3. crowns
4. branches
5. volcanoes (or volcanos)
6. lives
7. rodeos
8. salmons
9. trays
10. bunnies

Possessive Nouns

1. Tasha's dream is to be a pirate.
2. She read about Blackbeard's booty.
3. New Mexico's mountains contain hidden stashes of gold, Tasha says.
4. According to legend, the bandits' treasure has never been found.
5. In Mom and Dad's opinion, she's wasting her time.

Compound Nouns

1. fishtank
2. home run
3. tie-dyes, clothesline
4. raffle tickets
5. brother-in-law, lighthouse

Appositives

1. New Mexico, the "Land of Enchantment," has many lovely tourist attractions.
2. Santa Fe, my favorite city, is its capital.

3. A collection of southwestern art is housed in the Palace of Governors, a museum there.

4. The Palace of Governors, the oldest government building in the United States, was built in 1610.

5. My best friend Manuel wants to go there next summer.

PRONOUNS
Personal Pronouns
1. She is the school librarian. (subject)
2. People visit it all the time. (object)
3. They know how to use the card catalog. (subject)
4. Mrs. Szafir showed her where to find the audio-tapes. (object)
5. He asked if the library had any books about soccer. (subject)
6. The librarian showed Jacob where to find them. (object)
7. We go to the library every week. (subject)
8. Mrs. Szafir always helps us. (object)
9. It is the largest library in the world. (subject)
10. I told her that I will work there someday. (object)

Pronoun-Antecedent Agreement
1. Ashanti collects autographs. He has over 250 of them.
2. Ashanti treasures his autographs. He keeps them in a box.
3. Some autographs are rare. They are worth a lot of money.
4. Ashanti likes sports autographs the best. He especially likes to collect basketball players' signatures.
5. His sister collects coins. She thinks autographs are silly.
6. Ashanti and I disagree with her. We both think his hobby is great.
7. Tara wanted Shaquille O'Neal's autograph. She wrote him to ask for it.
8. Norah keeps track of both their collections. She likes to compare them.
9. Norah and I are old friends. We spend a lot of time together.
10. Mr. Crome looked at Tara's collection yesterday. He offered her one hundred dollars for it.

Possessive Pronouns
1. Her brother Michael plays in a rock group.
2. "Wildfire" is their name.
3. The bass guitar is his.
4. The drum set, though, is theirs.
5. I really like its melody.

Reflexive and Intensive Pronouns
1. The pilot herself checked the plane's engines before we left the airport. (intensive)
2. The flight attendants caught themselves as the plane dropped and recovered. (reflexive)
3. The plane steadied itself and continued uneventfully. (reflexive)
4. One passenger checked himself for splashed coffee. (reflexive)
5. The president of the airline himself apologized to us for the rough flight. (intensive)

Indefinite Pronouns
1. Nearly everyone at school is dressed strangely.
2. Somebody has declared today "Back to the '70s" Day.
3. Many put on bellbottom pants.
4. One of my friends wears a fringed leather vest.
5. Several look like the cast of an old TV show.

Interrogative and Demonstrative Pronouns
1. Who will be the leader of the discussion group?
2. That is the table where we'll sit.
3. Which of the three topics will we discuss?
4. Whose is this notebook?
5. Are those the notes from last week's meeting?
6. With whom did you go on vacation?
7. Was this your idea?
8. Is this the best map to follow?
9. That looks like the most detailed one.
10. Of these two roads, which do you think is quicker?

VERBS
Action and Linking Verbs
1. developed – action
2. is – linking
3. acts – action
4. sips – action
5. tastes – linking
6. looks – linking
7. wipes – action
8. mixes – action
9. receives – action
10. seems – linking

Predicate Nouns and Predicate Adjectives

1. J.R.R. Tolkien's real name **is** <u>John Ronald Reuel Tolkien</u>. (PN)
2. He **was** a <u>professor</u> of English language and literature. (PN)
3. Tolkien **appeared** <u>dignified</u> to his students. (PA)
4. He **became** <u>famous</u> all over the world for his novels. (PA)
5. His first novel **was** <u>The Hobbit</u>. (PN)
6. *The Hobbit* **is** a fantasy <u>novel</u>. (PN)
7. Bilbo Baggins **is** the main <u>character</u> of the story. (PN)
8. At first the plot of *The Hobbit* **seems** <u>complicated</u>. (PA)
9. Bilbo's companions **are** thirteen <u>dwarfs</u>. (PN)
10. The dwarfs' search for treasure **appears** <u>fruitless</u>. (PA)

Transitive and Intransitive Verbs

1. Shelly **took** a long <u>flight</u> to Arizona. *T*
2. She **visited** the <u>Grand Canyon</u> with a group of hikers. *T*
3. Everyone in the group **walked** quickly. *I*
4. One hiker **saw** a <u>rattlesnake</u> near the trail. *T*
5. Shelly **froze** instantly. *I*

Direct and Indirect Objects

1. me – *IO*; quilt – *DO*
2. Lee – *IO*; one – *DO*
3. us – *IO*; warmth – *DO*; beauty – *DO*
4. Mom – *IO*; Dad – *IO*; quilt – *DO*
5. design – *DO*

Active and Passive Verbs

1. (passive) Benjamin Banneker's grandmother taught him to read, write, and count.
2. (passive) He spent part of his childhood at a Quaker school.
3. (passive) At the age of 21, Banneker made a wooden clock.
4. (active)
5. (passive) In later years, Banneker wrote a plan for world peace.
6. (active)
7. (passive) George Washington asked Banneker to help plan the new city of Washington, D.C.
8. (passive) Pierre de L'Enfant created the first design.
9. (passive) President Washington did not like it.
10. (passive) Banneker completed the final design.

Principal Parts of Verbs

1. Paula <u>has</u> <u>said</u> that the Everglades is a 4,000-square-mile region of marshlands.
2. The Everglades National Park <u>was</u> <u>established</u> in 1947.
3. <u>Can</u> you <u>believe</u> all the varieties of plants and wildlife?
4. A century of draining and clearing <u>has</u> <u>threatened</u> the Everglades.
5. Ecologists <u>are</u> <u>working</u> in the marshlands.
6. Scientists <u>have</u> <u>studied</u> the water cycle for many years.
7. How much rain <u>does</u> the area <u>receive</u> each year?
8. Temperatures <u>have</u> rarely <u>dipped</u> below freezing.
9. The abundance of insects <u>can</u> <u>support</u> a wide variety of wildlife.
10. Paula and I <u>may</u> <u>apply</u> for jobs at the park.

Verb Tenses

1. Last week Alex played his guitar in a talent show. (past)
2. He dreams all the time about being a famous musician. (present)
3. Next summer Alex will go to a music camp. (future)
4. His sister attended the same camp two years ago. (past)
5. Now Alex hopes to form a band with some classmates. (present)
6. When I was younger, I created a guitar with a cigar box. (past)
7. For the strings I used rubber bands. (past)
8. My brother invited us to the concert yesterday. (past)
9. He will buy tickets for all of us tomorrow. (future)
10. Maybe I will take my cigarbox guitar. (future)

Present-Progressive and Past-Progressive Verbs

1. Mrs. Diaz <u>is instructing</u> her students about pollution.
2. The students <u>are studying</u> the subject.
3. We <u>were talking</u> about local litter problems.
4. Some students <u>are starting</u> a recycling drive.
5. Mike and Terry <u>were planning</u> a bottle drive.

Perfect Tenses

1. Marie <u>has edited</u> her social studies paper.
2. I <u>had finished</u> my rough draft.
3. We <u>will have discussed</u> our papers by Tuesday.
4. Susan <u>will have returned</u> from her vacation before the reports are due.
5. She <u>had worked</u> on her report before she left.

Irregular Verbs

1. Last month Hannah <u>bought</u> a book about Homer Price.
2. In the story, Homer <u>made</u> a donut machine.
3. The customers <u>had bought</u> only a few donuts before the machine broke down.
4. Hannah told me she <u>had felt</u> inspired to invent something.
5. She <u>had caught</u> "inventor's fever."

More Irregular Verbs

1. We <u>got</u> some plans for a deck.
2. Tom <u>had built</u> decks before.
3. He <u>had set</u> his tools down on the ground.
4. Jason and I <u>began</u> stacking the lumber.
5. Before we started, Tom <u>spoke</u> to us about job safety.
6. He <u>took</u> his cap off and put on a hardhat.
7. Selena <u>chose</u> a piece of wood for the first post.
8. Maggie <u>had broken</u> the seal on the box of nails as soon as we bought them.
9. I <u>had known</u> Maggie for a long time.
10. She <u>wore</u> her denim overalls for the deck project.

Singular and Plural Verbs

1. The workers carefully <u>dig</u> in the desert.
2. Dr. Shirazi <u>thinks</u> we will find some valuable treasures.
3. Every member of the three teams <u>knows</u> we will find something today.
4. Excitement suddenly <u>fills</u> the air.
5. Stone steps <u>lie</u> under the sand.
6. The stairway <u>leads</u> to a buried tomb.
7. Each of the workers <u>cleans</u> sand off a step.
8. The many broken pieces of the pot <u>rest</u> on the floor.
9. One of the pieces <u>scratches</u> Kit's finger.
10. The old clay <u>is</u> still sharp.

Subject-Verb Agreement

1. There <u>is</u> something interesting about this site.

2. To an archaeologist, a broken pot <u>represents</u> a treasure.
3. Here <u>are</u> some more paint pots!
4. <u>Do</u> ancient artifacts interest you?
5. Heat and sandstorms <u>slow</u> the archaeologists.
6. They <u>have</u> been working with Dr. Shirazi since noon.
7. The crew <u>spread</u> out in many directions.
8. Dr. Shirazi and I <u>inspect</u> the site carefully.
9. Neither the workers nor the foreman <u>shows</u> up the next day.
10. Neither the foreman nor the workers <u>show</u> up the next day.

ADJECTIVES AND ADVERBS
Adverbs

1. yesterday – visited, verb
2. extremely – interesting, adjective
3. extensively – spoke, verb; quite – extensively, adverb
4. Afterward – went, verb
5. northward – headed, verb

Adjectives and Adverbs

1. Mira writes *frequent* letters to her friends in India.
2. She *clearly* describes details about life in America.
3. Bharati, who misses Mira very much, *carefully* saves the letters.
4. Mira sends tapes of *current* music to Bharati.
5. Bharati is *really* interested in American pop and hip-hop bands.

More on Adjectives

1. <u>Stacey</u> felt **excited** (PA) about Thelma's **sixteenth** <u>birthday</u>.
2. She asked Thelma to pick out a **good** <u>restaurant</u>.
3. The **Chinese** <u>restaurant</u> looked **new** (PA) and smelled **wonderful.** (PA)
4. Both <u>girls</u> felt **hungry** (PA).
5. They ate two **delicious** <u>egg rolls</u>.
6. Thelma had **spicy** <u>noodles</u>.
7. She had to drink a **tall** <u>glass</u> of **ice** <u>water</u>, too.
8. The **main** <u>course</u> was **stir-fried** <u>broccoli</u> and **crispy** <u>tofu</u>.
9. Both girls ordered **sherbet** <u>coolers</u> for dessert.
10. The <u>meal</u> was **inexpensive** (PA) and **tasty** (PA).

Comparative and Superlative Adjectives

1. The snowy owl is the <u>most striking</u> of all owls.

2. The grass in the meadow is <u>greener</u> than the grass in the woods.
3. Saturday's hike was the <u>best</u> hike of the season.
4. The mosquitoes are <u>worse</u> today than yesterday.
5. Red-shouldered hawks have <u>more colorful</u> feathers than short-tailed hawks.
6. In folk tales, foxes are <u>more intelligent</u> than other creatures.
7. Br'er Fox is the <u>most popular</u> fox of all.
8. A spotted rabbit is <u>more unusual</u> than a white one.
9. A hare has <u>longer</u> ears than a rabbit.
10. Voles are actually <u>more common</u> than moles.

Definite and Indefinite Articles
1. *the* sandwich
2. *an* otter
3. *the* tetherball
4. *the* unicorns
5. *an* elevator

Proper Adjectives
1. an Arabian stallion
2. the Chinese people
3. a Polish exhibit
4. a South African city
5. the Brazilian coast

Adverbs/Double Negatives
1. The reptile show lasted <u>longer</u> than the bird show.
2. Of all the spectators, Lennie watched <u>most closely</u>.
3. The lizards behaved <u>better</u> than the snakes.
4. The flying dragon performed <u>most spectacularly</u> of all.
5. Sarah's iguana blinks slower than mine.
6. Yoko doesn't need any more shoes.
7. I can hardly count how many she has now.
8. She can scarcely fit them in her closet.
9. I can't remember ever meeting someone with a shoe collection like hers.
10. They have all been given to her; she doesn't have any that she bought.

PREPOSITIONS
Prepositional Phrases
1. One tale <u>of Cinderella</u> dates back <u>to ancient China</u>.
2. <u>In the Chinese version</u>, the heroine is named Yeh-hsien.
3. She wishes <u>on magic fish bones</u>.

4. <u>At the ball</u> Yeh-hsien drops a golden slipper.
5. A merchant finds the slipper and fits it <u>on Yeh-hsien's foot</u>.

Using Prepositional Phrases
1. Did you order that book for Claudia and *me*?
2. He had to walk around *you* to get to the door.
3. Kiko glanced at *us* as she left.
4. I don't recognize anyone except for *him* and *her*.
5. The line ends here, so you'll have to stand behind *me*.

Prepositional Phrases as Adjectives and Adverbs
1. When the movie ended, many people ran <u>for the exits</u>. (adverb)
2. Martin edited his work <u>after he finished</u>. (adverb)
3. Tamara loves hot dogs <u>with lots of mustard</u>. (adjective)
4. Members <u>of the media</u> asked the President questions. (adjective)
5. <u>Below the surface</u>, sharks lay in wait. (adverb)

CONJUNCTIONS
1. **Just as** the Brothers Grimm became famous in Germany, **so** did Louisa May Alcott find fame in America. (correlative)
2. **After** working as a seamstress, servant, and school-teacher, Louisa May Alcott became a famous writer. (subordinating)
3. **Although** she is best known for *Little Women*, Alcott wrote almost three hundred other works. (subordinating)
4. **Because** of its vividness and deep feeling, Alcott's *Little Women* is loved by millions. (subordinating)
5. Her father Bronson Alcott was well-educated, **but** he **and** his family were poor. but – (coordinating); and – (coordinating)

INTERJECTIONS
1. <u>Ouch!</u> I dropped my suitcase on my toe!
2. <u>Oh no!</u> The strap on my knapsack broke.
3. <u>Okay,</u> let's board the bus.
4. <u>Shhhh!</u> I'm trying to get some sleep.
5. <u>Hooray!</u> This section is over now!

CLAUSES AND VERBALS
Clauses
1. <u>When they reached North America</u>, the earliest inhabitants hunted or gathered. (adverb clause)
2. <u>What life was like for these early travelers</u> is largely unknown. (noun clause)
3. The land bridge, <u>which connected Asia and North America</u>, was covered with water when glaciers melted. (adjective clause)
4. I read <u>that Asia and America were once a single, large land mass</u>. (noun clause)
5. Early hunters used stone-tipped spears for hunting <u>because they had no metals</u>. (adverb clause)

Verbals and Verbal Phrases
1. A <u>glittering</u> audience gathered. (participle)
2. Kings, bishops, and courtiers all came <u>to watch</u>. (infinitive)
3. Lords and ladies enjoyed <u>showing off their finery</u>. (gerund)
4. <u>Pawing the ground</u>, the horses waited. (participle)
5. <u>To ensure fair play</u> was the umpires' job. (infinitive)
6. <u>Fighting in a dishonorable manner</u> brought disgrace to the knights. (gerund)
7. Because knights were often called into battle, the tournaments were a way of <u>practicing</u>. (participle)
8. The highest honor was <u>to win the king's praise</u>. (infinitive)
9. Knights also wanted <u>to impress the young ladies</u>. (infinitive)
10. <u>Challenging a knight to a joust</u> was heroic. (gerund)

CAPITALIZATION
Capitalization (1)
1. <u>Every November</u> our family gathers to celebrate <u>Thanksgiving</u>.
2. <u>Last</u> year we all went to <u>Grandpa Abe's</u> house.
3. <u>He</u> once sent a fan letter to the great ballplayer <u>Babe Ruth</u>.
4. <u>Ruth</u> wrote back, signing his letter, "<u>Your</u> pal, <u>Babe</u>."
5. "<u>I</u> heard these stories all the time," <u>Dad</u> said, "when <u>I</u> was a boy."

Capitalization (2)
1. Near the <u>Canadian</u> border you may hear people speaking <u>French</u>.
2. <u>Marco Porcino</u> lives on <u>Baltic Street</u> in <u>Brooklyn, New York</u>.
3. He celebrates his <u>Italian</u> heritage by visiting <u>New York's</u> historic sites.
4. <u>Marco's</u> grandfather sailed across the <u>Atlantic Ocean</u> from <u>Italy</u>.
5. <u>Ellis Island</u> is located in upper <u>New York Bay</u>.

Capitalization (3)
1. The citizens of <u>Massachusetts</u> are famous for being staunch <u>Democrats</u>.
2. The <u>Revolutionary War</u> began in <u>Lexington</u> and <u>Concord</u>.
3. A museum in <u>Hartford, Connecticut</u>, contains the desk on which <u>Abraham Lincoln</u> signed the <u>Emancipation Proclamation</u>.
4. The <u>American</u> national anthem is "<u>The Star-Spangled Banner</u>."
5. <u>Francis Scott Key</u> wrote it during the <u>War</u> of 1812.
6. My favorite song is "<u>Somewhere Over</u> the <u>Rainbow</u>."
7. It is from the movie *<u>The Wizard</u> of <u>Oz</u>*.
8. The movie came out in 1939, during the <u>Great Depression</u>.
9. The <u>Japanese</u> attacked <u>Pearl Harbor</u> in 1941, which began <u>America's</u> involvement in <u>World War</u> II.
10. The <u>United States War Department</u> grew during <u>World War</u> II.

PUNCTUATION
Periods/Question Marks/Exclamation Points
1. There are eight teams in our soccer league.
2. Tell me which team we will play next week.
3. Who is the captain of your soccer team?
4. How I love to play soccer!
5. Are you going to watch the game?
6. Kelly P. Jones is the best player on our team.
7. Wow! What an amazing goal she scored!
8. We have won every game so far this season.
9. I can't wait until the playoffs begin on Nov. 9!
10. Do you think we will win?

Commas

1. Did you know that Texas was the thirty-second state?
2. On our way to San Antonio, we visited Dallas, Austin, and Fort Worth.
3. On November 22, 1963, President John F. Kennedy was assassinated in Dallas.
4. In Fort Worth, Texas, we toured the Amon Carter Museum of Western Art.
5. Austin is the capital of Texas, and it is a major educational center.

Apostrophes, etc.

1. The director asked, "Have you ever seen <u>The Gong Show</u> on television?"
2. Mona's résumé lists the following talents: singing, acting, dancing.
3. The auditions are open; anybody may try out.
4. The waiting room was three-quarters full by 8:30.
5. At least forty-five people stood outside the door.
6. "Do you know any songs from the movie <u>Grease</u>?" Mr. Chaffee asked.
7. "I can't quite hear—let's see—can you sing a little louder?" he suggested.
8. Mona couldn't remember the lyrics, so she asked for help.
9. An assistant provided cue cards, cardboard signs with words printed on them.
10. "You've done a fine job," said the director.
11. Lena asked, "Have you seen the movie <u>Dr. Zhivago</u>?"
12. Kelly says she has seen it twenty-five times, but I don't believe her.
13. My great-grandmother lived in Germany's capital city, Berlin.
14. Did you know that Monica's father is Russian American?
15. <u>Peer Gynt</u>, a play set in Norway, was written by Ibsen.
16. Major cities in Scandinavia include the following: Stockholm, Oslo, and Copenhagen.
17. No, we arrived in Helsinki at 9:40 yesterday morning.
18. Every Finnish house seems to have a sauna—a small room with dry heat and a woodstove.
19. "I can't find the map," said Norma Jean.
20. "When did you have it last?" asked Jasmine.

PART SIX

Vocabulary and Spelling

CONTENTS

Vocabulary Strategies . . .222–237

Context Clues 224
Word Parts 226
Homophones and
Homographs 230
Idioms 231
Etymology 232
Using a Dictionary 234
Using a Thesaurus 236

Spelling Strategies 238–247

Basic Spelling Rules 241
Spelling Bugs 246

VOCABULARY STRATEGIES

How many thousands of words do you know? Your **vocabulary** is made up of all the words you know, including their definitions. With a great vocabulary you're able to communicate exactly what you mean. A good vocabulary will also help you understand what you read. In this section you'll find out about strategies that will help you figure out what words mean so you can learn more words faster.

Context Clues
Often you can figure out the meaning of an unfamiliar word by looking at the words around it–that is, the word's **context**.

Word Parts
Many words can be divided into a beginning, middle, and end. Knowing the meaning of its **word parts** can help you to figure out what a word means.

Homophones and Homographs

Homophones are words that sound the same but have different meanings and different spellings. **Homographs** are words that have the same spelling but mean different things.

Idioms

Idioms are sayings. They aren't supposed to be taken literally. Recognizing an idiom is the first step to figuring out what it means.

Etymology

Etymology means "the origins of a word." English is an amazing blend of words from other languages. Clues about a word's etymology can help you figure out its meaning.

A Dictionary

A **dictionary** is a reference book that lists words and gives their definitions.

A Thesaurus

A **thesaurus** is a reference book that lists synonyms. Any two words that have the same or similar meaning are synonyms. A thesaurus is a useful tool for finding just the right word for the meaning you are trying to express.

TAKE TIME TO LOOK AROUND

Often you can figure out the meaning of an unfamiliar word by looking for clues in the words surrounding it—that is, the word's **context.**

Imagine yourself in a strange new setting, a place where you don't have the foggiest idea how to behave. What would you do? You'd probably look around to figure out information about your surroundings. You can try the same thing with words you read. A word's context might offer the following kinds of clues:

▶ **Synonyms** or **Antonyms**   ▶ **Examples**

▶ **Definitions**   ▶ **Comparisons**

As you read these sentences, look for clues that will help you to figure out the meaning of each boldfaced word.

The actor played the part of a **melancholy** *character who was so sad he cried for most of the play.*

(If he was so sad that he cried, what might **melancholy** mean? *Melancholy* and *sad* are **synonyms**.)

The citizens of our **pluralistic**, *that is, varied, country are among our greatest assets.*

(If you know what *varied* means, you know what **pluralistic** means. This clue gives a **definition**.)

As our band's **percussionist**, *Melissa plays instruments such as drums and cymbals.*

(This sentence provides **examples**. You can form a good idea of what a **percussionist** means if you know what drums and cymbals are.

A writer's **pseudonym**, *like an alias, is meant to hide the person's true identity.*

(If you know what an *alias* is, you can figure out the meaning of **pseudonym**. This sentence provides a *comparison* between *alias* and *pseudonym*.)

How can you figure out the meaning of a word if a sentence has no clues—no synonyms, definitions, examples or comparisons? Sometimes the main idea of the sentence or paragraph can help you.

Read the passage below. What do you think **traversed** means?

The exhausted tourist had **traversed** *the rough and rocky countryside all afternoon. Her feet were sore. She wanted nothing more than to end her journey on the peaceful porch of her hotel.*

(If you think **traversed** means "walked" or "traveled," you're right. The general context of the passage— exhausted tourist, sore feet, end of the journey—suggests that the person had been walking or traveling.)

Can you figure out what **penitentiary** means?

When the suspect was found guilty of three counts of burglary, the judge sentenced him to five years in the state **penitentiary**.

(Here again, the word's *context* helps you. Where would someone have to go after being found guilty? To a prison—and that's what a **penitentiary** is.)

Figuring out the meaning of a word from general context can be more difficult than using context clues. Sometimes reading ahead or reviewing the sentences before an unfamiliar word may help. Here's another example to try:

What do you think **dismantle** means?

On the day after the carnival, the crew worked fast to **dismantle** the rides and booths. They packed all the pieces into the trucks and drove 200 miles to the next town, where they would put them together again.

(The crew is packing booths and big machines onto a truck, and you know they need to put them together again. So to dismantle must be "to take apart.")

keep in mind
The single best way to build your vocabulary is to read a lot.

PUTTING THE PIECES TOGETHER

Word parts are pieces of words—prefixes, bases, and suffixes.

Can you figure out the meaning of a word you don't know—without even using a dictionary? It's easier than you might think.

As you've seen, you can use *context clues*—words in the sentence or paragraph—to help you. But there's another way to figure out the meaning of an unfamiliar word. You can use the *structure* of the word—the way its pieces are put together—to figure out what the word means.

Many words consist of parts: the **prefix** (which comes at the beginning of the word), the **base** (the most basic piece of the word), and the **suffix** (which comes at the end of the word).

Take a look at the word **disappearance**:

prefix		base		suffix
dis	+	**appear**	+	**ance**
a prefix meaning "opposite"		a base that means "to become visible"		a suffix meaning "the state or act of"

If you put those pieces together, you can come up with a pretty good definition of the word *disappearance*: "the act of becoming invisible."

Some words have a prefix added to the base; some have a suffix added to the base; some, like *disappearance*, have both. These little pieces—prefixes and suffixes—play a big role in determining the word's meaning. So if you can learn the basic meaning of the most important prefixes and suffixes, you'll be able to determine the meanings of a great many words.

Here are some charts to help you with common prefixes and suffixes.

Prefixes

A prefix is one or more syllables that can be added to the beginning of a word or word part to form a new word.

Prefix	Meaning	Examples
anti-	against	*antislavery, antiwar*
auto-	self	*autobiography*
bi-	two	*bicycle, bilingual*
counter-	against	*counterattack*
dis-	opposite	*disappear, disagree*
equi-	equal	*equidistant*
extra-	outside, beyond	*extraordinary*
il-, im-, in-, ir-	not	*illegal, improper, inactive, irresponsible*
inter-	among, between	*international*
intra-	within	*intrastate, intramural*
mega-	large	*megaphone*
micro-	small	*microfilm, microscope*
mid-	middle	*midsize*
mis-	bad	*misbehave*
non-	not	*nonsense*
omni-	all	*omnipresent*
post-	after	*postgame*
pre-	before	*preheat*
pro-	for, in favor of	*pro-government*
re-	again	*repaint, replay*
semi-	half	*semicircle*
sub-	under	*subway*
tele-	distant	*telephone*
trans-	across	*transoceanic*
tri-	three	*triangle*
ultra-	beyond	*ultramodern*
un-	not	*unsure*
uni-	one	*unicycle*

Suffixes

A suffix is one or more syllables that can be added to the end of a word or word part to form a new word.

Suffixes	Meaning	Examples
-ance, -ence -ation, -ion, -tion -hood -ism -ity, -ty -ment -ness -ship -sion	State or quality of:	avoidance, independence starvation, suspicion, attention adulthood heroism necessity, honesty amusement goodness friendship tension
-er, -or, -ist	A person who:	singer, actor, scientist
-able, -ible	Capable of:	lovable, responsible
-al, -an, -ial -en -ic, -ical, -ish -like -some -y	Like, or relating to:	natural, suburban, social wooden poetic, historical, childish lifelike troublesome sunny
-ful	Filled with:	hopeful
-ily, -ly	In what manner:	steadily, quickly
-less	Without:	careless
-ology	Study of:	geology
-ward	In the direction of:	backward

Bases

A prefix or a suffix—or both—can be added to a base to make a new word. A base can be either a word or just a word part. Here are some common bases:

Base	Meaning	Examples
bio	life	biology, antibiotic
chron	time	chronology
dict	speak	dictate, predict
geo	Earth	geography, geology
graph	write	autograph
hydr	water	hydrant
loc	place	location
mem	mind	remember, memory
phone	sound	telephone
port	carry	import, transport
scop	see	microscope, telescope
scribe, script	write	describe, description
terr	earth, land	terrain, territory
viv, vit	alive	vivid, vitamin
volv	roll	revolve

Using Word Parts

When you see a word that's unfamiliar to you, you may be able to figure out its meaning by putting together its pieces. For example, think about the word *extraterrestrial.* From these charts you can tell that *extra-* means "outside or beyond," *terr* means "Earth or land," and *-ial* means "like or relating to." If you put these pieces together, you can figure out that the word means "outside of Earth." An *extraterrestrial* being (like in the movie *E.T.*) is a creature that comes from outside or beyond Earth.

THE SAME, ONLY DIFFERENT

Context clues can really help when you need to figure out the meaning of two special types of words: **homophones** and **homographs**.

Homophones are words that sound the same but have different spellings and different meanings.

Here are some examples:

to, too, two	beat, beet	bear, bare
earn, urn	I, eye	made, maid
heal, heel, he'll	rain, reign, rein	plain, plane

It's important to know the difference between homophones. Imagine what your reader might think if you wrote that you had "bear feet" instead of "bare feet"! Or if you said, "Eye want two go"! If you aren't sure which homophone is correct, look for context clues. If you need help with a homophone when you write or read, you can look up the word in a dictionary.

Homographs are words that are spelled the same but have different meanings.

In many cases **homographs** are spelled the same, but pronounced differently, as in these examples:

bass (a low voice)	or	bass (a fish)
content (things inside)	or	content (satisfied)
minute (60 seconds)	or	minute (tiny)

DON'T TAKE IT LITERALLY

An **idiom** is a saying that means something different from the literal meaning of its words.

Hit the roof is an idiom, for example. If someone said, "Uncle Leonard *hit the roof* when he heard what Joe did," you probably wouldn't think Uncle Leonard actually crashed into the top of the house. To *hit the roof* means to become very angry or upset. Context clues can be helpful when you need to figure out the meaning of an idiom.

Here are sentences which use some common idioms. Can you think of any others?

- ▶ You have to *draw the line* somewhere.
- ▶ Jake and I are *in the same boat.*
- ▶ Playing a game is a good way to *break the ice.*
- ▶ Could you *lend me a hand?*
- ▶ Why do you have to be *in my face* all the time?
- ▶ Your idea is *on the money.*
- ▶ I think we're *up the creek* this time.
- ▶ Peter was worried about the game, but Rick said it was *in the bag.*
- ▶ I don't want to work late tonight, but my boss has me *over a barrel.*
- ▶ Are you serious about this, or are you just *pulling my leg?*

IT'S HISTORY

The English language has developed from many other languages, and new words are being added all the time. Every word has a history, or **etymology**. Knowing the etymology of a word can help you understand its meaning.

Etymology tells where a word came from—and some word histories are fascinating. For example, did you know that the word *plumber* originally meant "lead worker"? *Plumbum* is the original Latin word for lead, and water pipes used to be made from lead. So a person who put water pipes in houses was known as a *plumber*.

Many of the roots you learned about came from Greek and Latin. Other words have been borrowed from other languages, such as German, French, and Spanish. The list below shows some words we use often and where they came from.

Germany	**France**	**North America**
kindergarten	route	igloo
pumpernickel	parrot	moccasin
wanderlust	gourmet	squash
Mexico	**China**	**Italy**
bronco	silk	spaghetti
taco	mandarin	pizza
salsa	tea	piano
Arabia	**Africa**	**India**
zero	gorilla	khaki
sherbet	banjo	dungarees
algebra	banana	pajamas

Words called **eponyms** have come from the names of people or places.

▶ **Boycott** is from Captain Charles Cunningham Boycott, an Irish landowner. In response to Boycott's cruel treatment, his farm tenants refused to do business with him. Since then, *boycott* has grown to mean "any group's refusal to buy, sell, or use a particular product."

▶ **Graham crackers** were invented in 1829 by Sylvester Graham, a vegetarian health-food enthusiast from Northampton, Massachusetts.

▶ **Hamburgers** are from Hamburg, Germany. In the 1850s German immigrants brought this food to the United States, where it quickly became one of the most popular American foods.

▶ **Sandwich** is from John Montagu, fourth Earl of Sandwich, who spent so much time playing cards that he didn't have time to eat full meals. During one famous 24-hour period, he didn't leave the table, and ate nothing but slices of meat and cheese on bread. This arrangement of bread and fillings became known as the *sandwich*.

Clipped words are shortened versions of longer words.

telephone ——> phone   refrigerator ——> fridge
veterinarian ——> vet   dormitory ——> dorm

Blended words have been blended together.

blue + print = blueprint   soft + ware = software
breakfast + lunch = brunch   time + table = timetable

Words called **acronyms** are formed by putting together the first letter of a group of several words. In recent years, many new acronyms have come from scientific discoveries.

RAM (**r**andom **a**ccess **m**emory)
laser (**l**ight **a**mplificiation by **s**timulated **e**mission of **r**adiation)
sonar (**so**und **n**avigation **a**nd **r**anging)

CHECK *it* OUT!

✔ *Words made by adding two complete words together, like sunglasses (sun + glasses) and earring (ear + ring) are called* **portmanteau words**. *Portmanteau is a French word meaning "a two-sided suit-case"—the two words travel together like they're in a suitcase. Suitcase itself is a port-manteau word!*

YOU COULD LOOK IT UP

For more on **spelling**,
see pages 238–247.

Sometimes you know what a word means, but you don't know how to spell it. Sometimes you know how to spell it, but you don't know what it means. In either case, you can use a **dictionary** to help you.

A dictionary is a reference book or computer file that lists words in alphabetical order. Each listed word is called an **entry word.** Most dictionaries give you the spelling, pronunciation, and definitions of each entry word; many also provide the etymology of each entry word, along with pictures and sample sentences to help illustrate the meaning of the word.

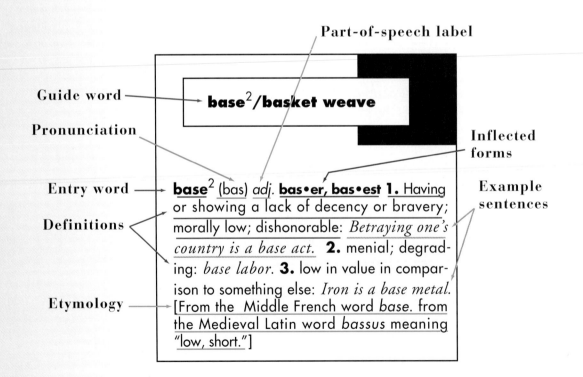

Part-of-speech label

Guide word

Pronunciation

Inflected forms

Entry word

Example sentences

Definitions

Etymology

base^2/**basket weave**

base^2 (bas) *adj.* **bas•er, bas•est 1.** Having or showing a lack of decency or bravery; morally low; dishonorable: *Betraying one's country is a base act.* **2.** menial; degrading: *base labor.* **3.** low in value in comparison to something else: *Iron is a base metal.* [From the Middle French word *base.* from the Medieval Latin word *bassus* meaning "low, short."]

THE ELEMENTS OF THE DICTIONARY

Guide words Are the first and last words on the page. They help you to find the word you're looking for.

Entry word Shows how a word is spelled. If the word is longer than one syllable, it's divided into syllables; dots are placed between syllables.

Respelling Shows how a word is pronounced. Use the **pronunciation key**—there's usually one inside the dictionary's front and back covers—to see the specific sounds of each letter.

Part-of-speech label Shows how the word can be used in a sentence, such as **n.** for noun, **v.** for verb, or **adj.** for adjective. Sometimes a word can be used as more than one part of speech.

Definitions Show the various meanings of a word. If there are more than one, the definitions are numbered, with the most widely used meaning listed first.

Example sentences Show how the word can be used in a sentence.

Inflected forms Show the plural form of nouns, the past and present participles of verbs, and the comparative and superlative forms of adjectives.

Etymology Gives the origin and history of the word.

CHECK it OUT!

✔ *Some words have similar definitions yet convey very different feelings or ideas—they have different connotations. The connotation of a word is the impression it conveys or suggests.*

For example, the words determined, stubborn, *and* pigheaded *all mean* to be fixed on a goal and unwilling to give in *but as you may know, their connotations are very different!*

LOOK FOR (SEARCH, SEEK, HUNT, EXPLORE) SYNONYMS

Are you bored with some of the words you use in your writing? Do you wish you knew more interesting words or words with more exact meanings to replace the ones you use all the time? Check out a **thesaurus**!

A thesaurus is a writer's reference—either a book or a computer program—that provides synonyms for many common words. It's a great tool to help you broaden your vocabulary and make your writing more lively.

In most thesauri, entry words are listed in alphabetical order, along with their synonyms. (Some thesauri also list a word's antonyms.) Some thesauri will also give you the part of speech, definition, and a sample sentence for each word.

Sometimes a thesaurus will also give you *cross-references*—directions to look under other entries. For example, if you look up the word *haste*, the thesaurus might provide the cross-reference, "See *activity*." This means that you should look up the entry for the word *activity*. The following entry will provide many more synonyms for the word *haste*.

Entry word ⟶ **HASTE [684]**

Part-of-speech labels

Nouns—haste, urgency; despatch, dispatch; acceleration, spurt, forced march, rush, dash; VELOCITY; precipitancy, precipitation, precipitousness; impatience, impetuosity; brusquerie; hurry, drive, scramble, bustle.

Verbs—1. haste, hasten, make haste, hurry, rush, dart, dash, whip on, push on, press; scurry, scuttle along, bustle, scramble, plunge, bestir oneself (see ACTIVITY), lose no time, make short work of; work against time. *Colloq.*, hurry up, hustle, make tracks, step on it. *Slang*, shake a leg, make it snappy, get a move on.

Cross-reference

2. speed, speed up, expedite; quicken, accelerate. *Slang*, step on the gas, give 'er the gun.

Adjectives—hasty, hurried, brusque; abrupt, cursory, precipitate, headlong, furious, boisterous, impulsive, impetuous, eager, impatient, hotheaded; feverish, breathless, pressed for time, hard-pressed, urgent.

Adverbs—hastily, precipitately, helter-skelter, slapdash, full-tilt, headlong; apace, amain; all at once (see INSTANTANEITY); at short notice, immediately (see EARLINESS); express, posthaste.

Antonym ⟶ *Antonym*, see SLOWNESS.

THE ELEMENTS OF THE THESAURUS

Entry word Is the word you look up to find its synonyms.

Part-of-speech label Tells you how the entry word is used in a sentence: as a noun, verb, adjective, and so on.

Definition Tells you what the entry word means.

Example sentence Shows you how the entry word might be used in a sentence.

Synonyms Are words whose meanings are the same or similar to the entry word.

Antonyms Are words whose meanings are the opposite of the entry word.

When you find a new word in a thesaurus, always look it up in a dictionary to double-check its meaning.

SPELLING STRATEGIES

When you spell a word correctly, your reader *knows* what you mean. When you spell a word incorrectly, your reader can only *guess.*

If you think spelling is unimportant, look at the following sentence:

Salt-n-Pepa are my favorite **wrappers**.

Huh? Is Salt-n-Pepa a kind of gift-paper? No—Salt-n-Pepa are rap singers, or **rappers**.

As you know, English is a tricky language because our words come from so many other languages. You can think of spelling as a code everyone agrees to use so we can communicate successfully with each other. The ways some words are spelled may appear to make little sense, but there are reasons behind them, whether the word entered our language thousands of years ago... or just recently (like *cyberspace*).

During the proofreading stage of your writing, be sure to check the spelling of each word you are unsure of how to spell—even if you wondered for just a moment. Remember, good spelling takes *patience* (and good doctors take *patients*).

Here are some steps to help you keep on top of spelling:

The Dictionary

If you aren't sure how to spell a word, look it up in the dictionary. When you don't know how a word is spelled, a trip through the dictionary can be frustrating—a little like looking for your glasses if you can't see without them. But after a few tries, checking the different ways you *think* the word might be spelled, you will usually find the word you're looking for. If not, try a related word that could lead you to your answer.

Problem: It sounds like **soshul studies**, but *it's not under s-o-s-h and you don't know where to turn*.

Solution: Think of related words—"In *soshul studies* we study *society*." A look at *society* shows **social studies** just a few listings above *society*.

Be sure to check the *definition* of the word along with its spelling. Some words that sound alike have different spellings and very different meanings (they're called homophones). What might your reader think if you wrote, "My favorite sticker cost ten **scents**"?

A Spelling Dictionary

When you learn a hard word or misspell a word in your writing, jot the correct spelling down in a notebook. This notebook will serve as your own spelling dictionary. When you use a new word or one you have misspelled before, you can check the spelling in your notebook. Pretty soon, you may find that you don't even have to turn to the notebook for some words!

more
INFO

For more on using a dictionary, *see pages 234–236.*

keep in mind

The more often you see a word's correct spelling, the more likely you are to remember it.

These catchy lines will help you remember how to spell some tough words:

✔ Weird: "**We** are w**e**ird."

✔ Cemetery: "**Three e's** are buried in the c**e**m**e**t**e**ry."

✔ To keep "**sta-tionery**" (the writing paper) straight from "stationary" (remaining still), remember that **stationery** contains an **e**—for **e**nvelope.

SPELLING STRATEGIES

Spell-Checkers

Many word-processing programs for computers have built-in spell-checkers. When you use the spell-checker, it automatically reviews every word in your document to see if it is spelled correctly. If a word is spelled incorrectly or if it's not familiar to the computer's built-in dictionary, the program asks you to check the word.

Spell-checkers can be very useful, but they're not perfect. They check words for spelling but not correct usage. For example, a spell-checker would find nothing wrong with the idea that something costs ten "scents."

Memory Aids

You can remember the spelling of some words with the help of memory aids—rhymes or sayings that can trigger your memory. You may have heard this one: "*I* before *e* except after *c*, or when sounded like *a*, as in *neighbor* and *weigh*." This rhyme can help you remember how to spell words with *ie* or *ei* combinations.

If you know a good memory aid, use it... and share it with friends. You can also make up your own. One student remembers how to spell **Manhattan** with this phrase:

"*A* **man** *in a* **hat** *with a* **tan**."

CRACKING THE CODE

Here are some guidelines you can learn to help crack the spelling "code." However, be warned: not all words follow these rules. Think of these guidelines as hints that will help you develop a sense of what's *usually* correct and what isn't.

Words with *ie* and *ei*

▶ Put the rhyme to work for you—"*I* before *e* except after *c*, or when sounded like *a*, as in *neighbor* and *weigh*." In most cases, a word is spelled with *ie* for the long *e* sound, except when the *e* sound follows the letter *c*:

brief		re**cei**ve
chief		**cei**ling
piece	but	con**cei**t
believe		per**cei**ve
wield		

▶ When the vowel sound is a long *a*, "as in *neighbor* and *weigh*," the word is usually spelled with *ei*.

eight	**wei**gh	s**lei**gh
weight	**nei**ghbor	f**rei**ght

However, some words are spelled with *ei* even when the vowel sound is not a long *a*:

either	s**ei**ze
neither	w**ei**rd

✔ *Try spelling a difficult word syllable by syllable, saying the word quietly to yourself as you write it. If you pronounce it correctly, your chances of spelling it correctly are improved. Check your dictionary for any spellings you're still not sure of.*

ADDING ENDINGS

Even if you know how to spell a word, what happens when you want to make it plural, change the verb tense, or change an adjective into an adverb? Spelling can be a challenge any time you add onto a word, so here are some rules (and, yes, some exceptions!) to help you add the right ending.

Adding -s and -es to nouns and verbs

▶ In many cases, you can make a noun plural or write certain forms of a verb by adding -s to a word without any other change in the spelling:

clock	*zebra*	*write*	*make*
clocks	*zebras*	*writes*	*makes*

▶ If the word ends with *ch, s, sh, ss, x,* or *z*, add -*es:*

porch	*moss*	*fax*	*buzz*
porches	*mosses*	*faxes*	*buzzes*

▶ For most nouns ending with a single *f*, change the *f* to *v* and add -*es:*

elf	*scarf*	*leaf*	*shelf*
elves	*scarves*	*leaves*	*shelves*

▶ However, there are some exceptions to this rule:

proof	*chief*	*roof*	*oaf*
proofs	*chiefs*	*roofs*	*oafs*

▶ For most words that end with *ff*, add -*s:*

staff	*cliff*	*stuff*	*gaff*
staffs	*cliffs*	*stuffs*	*gaffs*

Making plurals for words ending with o

▶ For most words that end with a consonant followed by *o*, add *es* to form the plural:

hero	*heroes*	*potato*	*potatoes*	*volcano*	*volcanoes*

▶ For most words that end with a vowel followed by *o*, add -*s* to form the plural:

video	videos	stereo	stereos	radio	radios

For most words ending with y

▶ If a word ends with a consonant followed by *y*, change the *y* to *ie* before adding an ending:

deny	hurry	lazy	melody
denies	hurried	laziest	melodies

For most words that end with a vowel followed by *y*, keep the *y* when adding an ending:

turkey	obey	spray	gray
turkeys	obeyed	spraying	grayer

But some verbs ending in *y* have an irregular past tense:

say	buy	pay	lay
said	bought	paid	laid

Irregular Nouns

▶ To form the plurals of some irregular nouns, change the spelling of the word:

child	mouse	ox	woman
children	mice	oxen	women

▶ For other nouns, especially the names of certain animals, the singular and plural forms are the same:

sheep	trout	deer	moose
sheep	trout	deer	moose

Doubling letters to form endings

▶ In most cases, if a one-syllable word ends with one vowel and one consonant (like -*ag* or -*in*), double the consonant when adding an ending that begins with a vowel:

tag	rip	thin	big
tagged	ripped	thinnest	bigger

▶ For most two-syllable words ending with one vowel and one consonant, double the consonant only if the accent falls on the second syllable:

bother	matter	refer	begin
bothering	mattered	but referred	beginning

▶ If a word ends with a silent *e*, drop the *e* when adding an ending that begins with a vowel:

ride	large	soothe	pale
riding	largest	soothing	paler

Adding suffixes

A suffix is an ending that changes a word's meaning or its function. For example, add the suffix *-ist* and you make the verb "type" into a noun, "typist." Or add the suffix *-less* and you've gone from "hope" to "hopeless." When you add a suffix, the spelling of the base word may change, so here are some guidelines:

▶ If the base word ends with a silent *e*, drop the *e* before adding a suffix that begins with a vowel:

operate	*type*	*move*	*response*
operator	*typist*	*movable*	*responsive*

▶ There are exceptions, such as *notice, noticeable.*
For most words ending with silent *e*, keep the *e* when adding a suffix that begins with a consonant:

hope	*care*	*amuse*	*shame*
hopeless	*careful*	*amusement*	*shameful*

Some exceptions to this last rule are words that end with *-dge*:

judge	*acknowledge*
judgment	*acknowledgment*

▶ When you add the suffix *-ness* (to form a noun) or *-ly* (to form an adjective) the spelling of the base word usually does not change:

kind	*pale*	*sharp*	*like*
kindly	*paleness*	*sharply*	*likeness*

Some exceptions to this last rule are certain one-syllable words ending with two vowels or a vowel and *y*:

gay	*true*	*day*	*due*
gaily	*truly*	*daily*	*duly*

▶ If a word ends with *y* and has more than one syllable, change the *y* to *i* before adding *-ness* or *-ly*:

cagey	*sunny*	*happy*	*lazy*
caginess	*sunnily*	*happily*	*laziness*

Adding prefixes

A prefix is an addition to the beginning of a word. Adding a prefix also changes a word's meaning. There's a world of difference, after all, between *spell* and *misspell!* (That's the whole point of this section.) When you add a prefix to a word, the spelling of the base word usually stays the same:

tell	*tie*	*state*	*biography*
retell	*untie*	*interstate*	*autobiography*

For more on homophones, *see page 230.*

Homophones

As you've already read, homophones are words that sound alike but have different meanings and different spellings. Be sure you know the meaning of the homophone you want to use. Knowing the meaning will help you spell it correctly.

Here are a few frequently used (and misused!) homophones:

to/too/two	*altar/alter*	*cellar/seller*
peace/piece	*ant/aunt*	*bough/bow*
forth/fourth	*base/bass*	*capital/capitol*
principle/principal	*loan/lone*	*cent/scent/sent*
stationary/stationery	*hair/hare*	*cite/sight/site*
through/threw	*foul/fowl*	*main/mane*
seam/seem	*oar/or/ore*	*scene/seen*
rap/wrap	*soar/sore*	*steal/steel*
toe/tow	*vain/vane/vein*	*which/witch*

LOOK OUT BELOW

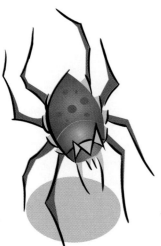

As you may have learned the hard way, many words do not follow spelling rules. Other words do follow the rules but are tricky to spell anyway. The best way to spell these "problem" words correctly is to memorize them.

Here's a list of words that seem to be the most troublesome. Try using this list and your dictionary whenever you are unsure of a word. Remember: The more often you see a word's correct spelling, the more likely you are to remember it.

abdomen	brilliant	desolate
absurd	bruise	develop
accommodate	business	diamond
ache	canoe	diaper
acknowledge	catastrophe	dilemma
acquire	category	disappear
agile	caught	disappoint
aisle	cemetery	eerie
ally	certain	elementary
amateur	chasm	elephant
analyze	chute	eligible
answer	cinnamon	embarrass
anxiety	colossal	enthusiasm
appearance	comparative	especially
appropriate	compatible	essential
asbestos	complexion	exceed
assistant	congratulate	excellent
athlete	cough	familiar
authoritative	courteous	fascinate
auxiliary	crease	feminine
awkward	criticize	fiery
bazaar	cylinder	fluorescent
bicycle	dandelion	foliage
boulevard	defenseless	foreign
breathe	descendant	forfeit

forty
fourth
fragile
frighten
gauge
gaunt
genius
genuine
government
graduate
grammar
grudge
height
hideous
icicle
independent
indispensable
initiative
institution
intellectual
interrupt
irresistible
isolate
jealousy
jubilant
judgment
kiln
label
laboratory
lacquer
ladle
lapel
lavender
lieutenant
lightning
linoleum
lullaby
maneuver

marriage
matinee
measles
mediocre
meteor
miscellaneous
misspell
mobile
mosaic
municipal
murmur
mystery
nausea
necessary
necessity
nickel
niece
nineteenth
ninetieth
ninety
ninth
obstacle
occasion
opportunity
orchid
pageant
parallel
particle
patent
peculiar
permissible
persuade
petal
pleasure
pliers
poison
prejudice
principal

principle
procedure
punctual
pyramid
realize
receive
reckless
recognize
recommend
relief
repetition
reservoir
responsible
restaurant
rhyme
rhythm
rhythmic
schedule
scissors
scour
secretary
seize
separate
similar
stationary
stationery
subdue
suburb
successful
sword
technical
tentacle
their
they're
throughout
tomorrow
toward
trapeze

treacherous
tread
treasure
trespass
truly
turbulent
typical
unique
utilize
variety
venom
vicinity
vise
waffle
weather
weight
weird
we're
whether
whim
wretched
wring
wrong
yacht
young
you're

247

PART SEVEN

Resources

CONTENTS

Writing Models . . 250–297

Persuasive Essay 251
Descriptive Essay 252
News Article 254
Feature Article 256
Editorial 258
Observational Report . . . 260
Research Report—Science 262
Research Report
—Social Studies 264
Compare/Contrast 266
Cause/Effect 268
Problem/Solution 270
How-to Guide 272
Autobiography 274

Biography 276
Interview 278
Character Sketch 280
Summary 282
Book Review 284
Story 286
Poem 288
Script 290
Personal Narrative 292
Business Letter 294
Friendly Letter 296

**Glossary of
Literary Terms** . . 298–307

Index 308–319

WRITING MODELS

Just as there are many kinds of music and art, there are many kinds of writing—and each one is a little different. A short story or a poem is very different from a research paper or a book review, and you need to use different strategies in writing them. But what *are* these strategies exactly?

In this section, you'll see model examples of many types of writing, along with helpful suggestions for how to read and write each kind yourself. By the time you're finished, you'll be ready to tackle just about any kind of writing you can imagine!

PERSUASIVE ESSAY

In a **persuasive essay**, you take a stand on a particular issue.

When you write a persuasive essay:
> Be sure you use specific reasons and examples to back up your argument.

When you read a persuasive essay:
> Identify the writer's main argument. Judge whether the examples truly support the argument.

THE OLD SCHOOLHOUSE: THE IDEAL CHOICE

Even in the title, the writer suggests an opinion.

The old schoolhouse should become our town's first shelter for the homeless and needy. The need for such a shelter in Monte Sereno is obvious. A recent article in the <u>Monte Sereno Gazette</u> reported a steady decline in affordable housing in town. Some people are having a hard time making ends meet. No one should have to live in the park.

The writer begins by clearly stating the topic and an opinion.

The writer offers specific reasons why the town needs a shelter.

The old schoolhouse is an ideal choice for the shelter. It has not been used since Pony Express School was built 13 years ago. It is a solid brick building, needing little in the way of repairs. It also has a kitchen area where hot meals can be made and a small cafeteria for eating. Shower facilities are available in the gym locker rooms.

The writer lists details that show why the schoolhouse is the right building. Notice how specific they are.

The project might be a good way to bring together the townspeople for a worthy cause. It is important to acknowledge that we are "our brother's keeper."

The essay ends by giving the reader a larger idea to think about.

In 1776 Thomas Paine published an essay that was so persuasive it helped convince Americans to fight the Revolutionary War. Published as a pamphlet, the essay "Common Sense" demanded that the Thirteen Colonies be granted complete independence from England. The pamphlet was a hit—hundreds of thousands of copies were printed and sold; in its first year 25 editions sold out.

DESCRIPTIVE ESSAY

In a **descriptive essay** you describe or explain a particular topic—a word, phrase, or idea.

When you write
a descriptive essay: ▶ Keep in mind that specific examples and particular details will help make your description clear and vivid.

When you read
a descriptive essay: ▶ Think about why the author is describing this particular topic. Is it an unusual topic? Or a common topic that the writer is looking at from a new angle?

SO I'M SUPPOSED TO WRITE AN ESSAY

The writer begins by naming what she is going to describe: an essay. Notice how her informal, humorous tone helps to get readers interested in the topic.

I have been given an assignment—to write an essay. That's great, except I'm not really sure what an essay is, so how can I write one? The only solution I could think of was to go digging in the library to find out everything I could about essays. What I found out is that no one is really sure about what exactly makes an essay, but I'll tell you what I learned.

The writer uses a specific example to show the root of the word "essay." A casual tone, which you'll notice remains consistent throughout, is used in many descriptive essays.

It all started with a French fellow named Michel de Montaigne. He was a philosopher, so he spent a great deal of time thinking and writing about the condition of the world and the people in it, but mostly he wrote about himself. His book was published with the title *Essais*, which is French for "attempts." These were his attempts to explain the condition of the world in short prose pieces. Well, the title caught on, and pretty soon anyone who wrote a short prose discussion of a narrowly limited topic was called an essayist.

Essays can be either formal or informal. The formal kind tend to be very serious and very long. For obvious reasons, these are not terribly popular. At their best, they are represented today in the form of thoughtful magazine articles.

The informal essay, in contrast, can be characterized by humor, rambling organization, personal opinions, and is relatively brief. Writers can complain, try to persuade, busily inform, express their opinions, tell anecdotes—almost anything goes. We can write them to our friends in the form of letters. We can read them every day in the guise of newspaper articles and editorials. Essays even appear on television at the end of a news program when some older man feels he must tell the world about what he thinks about—well, almost anything goes. Needless to say, everybody loves them. If you really want to charm your reader, you can't beat an informal—sometimes called personal—essay.

So what is an essay? Well, I've never really gone beyond saying that an essay is a brief prose discussion of a restricted topic. The nicest thing about this is that in the process, I've written one. My assignment is done.

Note how the writer has broken down the larger topic of "essay" into two smaller topics: formal essay and informal essay.

The writer concludes by summing up the general description of "essay" and adding a humorous twist.

The five senses are great tools to help you describe something vividly. In fact, a few scientists believe "the mind" does not exist at all—or at least not only in our brains. Instead, it travels through the body as hormones and enzymes—which help us to interpret the senses of touch, taste, smell, hearing, and vision.

NEWS ARTICLE

News articles are supposed to be factual, balanced, unbiased accounts of important events. They can have a local, national, or international focus.

When you write a news article:
Answer the 5 Ws: *who? what? when? where?* and *why?* Journalists try to include partial answers to as many of the 5 Ws as they can in the opening paragraph, or lead, of the story. Put information in order of importance and news value.

When you read a news article:
Focus on content. Pay attention to important facts. Be on the lookout for bias—is any important information missing? Do the sources quoted provide useful information?

The "title" of a news article is called a headline; like all good headlines, this one conveys what the article is about and grabs readers' attention.

The "lead," or introduction, answers as many of the 5 Ws as possible.

Rubbernecking moose family stops traffic

Minnetonka commuters had a drive on the wild side early today as a moose and her calf investigated rush-hour traffic on westbound Route 203, south of Minnetonka Wildlife Preserve, where the pair probably lives. Apparently drawn by aromas from a stalled bakery truck owned by Di Guglielmo Brothers' Bakery of Maplewood, the moose family wandered onto the highway at about 6:50 A.M., first sniffing the truck, then watching motorists throughout the morning commute.

The pair closed each westbound lane of traffic at various points over a 45-minute period. "I offered them some bread, but maybe they don't like sesame seeds," said bakery truck driver Mollie Williams, also of Maplewood. "We had a staring contest—and that baby moose definitely won."

Animal behaviorist Benjamin M. Kasmir, of Minnetonka State University's Veterinary School, said the rubbernecking behavior was "unusual" for moose, who are usually reclusive when protecting their young. Kas-

mir said the pair's usual terrain may have been dis turbed by loggers or other intruders. "The bakery truck may have been a draw, but the animals were probably more curious than hungry," Kasmir said. "Moose usually like more fiber in their diet."

State Trooper Francis Toby directed traffic around the curious animals. "They were definitely breaking no-pedestrian laws" for limited-access highways, Toby reports. "But we maintained one open lane throughout most of the incident, so we decided not to take them in for questioning."

Commuters took the slowdown in good humor. "It's one of the best things about living around here, being close to nature," said auto mechanic Matt Hart. "So I'm a couple minutes late to work. Big deal."

If possible, include quotes from witnesses and/or relevant experts.

After the two had had their fill of the highway scene, the moose calf followed its mother back into the preserve, and traffic flow quickly returned to normal. "I don't think you'll see any moose-related delays tomorrow," Kasmir predicted.

The article ends with less important information, and lets readers know whether they should expect to be affected by this news in the future.

FYI

Journalists refer to news articles as either *hard news* or *soft news*. If it's timely, essential information—like how Congress voted yesterday, or a crime spree in a city—it's *hard news*. *Soft news* is less crucial and not so linked to timeliness—an article about a 100-year-old citizen or a record-breaking unicyclist would be considered *soft news*.

FEATURE ARTICLE

A **feature article**, instead of reporting on an event, usually covers a topic in a more in-depth way, providing information in a highly readable format. Like news stories, features should be factual accounts.

When you write
a feature article: ▶

You can use a more conversational tone, but you should still answer the *5 Ws,* lead with a sentence that will grab attention while providing the basics of the story, and put information in order of importance.

When you read
a feature article: ▶

Look for answers to the *5 Ws :* who? what? when? where? and *why?*

Tom Sawyer: Still
WHITEWASHING

The lead paragraph pulls the reader in, and introduces the subject—notice that who? what? and where? are already answered.

Tom Sawyer is still whitewashing fences—sort of. A fan of writer Mark Twain, Vanessa Noel runs a fence-painting business called Tom Sawyer, Inc., based in Junction, Missouri. Junction is 12 miles down the Mississippi River from Hannibal, where Samuel L. Clemens, better known as Mark Twain, grew up. Twain wrote such classics as <u>The Adventures of Tom Sawyer</u> and <u>The Adventures of Huckleberry Finn</u>.

This paragraph offers information on why. It also quotes the subject of the article, which strengthens the human-interest angle.

"I got the idea for this when I was a kid and my dad read me <u>Tom Sawyer</u>," says Noel, 29, a graduate student in American literature. "When Tom tricks his pals into taking over his fence-painting chore, I said to my dad, 'I'll do it. That sounds like fun!' Before I knew it, I was hired to paint the fences around our farm. Later on, I figured it'd be a great way to save money for college."

Founded in 1983, Noel's business expanded rapidly, and she needed to hire helpers in a hurry. "I did just what Tom Sawyer did—talked my friends into wanting to paint—only I'm paying them. Tom never did that." Tom Sawyer, Inc., now employs six part-time painters, including Noel herself.

Business is booming, and Noel's schedule is booked solid from now through next fall. "I could actually use some more help with this stuff. I'm getting quite busy with school," she says. Noel is working on a graduate degree in American literature at Missouri State University. Is Tom Sawyer her thesis topic? "No," she says. "I read that book about 93 times when I was a kid. It's hilarious, and it's full of wisdom, but I'm onto new material now."

The writer relates what's next for the subject, and also provides more background information.

"Maybe somebody reading this will want to help me paint," Noel says. "After all, whitewashing is a lot of fun. Time goes faster if you've got a pal to talk to, though, or a Walkman," she admits.

One of the longest feature articles ever published later became a best-selling book. *The Fate of the Earth* by Jonathan Schell, which examines how living with the threat of nuclear war affects our lives, was originally published in three long installments in *The New Yorker* magazine in 1981.

EDITORIAL

An **editorial** is a persuasive essay that appears in a newspaper or magazine. The writer clearly states his or her opinion about a topic important to readers of that magazine or newspaper.

When you write an editorial: ▶ Choose a topic that you care about! Begin the editorial by introducing your topic and clearly stating your opinion about it. Support your opinion with facts and examples about the subject.

When you read an editorial: ▶ Make sure you identify the writer's opinion early on. Keep in mind that an editorial often gives only one side of the argument, so use your critical reading skills to decide whether you agree or disagree with the editorial.

Saving MORE Daylight

Try to state your opinion early in an editorial. That way, the reader will know right away what you think.

It's often a good idea to give some background to help educate the reader about the subject.

Daylight Saving Time is a clever plan in which clocks are set one hour ahead of standard time for a certain period in order to give everyone an hour more daylight in the evening. This extra hour of daylight is one of the joys of the warmer months, starting on the first Sunday in April and lasting until the last Sunday in October. However, I believe that Daylight Saving Time should begin earlier.

The United States has had a strange relationship with DST. First adopted here in 1918, Congress then repealed it in 1919. In spite of this repeal many cities continued to use daylight time. Then, during World War II, DST was again elected for use by some cities and states. It was not until 1967 that the U.S. Congress established the six-month April-through-October plan, and still state legislatures can vote to keep their states or even parts of their states on standard time.

The practicality of a longer Daylight Saving Time became apparent during 1974 and 1975. In an effort to conserve energy when oil was expensive, DST began on January 6 in 1974 and on February 23 in 1975. In 1976, as soon as the price of oil went down, the early schedule was abandoned for the old April plan.

Then in 1991, Operation Desert Storm made the world even more aware of the economic importance of oil. Must we conserve oil only when it is expensive? We are foolhardy if this is the case.

However, on a personal level, that extra hour of sunlight at the end of most of our days is very important. The sooner we start it in the year, the better. If the sun is up, we should be up. If we waste less energy in the process, let's count this as a bonus!

Notice how the writer establishes a connection between DST and oil conservation. This helps support his argument.

Unlike some other kinds of writing, an editorial is a good place to get personal. After all, you are stating your opinion.

FYI

Many newspapers have two pages of opinion pieces. The first page, the main editorial page, has pieces written in the *we* point of view. That's because the writer is speaking for the entire staff of the newspaper. The second page is called the "Op-Ed" page (because it's *op*posite the main *ed*itorial page). Here, writers may use the *I* point of view because they are offering personal opinions.

OBSERVATIONAL REPORT

An **observational report** provides factual information about something the writer has observed. The writer may or may not draw a conclusion about the information. Science reports are often written in this form.

When you write an observational report:
▶ Provide specific information about what you've observed in as objective a fashion as possible. Focus on describing what you saw, not how you feel about it. If you draw a conclusion, be sure it's well-supported.

When you read an observational report:
▶ Try to picture what the writer is describing. Focus on content, rather than writing style. If the writer draws a conclusion, judge whether the evidence supports it well.

The Effect of My Dog on Homework

The first paragraph introduces the topic and gives details about the writer's observations. This writer has chosen a casual tone; observational reports are often more formal.

After careful consideration of the evidence, I have come to the conclusion that my dog Mookie is opposed to homework. I cannot claim that my dog ever ate my homework, but he has walked on it with muddy paws and pulled other stunts that seem designed to prevent me from getting my homework done on time.

One day Mom let me keep Mookie in my room while I did my math homework. As I was figuring out a very complicated equation on my calculator, Mookie sat under my desk, chewing on my sneakers a bit, but generally behaving. I leaned down to pat his head, which was a big mistake. Mookie thought it was time to play. He jumped onto my lap and pressed his paw on the calculator, and I had to start my math homework all over again.

Another time, I made a three-dimensional clay map of New England, complete with mountains, valleys, and rivers. It took me three days to finish it. I knew it was great, and I went to get my sister, to show it to her. When we got back to my room, we found Mookie rolling around on top of my masterpiece. By the time we got him off the map, the Green Mountains looked more like the Great Plains!

At the end of last year, I had a term paper due in social studies. I decided to write it on our family computer. Someone must have told Mookie, because when I sat down to finish my paper, I found he had chewed right through the printer cable. It was Sunday night, so we couldn't get another cable, and I had to stay up late, copying the whole thing out by hand.

I know it's strange to think a pet could care one way or the other about homework, but after hearing about Mookie's behavior, perhaps you will agree that my dog disapproves of it.

Notice the focus on facts. Be sure to give examples of what you've observed. Visual details will help the reader picture your observations and will also support the conclusion if you've drawn one.

The last paragraph caps off the report and encourages the reader to interpret the information in a particular way.

It's harder to be objective about what you observe than you might think; we all tend to see what we want to see. After living among the natives of Samoa, the anthropologist Margaret Mead described Samoan society as very peaceful and happy. Another "professional observer," social scientist Derek Freeman, also visited Samoa. He claimed Samoan society is full of strife and violence and said Mead's view of Samoa is an example of wishful thinking. After reading their accounts, you might never guess the two were describing the very same society.

RESEARCH REPORT—SCIENCE

A **science research report** explains something about science or nature that you have learned from books, articles, or experiments.

When you write a science research report: ▶ State the main point, then develop the paper with information and examples from your research. Write in clear language so your reader can easily understand your topic—even if it is a complicated one.

When you read a science research report: ▶ Try to identify how the writer has presented the information. The writer of this essay has used comparison and contrast.

The title contains a lot of useful information, which will be developed more fully in the report.

This report is organized by comparison and contrast. The reader learns what the writer is comparing, and why (so you'll know which map to use when).

Perceiving the World: Globes and Mercator Maps

Globes and Mercator maps of the world show the same place, yet the world shown is somehow different. A globe is best for some types of reference, and a Mercator map is best for others. Because of this, it is important to understand how they are different.

The most accurate representation of the characteristics of Earth's surface is a globe. A globe can be tilted to correspond to the tilt of Earth's axis, and a globe can be made so that it will rotate. On a globe the relative sizes of the features and their locations are accurate.

The writer shows the advantages and disadvantages of the globe. Notice how specific the writer is in her examples and reasons. Providing specific information will help readers understand your material.

Using a globe, however, has many disadvantages. To begin with, a globe shows only half of Earth's surface at one time. Globes are usually too small to show much detail. On the other hand, most globes are too large and cumbersome to carry around as a ready reference. Because of a globe's rounded shape, it is awkward to chart or follow a straight line from one place to another.

Incidentally, a globe is not completely accurate because Earth is not truly round.

To explain the most important differences between a globe and a Mercator map of the world, it is necessary to understand the system of meridians and parallels. On a globe, meridians are north-south half-circles that begin at one pole and end at the other. These are used to measure longitude. Parallels are east-west lines drawn around a globe; these circles are used to measure latitude. The grid formed by meridians and parallels provides standard reference points. However, when making a two-dimensional map, such as a Mercator map, from a three dimensional globe, a mapmaker is essentially stretching and compressing the distance between them.

This spreading of the meridians and extending of the parallels would not distort sizes or distances of features at the equator. The farther a feature is from the equator, however, the greater the distortion. Thus areas nearer the poles, such as Greenland, are shown to be much larger than they should be.

Although distortion is the great disadvantage of a Mercator map, there are several important advantages. Like all maps, it is lightweight, foldable, and easily portable. A Mercator lets the viewer see the whole surface of the world at once. Because maps are flat, charting courses and measuring distances become easier.

When you're comparing and contrasting two subjects, it's important to help the reader understand both. Here the writer discusses the second item in the comparison—the Mercator map.

When you look at the world depicted on a globe or on a Mercator map, it's important to know what you are seeing and how each serves a different purpose.

The writer concludes by restating her main point: that a globe and a map are different.

You may think writing and science are very different things, but writing actually helped make science possible. The development of writing in Mesopotamia and Egypt several thousand years ago allowed people to record what they'd learned (by experiment or by accident!) and pass it on to later generations.

RESEARCH REPORT—SOCIAL STUDIES

A **social-studies research report** explains something about your society or other societies that you have learned from books or articles.

When you write a social-studies research report: ▶ Begin with your main point, then develop the paper with information and examples you have gotten from your research—books, newspapers, magazines, or interviews. You can organize a social studies report using any of the different forms you have learned about, such as compare and contrast, main idea and supporting detail, or classification.

When you read a social-studies research report: ▶ Try to identify how the writer has presented his or her information. In the following example, notice that the writer develops the topic by presenting historical information in time order.

The Origin of Agriculture

In the first paragraph, the writer introduces the topic—the origin of agriculture—and relates clearly what the report will say about it.

According to a new theory, the beginning of agriculture was the result of a change in climate and the depletion of natural resources.

These changes occurred in the Jordan Valley about 12,000 years ago when the climate of the mild summer months became hot and dry. The stress on the environment resulted in less available food and water because of shorter summers, shrinking lakes, and scarcer game.

If you're presenting a historical account, as this writer is, it's a good idea to organize the paper in time order.

The people in the region had always lived by hunting and by gathering foods they found growing in the wild. Now they, like the animals, were dramatically affected by the scarcity of food and water. As a result, they moved to areas near the Dead Sea, where food and water were more plentiful. The swelling population, however, soon made food scarce there also.

264

Some plants, primarily legumes and grains, were actually helped by the change in climate. The life cycles of these plants end in the spring. Because of their husks, seeds for these plants survived the summers, leaving them ready to germinate during the cool, wet winters. The flourishing grains became tougher, so that their seeds did not scatter when the plants were plucked. It was inevitable that people would learn to save some of the seeds of these wild grasses for planting, to cultivate the plants, and then to harvest these cereals.

Specific examples and physical details help the reader picture and understand your subject.

Archaeologists have discovered that a sophisticated culture formed in this area about 10,000 years ago. These people lived in well-built houses in a permanent settlement. They had a social organization that allowed them to control the storage and distribution of grain. They also had the technology of flint sickles and stone mortars. The increased food supplies made possible by agriculture led to the expansion of human population and thus to the formation of cities.

This writer presents research—archaeologists' discoveries—to help back up his theory. Notice that the writer gives specific examples to show what he means by "sophisticated culture."

Soon a spreading population carried the idea of agriculture east and north into Mesopotamia and what is now modern Turkey. Both agriculture and civilization were well under way.

The historical developments that the writer has shown lead to the conclusion.

"Social studies" is the study of people and their interactions. The word "social"—which is related to the word "society"—originally comes from the Latin word *socius*, which means "friend" or "companion."

COMPARE/CONTRAST

A **compare/contrast** essay emphasizes similarities and differences between two or more subjects.

When you write
a compare/contrast
essay: ▶

Your job is to explain how the subjects are alike and different. Organize information by outlining examples of similarities and then of differences, or by discussing various features of the subjects in an orderly way.

When you read
a compare/contrast
essay: ▶

Pay attention to the facts. As with all nonfiction, judge whether the writer supports his or her position.

ALLIGATORS AND CROCODILES

The first paragraph introduces the subjects, explains their basic similarities, and sets up a discussion of their differences.

Alligators and crocodiles are among the largest reptiles on Earth. They are both lizard-like reptiles from the animal family Crocodilia. Many people think alligators and crocodiles are the same, but they're wrong. As in most families, there are resemblances between the members of Crocodilia, but also quite a few differences. Crocodiles are bolder and more aggressive than alligators and nearly twice as big. Male crocodiles can reach 23 feet long. Full-grown alligators seldom exceed 12 feet in length.

Both alligators and crocodiles prefer swampy, warm environments. They spend about half their time in the water and half on land. When in water, they like to float just beneath the surface, with only their eyes, ears, and nostrils visible. Both are powerful swimmers with strong tails that help them to maneuver through the water.

This writer has organized her material by describing how individual features are alike or different. You might choose to outline all the traits of one subject, and then all the traits of the other, or to discuss all the differences before mentioning similarities.

Alligators have broad, short snouts, while crocodiles' snouts are long and tapering. When crocodiles close their mouths, their bottom teeth stick out, but you cannot see alligators' bottom teeth unless they open their mouths—in which case you'd better run!

266

Both animals have large, powerful jaws lined with many teeth, but neither attacks without reason. They use their jaws to catch and eat fish—and sometimes larger animals, too. Both animals can run surprisingly fast, considering the stubbiness of their legs.

Unfortunately, most members of the Crocodilia family are endangered, largely because people have hunted them, both out of fear and out of the desire to use their hides for shoes, belts, and wallets. Luckily, most alligators and crocodiles now live in protected areas, and their populations are once more on the rise.

Notice the emphasis on facts. This writer is not concerned with which animal she prefers. Be sure to stay focused on facts rather than opinions.

You can end like this writer does, with factual information and a last thought to take away. Or you can end with a summary of the main points. Be sure to end on a strong note.

FYI

Comparing and contrasting is a skill you use all the time. When you choose one candy bar over another, vote for one candidate over another, choose a class to take or a shirt to wear, you're comparing and contrasting. Many ads and television commercials compare and contrast things, too, often deceptively.

CAUSE/EFFECT

A **cause/effect** essay shows how one event or fact caused something else to happen.

When you write
a cause/effect essay: You need to show how one thing causes another. Be sure the links between things are clear.

When you read
a cause/effect essay: Look for the main points, and think about whether the chain of events is truly related—watch out for faulty logic.

Exercise *and* Energy Levels

The first paragraph introduces the topic and establishes the cause/effect relation.

When you're feeling listless and sleepy, you might think exercise is the last thing that could perk you up. Experts, however, say that exercise is perhaps the single best energy-booster there is.

This paragraph gives the reader more about the topic in general. It denies a common belief (in this case, that exercise tires people out), and replaces it with the assertion that most people get energy from exercise.

Many people believe it is better to skip their workouts on low-energy days. Some fatigue, however, actually stems from the need to move. This is called "sedentary inertia" or "exercise deficiency." If that's what's behind your fatigue, exercise is certainly the best answer. Aerobic exercise such as running or swimming—in moderation—can pick you up. Most people experience an improvement in mood and energy level following a moderate workout. You don't need to run five miles to reap the energy-enhancing benefits of exercise; studies claim that even a brisk ten-minute walk can help you feel more alert for over an hour.

This paragraph gives the reader information about a secondary point—how exercise affects the mind and mood.

If anxiety or mild depression is at the root of your fatigue, then exercise might be just the ticket to raising your energy supply. Some studies suggest that exercise produces chemical and electrical changes in the brain that make you more alert and brighten your mood. Besides giving you more energy, exercise naturally reduces muscle tension, boosts circulation, and reduces your body's stress responses. A workout can also give you a healthy feeling of accomplishment.

There are times, however, when exercise won't pick you up. If you're sick with a cold, flu, or more serious illness, or if your fatigue results from lack of sleep or an unhealthy diet, exercise probably won't lift your energy level much. Before setting up a regular exercise routine, it's probably a good idea to see a doctor.

If you exercise regularly and eat a well-balanced diet, you will probably have plenty of energy. Days when you feel groggy are probably the times when exercise will help you the most.

Now the writer gives the reader information about a related point— that exercise is only one factor that affects energy levels.

The last paragraph summarizes the message and gives the reader a useful, easy-to-remember piece of advice.

FYI

Is there an identifiable cause for everything that happens, or do some things happen at random? The answer isn't as easy as you may think—physicists don't always agree on an answer. Some are researching proofs of "chaos" theory—the idea that events can be random. Others argue that at least in theory, there's a reason for everything. Most physicists, however, think that both are true, depending on the angle of observation.

PROBLEM/SOLUTION

A **problem/solution essay** presents a problem and then describes one or more possible or proven solutions to that problem.

When you write a problem/solution essay: Be sure to describe the problem before launching into possible solutions, and be sure the solution or solutions you present actually address the problem.

When you read a problem/solution essay: Pay attention to how (and whether) the solutions presented fix the problem the writer has described.

Paper-Route *Blues*

The first few paragraphs should provide details about the situation—introducing the who, what, when, where, and why of the problem.

I'm a busy guy, especially in the afternoons. I play soccer and track, and after sports practice every afternoon, I deliver *The Springfield Eagle* to 26 houses. It's always a challenge to complete my route before dinner. My mom works nights, so she especially likes to have the whole family together for dinner. We eat at 5:30 sharp. For two years my schedule ran smooth as silk. Then came Mrs. Cove.

About three months ago Mrs. Cove moved into a house at the end of Manor Road. She is older than my grandmother and lives alone. After she subscribed to the paper, I began delivering it seven days a week. Mrs. Cove would come outside to wave when I delivered her paper. One day she offered to let me ride my bike through her sprinkler. After that we got to be friends. The only problem was that, because I was talking to Mrs. Cove, my route began taking longer and longer.

The first day I was late for dinner. I told my mom why, and she didn't mind. She said it was nice of me to visit with Mrs. Cove. After the fourth time Mom said I had to find a way to deal with my problem. I couldn't stand the idea of leaving Mrs. Cove on her porch feeling lonely. I thought about this for a long time and finally came up with a solution. I told Mrs. Cove that instead of a little visit every day, I'd come over to see her for an hour on Saturdays after my route was done.

For the problem this writer has outlined, one solution is enough. More complex problems, though, might call for several possible solutions.

She still comes to the window every day and waves, and when I see her warm, crinkly smile, I know she's planning whatever fun we will have that Saturday. So far she's taught me how to make newspaper hats and apple tarts. Once we painted her window sills. I have enough time to get my route done before dinner now. My mom thinks I'm terrific, since I'm nice to Mrs. Cove—*and* I always show up on time for dinner.

So the problem is solved. Of course, not all problems can be solved quite so easily. An essay about Earth's thinning ozone layer, for instance, might include solutions that could require years to take effect.

What does your math textbook have in common with *Dear Abby?* They both follow a problem/solution format. As you can see, there are many ways to present problems and solutions!

HOW-TO GUIDE

A **how-to guide** shows the reader how to do something correctly.

When you write a how-to guide: ▶ Make sure you understand every step of the process. Then carefully describe each step in time order.

When you read a how-to guide: ▶ First read the entire guide, to make sure you understand the overall process. Then proceed carefully, making sure to complete each step before moving on to the next.

A LAKOTA NATION GAME

In the first paragraph, state what you will be explaining in the how-to guide.

"Stop" is a dance-step game originally played by children of the Lakota nation. The game is easy to organize because it needs little preparation and only a few materials. It can be played in large or small groups and by people of all ages.

Make sure to describe all the materials the reader will need.

To play, you will need one or more drums. If a ready-made drum is not available, you can easily make one. Find a large, empty aluminum can or any large cylinder, like an oatmeal container, and make sure one end is open. Turn the cylinder upside down, and you have your drum. You can also use an upside-down pail. Cans and pails of different sizes will make different musical tones when struck with your hand: the greater number of different sounds, the more interesting the game.

Gather together the game players and choose one player to beat the drums. The drummer creates a steady rhythm, fast or slow, and all the other players must dance or perform exaggerated leg and arm movements to the beat of the music. At any moment the drummer may suddenly stop beating the drums. When this happens all the dancers must "freeze" positions. Those who cannot hold their positions must sit down, they are eliminated from the game. The drummer resumes drumming the beat, and the dancing continues. The last dancer left standing wins the game and becomes the next drummer.

Remember: In a how-to guide, having a beautiful writing style is not as important as being clear and concise. Use short, easily understood sentences. Avoid figurative language like metaphors and similes.

You use how-to guides all the time—perhaps more than you might suspect. Every time you give someone directions, you're composing a kind of how-to guide. Recipes are really how-to guides too. What are some other how-to guides you use in your daily life?

273

AUTOBIOGRAPHY

In an **autobiography** the author tells a true story about all or part of his or her life.

When you write an autobiography: ▶ Think about some of the most important events in your life. What do you remember about them? What was their meaning to you? What would be the best way to describe them to someone else?

When you read an autobiography: ▶ Think about why the author chose to include these particular events. What makes them so important? What can you learn about the author from them?

In the Heart of the MOUNTAINS

One good way to begin an autobiography is by describing your home; this provides the setting for the rest of the story.

Although I, Bill Eagle, was born in Chicago, I have lived from my earli-est childhood on the Indian reservation in Cherokee, North Carolina, deep in the heart of the Great Smoky Mountains.

Autobiographies often include a discussion of the author's family. Sometimes an autobiography will tell about the lives of the author's parents, as a way to set the stage for the story of the author's own life.

My father, Tom, is a full-blooded Cherokee who was lured to the big city to work in construction. When he was in Chicago, he met my mother Lila, a city girl who had never seen a mountain in her life. Shortly after I was born, they decided to move back to the area where my father had grown up and where he had been offered a job as a forest ranger.

Being the son of a forest ranger is very exciting. In the summers I often spend the days with my father as he makes his rounds. This often takes us on back roads and trails deep into the mountains and far away from Cherokee, which is filled with tourists during the summer months. I help my father do such things as mark trails for hikers and plant seedlings in areas where the soil has eroded. The most exciting event is when we pay a visit to the watchtowers where rangers spend the days watching for forest fires. From these great wooden towers high on the mountain tops, I can see for miles and miles across the hazy blue valleys that give the Smoky Mountains their name.

This writer describes himself by discussing the things he most likes to do.

My whole life is not spent on the trails with Dad. I have a busy life at school. I am the best center on the school basketball team. At home I help my Mom and play with Jason, my little brother. The best part of my year, however, is being with Dad deep in the glades and woods in the heart of the mountains.

The writer reveals more about himself, discussing his life at school and at home.

The line between autobiography and fiction is fuzzier than you might think. Autobiographies are often written to explain and justify things the authors have done, so sometimes he or she may bend the truth to present a more appealing story to the reader. And much fiction, of course, has autobiographical elements in it. Many novels are written in the first-person point of view, which makes it seem as though the main character is telling his or her own autobiography.

BIOGRAPHY

A **biography** is the true story of all or part of someone's life.

When you write a biography: ▶ Make choices about what to include. What were this person's most important achievements? What were the most important events in his or her life?

When you read a biography: ▶ Think about why the author chose these particular events to describe. What do they reveal about the subject of the biography?

FATHER OF India

When you're writing a biography—especially a short biography—it's often useful to sum up your subject's most important achievements in the opening paragraph.

Mohandas Karamchand Gandhi is considered by the people of India to be the father of their nation. He helped to free India from control by the British by using an unusual form of protest and resistance: nonviolence. He was also responsible for many social and economic reforms in India. He was killed by an Indian extremist.

Biographies are usually organized chronologically (in time order).

Gandhi was born in 1869 into a merchant family. After being educated in India, he went to England in 1888 to study law. In 1891 he returned to India to practice law but had a hard time earning a living. In 1893 he went to South Africa to do some work with an Indian law firm. Gandhi soon became a successful lawyer and worked for the rights of Indians in South Africa. He had only planned to stay one year but remained for 21.

In South Africa Gandhi experimented with forms of civil disobedience and nonviolent action. When he returned to India, he again used nonviolent techniques to help Indian peasants and mill workers. Within five years of his return to India, Gandhi became the leader of the Indian nationalist movement.

Gandhi worked hard all his life to help India gain independence from Britain. One method he used was to fast until changes he wanted were made. He led a fight against the government's treatment of the caste, or group of people, called "Untouchables." He also promoted women's rights, basic education, village and home industries, and Hindu-Moslem equality. Gandhi was often jailed for his efforts. Great Britain finally granted freedom to India in 1947. Less than a year later Gandhi was shot to death by an upper class Hindu separatist.

His people had called Gandhi *the Mahatma,* an honorary title meaning "great-souled." Gandhi searched all his life for truth, which can be seen in the title of his autobiography, *The Story of My Experiments with Truth.* He spent his life struggling to gain rights for the oppressed and promoting peace and equality among all classes, castes, races, and religions.

It's often useful to sum up the subject's main contributions in the closing paragraph.

FYI

In ancient Greece and Rome, the earliest biographers often glorified their subjects, describing them as noble people who lived moral lives. Today, though, biographies usually present a more well-rounded view, showing their subjects' strengths *and* flaws. In fact, some people claim that many modern biographies focus *too* much on bad qualities or even do "hatchet jobs," presenting their subjects in the worst light possible. The writer Joyce Carol Oates has termed these books "pathography," meaning literally "writing about disease."

INTERVIEW

An **interview** is a record of questions and answers between a journalist and his or her subject.

When you write an interview: ▶ Think about the information you want to learn. Prepare a list of questions beforehand. It's a good idea to use a tape recorder, so that you have an exact record of the interview.

When you read an interview: ▶ Think about the questions the interviewer asks. Do they help reveal important information? Would you have asked different questions?

Abby Schirmer Finally Speaks!

Writers often begin an interview with a general paragraph providing basic information to the reader. They also usually mention when and where the interview took place.

One of the most controversial issues of this school year arose when Principal Gilbert ruled that class valedictorian Abby Schirmer could not deliver her commencement address; she had given him a text of the speech, and he decided that it was not appropriate. We asked both Abby and Principal Gilbert for interviews. Principal Gilbert refused to grant an interview; Abby, however, agreed to speak with us. We met with her in the cafeteria last week to talk over the controversy.

If you listen closely when people speak, you'll hear a lot of hesitations, broken sentences, and poor grammar. It's okay to "clean this up" in your written interview—but it's never okay to add things your subject didn't say or to delete important information.

Gettysburg High Gazette: What were you going to say in your address?

Abby Schirmer: Last summer I spent some time traveling in Brazil. I saw the worst poverty I had ever seen—people living in cardboard shacks, begging for food on the streets. It was very upsetting. I was going to talk about some of this in my address.

Gazette: Why did you want to talk about this in your address?

AS: It seems to me that, as young people, we have a responsibility to create a world that's better than the one we've been given. I was simply going to talk about one of the very serious issues we're faced with today—world poverty—and urge my classmates to think about ways of trying to deal with it.

Gazette: How did you find out that Principal Gilbert was not going to let you say this?

An interview's questions are often printed in italics. Often, the interviewer is named only as the newspaper or magazine in which the interview is printed.

AS: I was called to the principal's office one afternoon and when I got there, he told me that he wasn't going to let me give my address. He didn't give me specifics, but he said that he didn't think it was an appropriate subject for a commencement address.

Gazette: How did you feel when he said this?

AS: I couldn't believe it. I walked out of his office in a daze. But then later on, I got angry. I don't think he has the right to tell me what I can and can't say in my commencement address.

Gazette: What's been the reaction in school since this all came out? Has any of this been difficult for you?

Ask the questions you think your readers would be most interested in having answered.

AS: No, not really. A lot of people have come up to me and said they wished I had been allowed to speak. Others have told me they agree with Principal Gilbert, but no one has said anything to make me change my mind.

Gazette: Including Principal Gilbert?

AS: Including Principal Gilbert. I thought I was right then, and I still think so.

The best stories can come from the unlikeliest sources. New York journalist Jimmy Breslin believes in what he calls the "gravedigger theory" of interviewing. After President John Kennedy's death, when other journalists were interviewing famous people, Breslin chose to interview the President's gravedigger—he felt this provided an important, and otherwise unexamined, perspective on the death.

CHARACTER SKETCH

In a **character sketch** you paint a portrait of someone with words.

When you write a character sketch: ▶ Think carefully about what the character looks like; how he or she talks; the kind of clothes he or she wears; or a particular incident that reveals his or her personality. What details can you include to describe this character vividly?

When you read a character sketch: ▶ Pay attention to the details the writer uses to help you see and hear the character. Also, be sure to note the relationship the writer has to the character he or she is writing about. That relationship might help you better understand not only the character but also the writer.

You can use the title to present an impression of, or an attitude toward, the character right away.

My Favorite AUNT!

The writer begins by giving a detailed physical description, so we can picture Aunt Sophie.

Aunt Sophie, my father's older sister, is 67, but the weird thing is, she seems like she could be my age. She wears jeans, a T-shirt, and tennis shoes. Most of the time her clothes and hands are spattered with paint because she is an artist. Sometimes she even wears a baseball hat to keep paint out of her silver hair.

"Don't you mean gray?" Dad jokes when she talks about her silver hair.

"No," she insists. "Gray is the color of a stormy sky. Silver is the color of a precious metal. I'm more like a precious metal than a stormy sky."

The words and actions of other people can help shed light on the main character.

"Oh, no, Sophie," Dad says, laughing. "You're more like a stormy sky."

Dad is right about that. She shouts and yells as easily as most people talk. Yesterday we visited her apartment in the city, and I told her how bad the traffic had been.

"Traffic!" she bellowed. "There's always traffic. No one ever gets anywhere because they're too busy trying to go somewhere else!"

By using dialog, the writer lets the reader hear Aunt Sophie, which makes the picture even more vivid.

Aunt Sophie doesn't even have a car. She lives downtown in a big loft where she does her painting. The apartment, like Aunt Sophie herself, is streaked with paint and filled with energy. I love visiting her and seeing the new paintings she's working on. Her latest one is my favorite. It's a painting of me!

The writer ends with a twist—which is fun for the reader.

 Artists sometimes make preliminary sketches in order to capture the essence or shape of a figure before developing it more fully in a painting. Writers can use character sketches for the same purpose: to explore someone they might develop more fully in a story or novel.

SUMMARY

A **summary** is a brief overview of something you've read. Most summaries cover the material in the same order the book does.

When you write a summary: ▶ Convey a balanced overview of what you've read. It's *not* a book review, so don't include your own opinion on the topic and/or the writing style. Be brief; don't rewrite the book or story you've read!

When you read a summary: ▶ Focus on content, rather than on the writer's style or how much you liked the book or story summarized.

A SUMMARY OF

RAYMOND'S RUN

The introductory paragraph conveys the gist, or main idea, of the story—you learn a bit about what happens, what it might mean, and who the main characters are.

"Raymond's Run," by Toni Cade Bambara, is a story about a champion runner who learns there are more important things than winning a race. The main character is a young girl named Squeaky. Other story characters include her older brother, Raymond, and a new girl in the neighborhood, Gretchen.

The story begins with Squeaky preparing for a big race. She is practicing her breathing techniques, and Raymond, whom she takes care of, tags along. They meet a few of Squeaky's classmates who taunt her about Raymond not being "quite right." The classmates also say the new girl Gretchen will beat Squeaky at the race. Squeaky defends Raymond and continues training.

During the race Squeaky decides two important things. She gains respect for Gretchen, who takes running as seriously as Squeaky does. Squeaky also notices that Raymond runs very fast. She decides to retire as a runner and train her brother to become a champion. Then Raymond can have ribbons, medals, and respect of his own. As Squeaky and Gretchen wait for the race results, they smile at each other in friendship.

This paragraph provides more details. It often makes sense to present events in the same order the story or article does.

This paragraph sums up the main events of the story. Notice that the writer has told you about the whole story without telling whether she liked it. A summary is supposed to be a reliable, short overview of content, not a reaction to it.

Don't mix up *summary* and *summery*. They sound alike, but have very different meanings. *Summary* comes from the Latin *summa*, which means sum. *Summery* comes from the Sanskrit word *sama*, which means "season" or "year."

BOOK REVIEW

In a **book review,** the reviewer describes a book's strengths and weaknesses, and conveys information a potential reader might like to know. A book review is not a summary. A summary is an objective overview of a book's contents; a review focuses on a book's merits or lack of them.

When you write a book review: ▶ Discuss the book's strengths and weaknesses. If it's a nonfiction book, does it provide authoritative information? If it's literature, does it hold your interest? Support your opinions with specific examples from the book.

When you read a book review: ▶ Consider whether you'd enjoy reading the book itself. Does the reviewer give you a favorable impression of the book? Are the reviewer's comments—positive and negative—well-supported by examples?

A Review of Patricia MacLachlan's Novel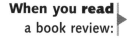

The reviewer mentions the book's author and title, along with what kind of book it is (a novel). She gives a hint of the book's subject matter, and lets you know she thinks it's a good book.

Patricia MacLachlan's novel *Journey* is not about a trip, but about what happens to those who are left behind. It's a wonderful, wise story about how a family adjusts to change. The main character, Journey, is someone almost any kid could relate to. He's smart and sensitive and full of an interesting blend of confidence and insecurity.

When Journey is 11, his mother takes off, leaving Journey and his teenage sister Cat with their grandparents. The members of the family are left to grapple with what they mean to each other and how they will fill the empty space left in their lives. Journey's grandfather takes lots of photographs. His grandmother raises a garden twice as big as before. Cat tries to take her mother's disappearance in stride by telling herself not to care anymore. Journey seems to take it the hardest. For a long time, he can't feel angry at his mother. All he can do is wonder why she left and pretend she'll be coming back soon.

Photographs help Journey come to some important realizations. He searches family photographs for hidden truths. After he finds a box of torn-up baby pictures, his grandfather admits that Journey's mother tore them up. Journey finally understands that she is not coming back, but it doesn't destroy him. When she calls one day, Journey is able to handle speaking with her.

The summary she provides both supports her opinion, and encourages people to read the book.

The story sounds very sad, but there are some happy surprises. By the end of the book, Journey, Cat, and their grandparents find a new strength within themselves and with each other. I found myself wishing the author told more about how Cat adjusts, but overall the book is well-rounded. Patricia MacLachlan's writing is simple but very moving. As Journey's grandfather says, "A thing doesn't have to be perfect to be fine. . . . Things can be good enough." Along with Journey, we learn that people can be happy even if they have problems.

When you write a review, tell your readers what the book offers— and what it doesn't. Support your ideas with examples your readers can get a handle on.

Book reviews can be funny—and they don't necessarily have to be nice. Here's an excerpt from a rather mischievous review by a writer famous for her wordplay:

This is not a novel to be tossed aside lightly. It should be thrown with great force.

—Dorothy Parker

STORY

A **story** is a series of made-up events with a beginning, middle, and end. Beyond that it can be almost anything: a suspenseful mystery, a heart-stopping ghost story, a comedy, a romance—whatever you, the writer, want it to be.

When you write a story: ▶ Keep in mind that you are creating a new world for the reader. Use details from the five senses to help bring that world to life.

When you read a story: ▶ See if you can identify the main characters, the setting, and the conflict. Keep in mind other elements of fiction that the writer uses to make the story rich and believable, such as point of view, flashback, and dialog.

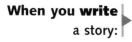

THE OLD HOUSE

The writer introduces the main characters and the setting in the opening paragraph, catching the reader's interest right away.

Liz and I had always wondered about the old house that stood at the end of our street. It was dark and ramshackle; the trees and bushes that surrounded it had grown wild and almost hid the fact that the house was there. Liz said that no one had lived there for as long as she could remember. In our minds it was a place of great mystery.

Late one afternoon as Liz and I walked back from the library, we passed the house. "Let's see if we can look inside," Liz suggested mischievously.

Here the conflict begins. Every short story contains conflict of some kind. We read stories to see how the conflict is resolved.

"Oh, no. Do you really think we should?" I responded. In my heart I didn't think so.

Sensory detail (like sound and touch) helps your reader experience the story.

Liz took the initiative. She began to work her way through the shrubbery at the side of the house. I timidly followed. When a branch snapped back in my face, I stopped to rub my eyes, which were teary. All of a sudden I heard Liz cry out. Then she was gone.

I panicked. "Oh, Liz, Liz, Liz," I cried. Through my tears I could not see a trace of her. I was trapped on all sides by branches and undergrowth. I turned and ran back toward the street. Just then I heard a giggle. It was Liz.

My joy at seeing her was tempered by the anger I felt because I knew that she had tricked me. "Oh, Liz, what happened? You're terrible to tease me this way."

"Calm down, calm down," Liz said, becoming suddenly serious. "I did this to teach you a lesson. You must learn not to do something that you don't want to do just because someone else does."

"But how did you disappear like that?" I asked.

"Oh, that was easy," smiled Liz. She told me that yesterday she stopped by the house and cut a low path into the tangle of bushes. That was how she could get out so quickly.

"Do you mean you planned this whole thing?" I asked, ready to be really mad.

"No, I really did want to peek into the house yesterday, but after I started, I realized how dangerous it was and I abandoned the project."

It took me several days before I forgave Liz for tricking me, but I did remember her lesson.

One of the most legendary storytellers was herself a fictional character: Scheherazade. She appears in a collection of tales gathered together in the 1500s from Arabia, Egypt, India, and Persia. It is called *Arabian Nights* or *A Thousand and One Nights.* The story about her is perhaps the best one of all. Her evil husband plotted to kill her, but Scheherazade begged him to let her tell a story first. He liked that story so much he postponed her execution so that he could hear another story on the next night. A thousand and one nights passed in this way until the husband could no more imagine executing her than doing without her wonderful stories for the rest of his life. In the meantime he had fallen in love with her and, for all these reasons, decided to let her live after all.

POEM

A **poem** is a work written in verse form—but it's as flexible as your own imagination.

When you write a poem: Think about what you most want to say. Do you want to tell a story, describe an image, reveal your feelings about something? What kind of poem would best get this across?

When you read a poem: Think about what the poet is trying to say. How does he or she communicate this? Reading a poem out loud is a great way to really *hear* its sounds and rhythms.

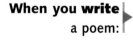

The Quest for the Chococicle

The whole house was dark
As Tim crept down the stair;
He peeked round the corner
And no one was there.
He stared across the hallway
And into the gloom
Of what was the kitchen,
His favorite room.
And deep in the freezer,
He knew there to dwell
The last Chococicle—
And would it taste swell!

This poem uses a regular rhyme pattern. However, many poems don't rhyme at all.

He crossed to the kitchen
Without making a sound,
When a hum and a whistle
Proved Mom was around!
She breezed down the hallway,
Still humming her song,
And she flicked on a light
As she glided along.
Tim's heart filled with panic
As he slipped past the door,

This type of poem is called a narrative poem, because it tells a story. Narrative poems are often longer than other kinds of poems.

Mom entered the kitchen,
And what do you think?
Did she head for the stove
Or go to the sink?
No, she went to the freezer
And opened the door
To seize the Chococicle—
But there—no more!
Then Mom stopped her
        humming
And let out a sigh,
And mumbled, "Oh, drat"
And, "Kiss that good-bye."

Then a screen door banged
        loudly,
And Dad shuffled in
With a smile on his face,
A brown smudge on his chin.
And Tim got the giggles
When he saw this sight,
And they all started laughing
In the middle of the night.
And Dad bowed with relish
And presented the stick
To Mom as a trophy—
And she gave it a lick.

Then they all went together,
And climbed up the stairs,
And returned to their beds
To resay their prayers.
And what did they dream of?
Well, I bet you know—
It's brown and it's sticky
And cold as the snow.

A stanza is a group of lines in a poem. This poem uses 12-line stanzas. Notice, though, that the final stanza is only eight lines. The stanzas of your poem don't all have to be the same length. And many poems—particularly poems that don't rhyme—are not written in stanzas.

Poetry existed even before writing. The first poems were memorized and recited aloud. Even today, poems are told by peoples who do not use a written language. Poetry is truly universal. Every society has poetry.

SCRIPT

A **script** is the written text of a play or movie.

When you write a script: ▶ You are telling a story with dialog alone. There is not a narrator present as there is in a story. Instead, you must convey all the action, emotion and thought through the characters.

When you read a script: ▶ Try to picture it being performed on a stage. Reading parts aloud with others can help you get a better sense of the characters and action.

At the start, the writer describes the setting (including time) and characters. These notes convey important information to the actors and those designing the scenery.

SETTING: The hat department of a men's clothing store.	**TIME:** The present.

CHARACTERS:

Salesclerk—a slender, nervous man who is very busy keeping the shop tidy.

Customer—a slightly rumpled older woman who is carrying a large straw handbag.

The department manager (a nonspeaking role).

Stage directions, which indicate a character's actions, are set off in parentheses and italics. This lets the reader know they are not part of the dialog.

Customer (*poking at the salesclerk with her walking cane*): Young man, young man. Would you please help me?

Salesclerk (*flustered*): Yes, may I help you?

Customer: Yes, I'd like to see some hats.

Salesclerk (*looking to see if she has a male companion*): Oh, yes. Hats. Is this hat for—you?

Customer: Of course not. Do I look as if I would wear a man's hat? Don't be impertinent. The hat I need happens to be for Edgar.

Salesclerk: Well, er—yes. Uh—would you like a felt hat or something in straw?

Customer: Straw would be nice, I think.

Salesclerk: Please step this way. *(He moves to where the straw hats are displayed.)* Now here we have a nice Panama of the finest quality. Or if you want something more sporting, a boater will fit the bill.

Notice how the dialog carries the action along.

Customer: Oh, they're both lovely—I just don't know. Would you try it on, to give me an idea?

Salesclerk: Uh, well, ah—oh, all right. *(He self-consciously puts on the sporty hat.)* There!

Sometimes the writer uses the stage directions to convey a character's tone or expression. This can help actors understand their roles and help give readers a window into the characters' minds.

Customer: Very nice indeed. Now could you crouch down for a minute? Edgar is rather short.

Salesclerk: Madame.

Customer: Just for a minute . . .

Salesclerk: Oh, all right. *(He crouches ridiculously.)*

Customer: Could you turn a bit to the right?

Salesclerk: Madame, really!

Customer: Just a bit . . .

Salesclerk: Oh, okay. Just a bit. *(As he awkwardly bounces up and down in his crouched position, the department manager quietly appears on the scene.)*

Customer: No, no. To the right. *(As the clerk reverses his bouncing, wheeling to the right, the customer addresses Edgar, a tiny dog in her large handbag.)* No, Edgar, I don't think so. Thank you anyway, young man. *(As she is leaving.)* And you really must learn your left from your right.

As a good story sometimes does, this scene ends with a surprising twist.

FYI

One of the greatest playwrights ever, William Shakespeare, wrote:

All the world's a stage,
And all the men and women merely players:

They have their exits and their entrances,
And one man in time plays many parts.

—As You Like It

PERSONAL NARRATIVE

Personal means *having to do with a person*. *Narrative* means *story*. So a **personal narrative** is a story you tell about yourself—except that instead of making it up, you tell a true story. Most personal narratives are written in a casual style and reveal something about the writer's personality.

When you write a personal narrative essay: ▶ Be sure to convey enough information for the reader—remember, *you* know what happened, but *your readers* don't until you tell them.

When you read a personal narrative essay: ▶ Pay attention to the events of the story. What can you learn about the writer's personality?

The first paragraph pulls the reader in with an overview of the story— a good choice here, but there are many ways to tell a story, so don't assume this is the only way to go.

Not many people know what it's like to be privately famous, but I do. I spent an afternoon as the school mascot, Hopkin the Kangaroo, at a football game last fall. I hopped around the bleachers, signed autographs, and even did a cartwheel with the Hopkintown Middle School cheerleaders at half-time.

My brother Ross was usually Hopkin, though no one was supposed to know that—there's a lottery every June to see who will be Hopkin the next fall. The winner is sworn to secrecy. Ross even hid his costume in a box under his bed so his friends wouldn't see it.

I was eating peanut-butter toast one Saturday morning when Ross shuffled into the kitchen with his costume over his arm. When he croaked out "good morning," I made fun of him, but it turned out he wasn't faking. He had laryngitis and needed an understudy. My heart started beating like crazy. "Definitely!" I said. We went into the backyard to perfect my jumping style. He taught me how to look and breathe through a hole in Hopkin's mouth. The hardest part was doing cartwheels without letting Hopkin's head fall off!

My dad dropped me off about ten minutes before kick-off. The bleachers were packed. As I hopped onto the field, the crowd started cheering. I turned around to see what for, and then realized it was *me!* Or more precisely, Hopkin.

It was over so fast I never even had a chance to get nervous. The only proof I have of my private fame is a photo in the school paper, showing Hopkin getting a hug from the cheerleaders. If you look closely at his ankles, you can see a little sliver of my favorite striped socks. It was a blast—but next time I want to be famous in a more high-profile way.

It's okay to use a natural, casual tone. Bring your personality to your personal essays. Your distinctive writing style is called your writer's voice.

You can make your readers feel as if they're right there with you by including vivid details.

Since your aim is to reveal something about yourself, feel free to include your reactions to the events you relate.

FYI

Long before there were home movies or video cameras there was personal narrative. It used to be the only way history could be passed down through generations, so the art of personal storytelling was very important. We now have all kinds of ways to record information, but oral storytelling is still popular. Some people even make their living telling stories about themselves.

BUSINESS LETTER

In a **business letter** you communicate to a person (or sometimes to a group of people) in a formal way about a nonpersonal matter, such as business or politics.

When you write a business letter: ▶ Type it neatly. Include the recipient's full name and address and type your own name and address beneath your signature. Make sure the envelope is as neat as the letter itself.

When you read a business letter: ▶ Pay attention to important information. Keep in mind that people or companies write business letters to get ahead in some way, so be sure to read between the lines.

The name and address of the person to whom you're writing goes above the greeting. Include job title if you know it.

In a business letter, end the greeting with a colon, not a comma.

Remember: The person to whom you're writing is probably very busy— so it's a good idea to state the main idea of your letter right in the opening paragraph.

3675 Rossen Street
Caxton, Arizona 83269

March 15, 1993

Ms. Alison Wagner
Superintendent of Schools
903 North Oakdale Road, Room 222
Caxton, Arizona 83627

Dear Ms. Wagner:

I am writing to you on behalf of the Madison School seventh grade students. We would like to tell you about our World Culture Day on Saturday, May 8, from 11:00 A.M. to 4:00 P.M. and invite you to attend. (Rain date: Saturday, May 15.) The activities will be held in the Madison School auditorium and playground. Admission is $1; arts, crafts, and food will be available for purchase. All proceeds will be donated to the Madison School Sports Equipment Fund.

294

Many diverse cultures will be represented on this day. Among the artistic offerings is a booth that will give lessons in origami, the Japanese art of paper folding. A demonstration of Navajo weaving will be presented at another booth. Early American quilt-making will also be demonstrated.

Booths will serve foods from many nations. A chili relleno dish from Mexico, a mushroom crepe dish from France, and a Cajun-style chicken dish from the Louisiana Bayou are just some of the delicious selections we are planning.

The students of Madison School understand how busy you must be with your many responsibilities as school superintendent. We do hope, however, that you can spend some time with us on World Culture Day.

It's also a good idea to restate your main idea in the closing paragraph.

Sincerely yours,
Tomas Ramos, President
Madison Student Council

A business letter doesn't have to be about business. A letter expressing your political views is a business letter too. Did you know that your elected representatives in Washington have employees whose only job is to respond to letters sent by the people in their districts? When an important issue is up for a vote, a politician's office might receive hundreds of letters in a single day!

FRIENDLY LETTER

In a **friendly letter** you share personal news, discuss things you've been thinking about or feeling—or just keep in touch.

When you write a friendly letter: It can be handwritten—just make sure it's legible!

When you read a friendly letter: Consider yourself lucky! Think about writing back soon, before you forget what you want to say in response.

A Letter from Rick

1610 East Boston Terrace
Seattle, Washington 98112
April 26, 1998

Dear Renu,

It was great to receive your letter. I hadn't heard from you in so long, I was wondering if you even re-membered who I was! Hey, guess what: for once, I actually have a lot of news.

First things first. Do you remember my beagle, Barney? Well, she had puppies—four of them! Two are almost all brown, with little patches of black and grey. There's another one who looks a lot like Bar-ney. And last, there's my personal favorite: she's mostly white, with brown speckles on her back and sides. I know it's totally corny, but I couldn't resist calling her Spot.

In a friendly letter, end the greeting with a comma or a dash—not a colon, as in a business letter.

Most friendly letters are written in an informal tone, similar to the kind you would use in every-day conversation.

*A Letter
from Rick*

The other big news is that I was elected vice-president of the seventh grade. I had serious competition from Joseph Parks, and I have to admit it was a very close race. But I promised a few things to a few people, and I guess that made the difference.

How's everything in your new school? Mr. Tanabe's English class really misses you. You wrote better limericks than anyone else. How about coming back for a visit sometime soon? I can't keep your seat in the lunchroom reserved forever!

Your friend,

Rick

Just as in any personal conversation, in a friendly letter you tell the other person what's going on with you; and most likely you'll want to know what's going on with them too.

FYI

Personal letters are, unfortunately, becoming increasingly rare. The United States Postal Service reports that in 1993, personal (household-to-household) mail was only 3.8 percent of all mail—or about 1.3 pieces of mail per household per week.

GLOSSARY OF LITERARY TERMS

Acts The main divisions of a play. (See also *Drama, Scenes.*)

Allegory A literary work in which different elements, such as characters or settings, have symbolic meanings.

Alliteration The repetition of consonant sounds, usually at the beginnings of words. (See also *Poetry.*)

Allusion A reference within a literary work to a character or situation in another literary work or work of art.

Anecdote A short, often amusing story based on an incident in a person's life.

Antagonist The character or force that opposes the protagonist, or hero, in a work of literature. (See also *Character, Protagonist.*)

Assonance The repetition of a vowel sound in words within a sentence or line of verse. (See also *Poetry.*)

Audience The group of people who read a literary work or watch a play, film, or television program.

Author's Point of View The author's point of view is his or her attitude toward the subject of the written work. (See also *Author's Purpose.*)

Author's Purpose The author's purpose is his or her reason for writing a particular work. An author's purpose may be to inform, to persuade, to entertain, to express an opinion, or a combination of these purposes. (See also *Author's Point of View.*)

Autobiography The story of a person's life written by that person. (See also *Anecdote, Biography, Narrative Point of View, Subject, Subjective Details.*)

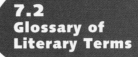

Biography The story of a person's life written by another person. (See also *Autobiography, Subject.*)

Character A person, an animal, or a personified object that plays a role in the action of a literary work. A **round character** is one for whom an author has created a fully developed physical appearance and personality. A **flat character** is one who is not fully developed. (See also *Antagonist, Hero/Heroine, Protagonist.*)

Characterization The techniques authors use to present and develop characters. In **direct characterization,** authors comment in a straightforward manner on the nature of a character. In **indirect characterization,** authors allow readers to draw conclusions about characters based upon the characters own words and acts, as well as upon how other characters react to them. (See also *Character Traits, Character: Motivation.*)

Character: Motivation The reasons fictional characters act, think, or feel certain ways. (See also *Character Traits.*)

Character's Point of View A character's perspective on plot events or other characters.

Character Traits The personal qualities that distinguish one literary character from another. (See also *Character, Characterization, Character: Motivation.*)

Chronological Order The order in which events happen in time.

Circular Story A story that begins and ends with the same or a similar event. (See also *Short Story.*)

Climax (See *Plot.*)

Colloquialisms Expressions that are used in informal conversation. (See also *Dialect.*)

Complications (See *Plot.*)

Conflict The struggle between opposing characters or forces that is central to the action of a literary work. **External conflicts** are those in which a character struggles against another character, society, or force of nature. **Internal conflicts** are those in which a character struggles with an issue or problem within his or her mind. (See also *Plot.*)

Connotation The emotional meaning associated with a word and that adds to its literal meaning. (See also *Denotation*.)

Denotation The literal dictionary meaning of a word. (See also *Connotation*.)

Descriptive Details Specific instances in a literary work in which an author uses sensory language to create vivid images of characters, events, or places. (See also *Figurative Language*.)

Dialect A form of language spoken by a particular group of people or in a specific geographical area. Dialect differs from standard spoken English in its spelling, word use, and pronunciation. (See also *Colloquialisms*.)

Dialog The conversation between characters in a literary work. Usually, dialog is enclosed in quotation marks and tells the exact words a character says. Sometimes, as in drama, quotation marks are not used to enclose dialog. Instead, the words spoken by the actors come after their characters' names. (See also *Drama, Monolog*.)

Direct Address A literary device that enables an author or a literary character to talk directly to an audience.

Drama A genre of literature meant to be performed before an audience. In drama, the story is told through characters' dialog and actions. (See also *Acts, Dialog, Monolog, Scenes, Stage Directions*.)

Episode An event or incident that forms a distinct part of a story and may or may not relate to the plot.

Epistolary Literature Literature that is written in the form of a letter or a series of letters.

Essay A short work of nonfiction that focuses on a single subject. There are two general types of essays: **formal essays** are objective, or impersonal, and serious in tone; **informal essays** are subjective, or personal, and light in tone.

Exaggeration The deliberate overstatement of an idea for emphasis or for a humorous effect.

Exposition Writing that explains, analyzes, or defines.

Fables Brief stories that teach morals. Most fables tell about animal characters that behave like people. (See also *Folklore, Moral*.)

Facts Statements that can be proven true. (See also *Nonfiction, Opinions.*)

Fairy Tales Stories about fanciful characters with unusual abilities. Typical characters in fairy tales include giants, monsters, dragons, gnomes, evil beings, and talking animals. (See also *Folklore.*)

Falling Action (See *Plot.*)

Fantasy A type of literature that takes place in an unreal, imaginary world characterized by magical or supernatural elements. (See also *Realistic Fiction.*)

Fiction Prose writing that tells an imaginary story in the form of a short story or novel. (See also *Nonfiction, Novel, Short Story.*)

Figurative Language Language that uses imagery and figures of speech to create original and colorful descriptions. Simile, metaphor, and personification are the most commonly used types of figurative language. (See also *Descriptive Details, Hyperbole, Imagery, Metaphor, Personification, Poetry, Simile, Style.*)

Flashback A scene or an image that interrupts the present action in a story or play to describe an event or events that took place earlier. (See also *Foreshadowing.*)

Folk Hero The major character in a folk tale, whose courageous action and brave deeds are responsible for bringing the story to a happy conclusion. (See also *Folk Tale.*)

Folklore Stories, songs, and poems that have been handed down within a culture from one generation to another. Kinds of folklore include folk tales, fairy tales, tall tales, fables, myths, and legends.

Folk Tale An entertaining story that has been passed along orally from one generation to the next. These stories usually contain a hero or heroine and common folk who often are shown to have better values than their wealthier, more powerful neighbors. (See also *Folk Hero, Folklore.*)

Foreshadowing The literary technique authors use to hint at events that will take place later in a story. (See also *Flashback.*)

Frame Story A story that contains another story. (See also *Short Story*.)

Genre A category of literature having certain characteristics. Examples of genre include: biography, drama, poetry, and short story.

Haiku An unrhymed poem of Japanese origin that usually expresses a single thought about nature. A haiku consists of three lines made up of seventeen syllables; five syllables in the first and third lines, and seven syllables in the second line. (See also *Poetry*.)

Hero/Heroine The central character in a literary work who is often admired for exemplary personal qualities, such as bravery and nobility. (See also *Character*.)

Historical Fiction A type of fiction that is based on historical events and characters. (See also *Fiction*.)

Humor The characteristic of writing that makes it funny or amusing.

Hyperbole A statement that is exaggerated or overstated to emphasize a point or to create a humorous effect. (See also *Exaggeration, Figurative Language*.)

Imagery Words and phrases that appeal to the senses and that are used to create vivid descriptions. (See also *Figurative Language, Sensory Language*.)

Interview A conversation, usually in a question-and-answer format, between a reporter or writer and another person. The person who asks the questions is the **interviewer.** The person who answers the questions is the **subject.**

Irony The effect created when there is a sharp contrast between what is expected to happen and what actually happens or between what is stated and what is meant.

Legends Stories handed down through generations that describe the heroic actions of characters. Legends sometimes tell about real historical figures in fictionalized situations. (See also *Folklore*.)

Limerick A humorous verse, or poem, written in one five-line stanza with a regular scheme of rhyme and meter.

Lyric Poem A brief poem that expresses a personal thought or emotion, usually through the use of vivid images and a musical rhythm. (See also *Narrative Poem, Poetry.*)

Main Idea The main idea is the central idea of a work of nonfiction. The main idea may also refer to the most important idea contained within a paragraph. (See also *Supporting Details.*)

Metaphor Figurative language that suggests a comparison between two things that are not usually considered to be alike. (See also *Figurative Language, Poetry.*)

Meter The pattern of rhythm in lines of poetry. (See also *Rhythm.*)

Monolog A long speech delivered by a character in a literary work. (See also *Dialog, Drama.*)

Mood The emotional effect or feeling that an author creates in a literary work.

Moral A lesson about life that is taught in a fable. (See also *Fable.*)

Myths Stories set in ancient times that explain important natural events, such as the formation of the earth or the creation of the seasons. Greek and Roman myths describe the actions of gods, goddesses, and mortal heroes and heroines. (See also *Folklore.*)

Narrator The teller of a story. (See also *Narrative Point of View.*)

Narrative Nonfiction A type of writing that tells a story about real people, places, and events.

Narrative Poem A poem that tells a story. (See also *Lyric Poem, Poetry.*)

Narrative Point of View The perspective from which an author tells a story. There are two main types of point of view: first person and third person. In the **first-person point of view,** the narrator is a character in the story and uses first-person pronouns, such as I, me, and we. In the **third-person point of view,** the narrator is an outside observer, rather than a story character, and uses third-person pronouns, such as *he* and *she*. The third-person point of view can be subdivided into two types: limited and omniscient. In the **limited point of view,** the narrator focuses on the thoughts, actions, and feelings of one character. In the **omniscient point of view,** the narrator can reveal the thoughts, actions, and feelings of all the characters. (See also *Narrator.*)

Nonfiction Prose writing that tells about real people, places, and events. Examples of nonfiction include articles, essays, diaries, news stories, letters, biographies, autobiographies, and reviews. (See also *Facts, Fiction, Opinions.*)

Novel A novel is a fictional story of considerable length containing detailed treatments of characters and/or complicated plots. (See also *Fiction, Short Story.*)

Objective Details Small bits of information that can be observed or measured and are not based solely on an author's thoughts or opinions. (See also *Subjective Details.*)

Onomatopoeia A literary technique involving the use of words in which the sound of a word suggests or imitates its meaning. (See also *Poetry.*)

Opinions Statements based on a person's beliefs, feelings, or thoughts about what is true rather than on what can be proven to be true. (See also *Facts, Nonfiction.*)

Parody A humorous imitation of a serious literary work or of an author's writing style. (See also *Style.*)

Personification Figurative language in which animals or objects are given human characteristics.

Persuasion A type of writing in which an author tries to convince an audience to believe or accept the ideas being presented. (See also *Propaganda.*)

Play (See *Drama.*)

Plot The series of related events in a literary work. Most plots follow a pattern. The **exposition** introduces the characters and the problems, or **complications,** they face. The part of the story in which the conflict grows is called the **rising action.** The turning point in the story, or the point at which the conflict is resolved and the story outcome is clear, is called the **climax.** The **falling action** describes the events that take place after the climax. The falling action includes the **resolution,** or the outcome of the conflict that is developed in the plot. (See also *Conflict.*)

Poetry A type of literature that expresses ideas and feelings by relying on compact, often musical language that appeals to readers' senses and ignites their emotions. (See also *Alliteration, Assonance, Figurative Language, Haiku, Imagery, Lyric Poem, Metaphor, Narrative Poem, Onomatopoeia, Refrain, Rhyme, Rhythm, Simile, Speaker, Stanza.*)

Propaganda Information and ideas presented in order to persuade people to do or believe something that may or may not be true. (See also *Persuasion.*)

Prose The kind of everyday writing or speech that does not have the rhyme or rhythm patterns of poetry.

Protagonist The central character in a literary work. (See also *Antagonist, Character.*)

Realistic Fiction A type of fiction that tells an imaginary story about characters and places that could actually exist and events that could actually happen. (See *Fantasy.*)

Refrain A repeated line or phrase in a poem that creates recurring rhythm and produces a musical quality. (See also *Poetry.*)

Repetition A literary technique that involves repeating a word or phrase for emphasis or to create a rhythm or particular emotional effect.

Resolution (See *Plot.*)

Rhyme A literary technique involving the repetition of the same or similar sounds. When two words rhyme, the accented syllables and all the sounds following these syllables sound the same. The most common form of rhyme, **end rhyme,** occurs when words at the ends of several lines of poetry rhyme. In **internal rhyme,** the rhymes occur within lines of poetry. (See also *Poetry.*)

Rhythm A pattern of sounds or beats created by the arrangement of accented and unaccented words or syllables, especially in poetry. (See also *Poetry.*)

Rising Action (See *Plot.*)

Scenes The divisions within acts in a play. (See also *Acts, Drama.*)

Science Fiction A type of imaginary story that involves up-to-date or futuristic scientific developments and technology.

Sensory Language Descriptive language that appeals to one or more of the five senses: sight, hearing, smell, touch, and taste. Authors use sensory language to create vivid word pictures that heighten an audience's interest. (See *Imagery*.)

Setting Setting is the time and place in which the action of a literary work unfolds.

Short Story A brief work of fiction that can usually be read in one sitting. (See also *Circular Story, Fiction, Frame Story, Novel*.)

Simile Figurative language that makes a direct comparison between two apparently unlike things; uses the words *like* or *as*.

Slang Nonstandard or unconventional speech used by speakers for informal or humorous expression.

Speaker In poetry, the voice that talks to the reader. The speaker is comparable to a narrator in a work of fiction. (See also *Narrator*.)

Stage Directions The means by which actors know where and how to move and speak. Stage directions are set off from dialog by parentheses and/or italics. They often describe scenery, props, and lighting. (See also *Drama*.)

Stanza A group of lines in a poem that is the equivalent of a paragraph in prose writing. (See also *Poetry*.)

Style The distinctive way an author writes. An author's style is shaped by many elements, including word choice, sentence patterns and length, figurative language, and tone. (See also *Figurative Language, Parody, Tone*.)

Subject The person whose life is presented in an autobiography or a biography or who is profiled in an interview or a news article. A subject may be famous or little known, alive or dead, but he or she is always someone who has actually lived. (See also *Autobiography, Biography, Interview*.)

Subjective Details Small bits of information that are based on personal feelings and opinions rather than on what can be observed and/or proven to be true. (See also *Objective Details.*)

Supporting Details Specific bits of information that directly relate to the main idea in a piece of nonfiction writing. (See also *Main Idea.*)

Surprise Ending An unexpected twist in the ending of a literary work.

Suspense Curiosity about what might happen next in a literary work.

Symbolism A literary technique involving the use of an object, event, or character to represent an idea more general or broader than itself.

Tall Tales Humorous stories that exaggerate characters and events beyond belief. (See also *Folklore.*)

Teleplay A drama written for television. (See also *Drama.*)

Theme The underlying idea or message about life or human nature contained in a literary work. A **stated theme** is one the author puts directly into words. An **unstated,** or **implied theme** is one readers must determine on their own by analyzing other story elements.

Tone An author's attitude toward his or her subject.

Tragedy A dramatic work in which the main character faces a moral struggle and is destroyed because of his or her own actions.

Trickster Tales Stories that describe how clever animals or people play tricks on or otherwise take advantage of animals or people. (See also *Folklore.*)

Acts, 67
Action, in plot, 57
Action verbs, 162, 163, 165, 166, 167
Active reading strategies
  asking questions, 36
  forming a group, 37
  K-W-L, 41
  making a connection, 36
  predicting, 41
  previewing, 40
  writing a response, 37
Active voice, 167
Adjectives
  adding *ly*, 179
  articles, 184
    definite, 184
    indefinite, 184
  as modifiers, 161, 178, 179-180
  clauses, 195
  comparative form, 182-183
  demonstrative, 161
  distinguished from
    adverbs, 178-180
  irregular, 182
  participles as, 196
  placement, 181
  predicate, 164, 181
  prepositional phrases as, 191
  proper, 185
  superlative form, 182-183
  verbs as, 181, 196-197
Adverbs
  as modifiers, 179-180
  comparative, 186, 187
  distinguished from
    adjectives, 178-180
  double negatives, 187
  irregular, 187
  kinds, 179
  prepositional phrases as, 191
  superlative, 186, 187
  verbs as, 196-197
Advertising, 100-101
After-reading strategies
  reflecting, 47

  summarizing, 46
  talking it over, 47
Agreement
  pronoun-antecedent, 156, 159
  subject-verb, 175, 176-177
All, none, always, never, must, 39
Alliteration, in poetry, 65
Almanacs, 120
Although/because, 143
Analyzing, 22
Antagonist, 56
Antecedent of pronoun, 154, 158
Anthology, making, 13
Antonyms, 237
Apostrophe, 151, 157, 207
Appositive phrase, 153
Appositives, 153
Arguments, developing, 19, 258-259
Articles (parts of speech), 184
As/like, 65
Audience
  defining, 6
  targeting, 6, 9, 20-21, 22-23, 76, 81
  understanding, 6, 19
  writing style and, 6
Audiotapes, using, 75, 83, 84
Audiovisual resources, 77
Author's point of view, 19, 34, 38, 58-59
Author's purpose, 20-23, 43
Autobiography, model, 274-275

Backup, on computers, 124
Ballads, 61
Bandwagon technique, 82
Bar graphs, 121
Base word, 226, 229
***Be,* conjugation of,** 173, 175
Before-reading strategies
  K-W-L, 41
  predicting, 41
  previewing, 40
Bias, recognizing, 82, 254
Biography, model, 276-277
Body of a report, 262-263, 264-265

Book review, model, 284-285
Book, parts of, 111-112
  bibliography, 112
  copyright page, 111-112
  glossary, 112
  index, 112
  table of contents, 111-112
  title page, 111-112
Brainstorming, 5, 7, 30, 73
Business letter, model, 294-295

Capitalization
  brand names, 201
  dates, 199
  ethnic groups, 200
  events, 199
  family titles, 199
  for first words, 198
  geography, 200
  historical events, 201
  holidays, 199
  initials of people, 199
  languages, 200
  letter greetings, 198
  names of animals, 199
  names of buildings, bridges,
    monuments, 200
  names of heavenly bodies, 200
  names of people, 199
  nationalities, 200
  organizations, 201
  places, 185, 200
  poetry, 198
  pronoun "I", 198
  quotations, 198
  streets, 200
  times, 199
  titles, 199
Card Catalog, 105, 109, 110
Cartoon, drawing, 13
Catalog,
  card, 109
  computer, 110
  numbering of, 106-107
Cause/Effect

essay, 22
faulty, 39
information pattern, 48, 51
model, 268-269
organization by, 80
CD ROM, 123, 124
Character sketch, model, 280-281
Character, story, 56, 66, 280-281,
286, 290
Charts, 50, 121. *See also*
Graphic organizers.
Checklists
audience, 6
previewing, 40
revising, 11
study strategies, 130
using, 130
Chronological order, 8, 16, 264, 276
Circle graph, 122
Classification, 48, 50
Clauses, 192, 194-196
adjectives, 195
adverb, 195
dependent, 194-195
noun, 195
independent, 194
use with subordinating
conjunctions, 192, 194
Climax, 57
Cluster maps, 8, 45
Colon, usage, 208, 294
Commands, computer, 124-125
Comma, usage, 142, 144, 145, 146,
153, 193, 204-206
after interjections, 193
appositives and clauses, 205
direct address, 205
direct quotations, 205
in letters, 206
interrupters, 205
introducing a sentence, 204
places, dates, and titles, 206
separating items, 204
Communication skills, 72-87

Comparative forms
of adjectives, 182-183
of adverbs, 186-187
Comparison/contrast
essays, 22
information patterns, 48, 52
model, 266-267
research reports, 262-263, 264-265
using diagrams for, 8, 51, 52, 80
Complete predicate, 140
Complete subject, 140
Complex sentence, 140
Compound nouns, 152
Compound predicate, 142
Compound prepositions, 188
Compound sentences, 144, 146
Compound subject, 142, 177
Comprehension strategies
cause/effect, 22, 39, 48, 51, 80,
269-269
classification, 48, 50
comparison/contrast, 22, 48, 52,
266-267
evaluating evidence and sources of
information, 23, 254-255
evaluating fact and opinion, 23, 34,
39, 251, 254-255, 258-259, 266-267
evaluating important and
unimportant information, 23
main idea and supporting
details, 48, 49, 251, 263-263,
264-265
making judgments, 23, 251, 260-
261, 266-267
problem/solution, 48, 53, 270-271
steps in a process, 272-273
summarizing, 267, 269, 282-283
Computer
catalog, 105, 110
commands, 124-125
cut and paste, 125
delete, 125
find, 125
open, 125

print, 125
quit, 125
save, 125
tab, 125
components, 124
hardware
keyboard, 124
modem, 124
monitor, 124
mouse, 124
printer, 124
in libraries, 105, 110
online research, 123
terms
backup, 124
byte, 124
character, 125
command, 125
disk, 125
document, 125
font, 125
format, 125
function, 125
memory, 125
menu, 125
software, 125
visual aids, 121-122
Conclusion
speech, 78-79
writing, 253, 255, 261, 263, 265,
267, 269, 277, 281, 283
Conflict
character, 56, 286
plot, 57, 286
Conjugation of verbs, 170-174
Conjunctions, 142, 144, 146, 147,
192, 194
Context clues, 222, 224-225
Contractions, 157, 160
Copyright page, 111-112
Correlative conjunctions, 192
Critical reading, 34, 38-39
differentiating between facts and
opinions, 34, 39

evaluating sources of information, 38
faulty logic, 39
  either/or thinking, 39
  faulty cause and effect, 39
  overgeneralization, 39
identifying writer's point of view, 38
Critical seeing/viewing, 98-99, 100-102
Critical thinking, 22-23, 34, 38-39, 98-99
Critical writing, 22-23
analyzing, 22
comparison/contrast, 22
differentiating between fact and opinion, 23
evaluating, 23
  evaluating evidence and sources of information, 23
  evaluating important and unimportant information, 23
making judgments, 23
synthesizing, 23
understanding, 22-23

Dash, use of, 210
Databases, 123
Debate
formal, 85
guidelines for, 86
judges, 85
moderator, 85
rebuttal, 85
strategies, 87
Decisions, making, 23, 251, 260-261
Declarative sentences, 139
Definite article, 184
Definitions
dictionary, 235
thesaurus, 237
Demonstrative pronouns, 160, 161
Descriptive essay, model, 252-253
Descriptive writing
figurative language, 17

sensory details, 17, 286
types of, 15, 17, 21
Details, in writing, 251, 254, 256, 260, 261. 262, 264, 265, 270, 286, 293
Dewey Decimal System, 106-107
Diagrams, 8, 51, 53, 80
Dialog, 31, 66, 290-291
Dialog journal, 31
Dictionaries, 113, 224, 234-235
definitions, 235
entry word, 234, 235
etymology, 235
example sentence, 235
guide word, 235
inflected forms, 235
part-of-speech label, 235
respelling, 235
Differences and similarities, 8, 48, 52, 80, 262-263, 266-267
Direct object, 165-166
Directions, 132
Double negative, 187
Drafting, 9
Drama, 55, 66-67
acts, 67
basics, 66
characters, 66, 290-291
dialog, 66-67, 290-291
elements, 66-67
pantomime, 67
props, 67
scenes, 67
script, 66-67, 290-291
stage directions, 66-67, 290-291
structure, 67
During-reading strategies
ask questions, 42
determining author's purpose, 43
SQ-3R plan, 44

Editing, 3
Editorial, model, 258-259
ei, ie, 241

Either/or **thinking,** 39
Emotional content of words, 55, 58, 60, 61, 62, 65, 79, 193
Encyclopedias, 114-115
End rhyme, 64
Endings
adding *s* and *es,* 242
comparative and superlative forms of adjectives, 182
comparative and superlative forms of adverbs, 186
irregular verbs, 173-174
nouns ending in *f,* 242
verb principal parts, 169
words ending in *ch, s, sh, ss, x, z* 242
words ending in *ff,* 242
words ending in *y,* 242-243
Entertaining writing, 21, 43, 252-253
Entry words, 114-115
Eponyms, 233
er, est, 182-183, 186
Errors in form, 12
Essays
cause and effect, 268-269
comparison and contrast, 266-267
critical reading of, 266-267, 268-269
descriptive, 252-253
entertaining, 252-253
ending of, 267, 269
lead paragraphs, 266, 268
persuasive, 251, 258-259
Etymology. 223, 232-235
Evaluating, 23
Events, order of, 16, 57, 80, 256-257, 268-279
Exclamation points, usage, 139, 193, 203
Exclamatory sentences, 139
Explanatory writing, 20, 43
Exposition, in plot, 57
Expository writing, 262-263, 264-265, 276-277

focus of, 18
inclusion of facts, 18
organization of information, 18
precise language in, 18
to explain, 18
to inform, 18
types of, 18

Fact or opinion, differentiating, 23, 34, 39, 251, 254-255, 258-259, 266-267
Fallacies, 39, 82
either/or fallacy, 39
faulty cause and effect, 39
overgeneralization, 39
Falling action, 57
Faulty logic
either/or thinking, 39
faulty cause and effect, 39, 268
faulty reasoning, 82
overgeneralization, 39
Faulty reasoning technique, 82
Feature article, model, 256-257
Fiction, reading
basic elements, 54-59
characters, 54, 56
conflict, 56
protagonist, 56
plot, 54, 57
climax, 57
conflict, 57
falling action, 57
rising action, 57
sequence of events, 57
setting, 54, 56
theme, 57
techniques, 58-59
figurative language, 58
flashback, 58
foreshadowing, 58
point of view, 58
first, 58
third, 58

sensory language, 58
Figurative language, 17, 58, 60, 65, 273
First drafts, 9
First-person point of view, 58
Flashback, 58
Foreshadowing, 58
Fragments, sentence, 146-147
Free verse, 63
Freewriting, 7. *See also* Writing process.
Friendly letter, model, 296-297
Future tense, 170

Gender, pronoun and noun, 156
Gerund, 196-197
Gerund phrases, 196-197
Grammar, mechanics, and usage
defining grammar and mechanics, 136-137
parts of speech
adjectives, 161, 178-187, 195, 196-197
adverbs, 179-180, 186, 187, 191, 196-197
articles, 184
clauses, 192, 194-196
adjective, 195
adverb, 195
dependent, 194-195
noun, 195
independent, 194
use with subordinating conjunctions, 192, 194
conjunctions, 142, 144, 146, 147, 188-193
contractions, 157, 160
gerunds/gerund phrases, 197
infinitive/infinitive phrases, 197
interjections, 193
nouns, 148-153, 165, 166, 197
prepositions, 160, 188-193
prepositional phrases, 166, 189, 190-191

pronouns, 154-161, 189, 190
antecedents, 154, 156, 158, 159
agreement, 156
as indirect object, 166
as object of verb, 155
as subject of sentence, 155
gender, 156, 159
neuter, 156
number, 156
demonstrative, 160, 161
indefinite, 159
intensive, 158
interrogative, 160
object of preposition, 155, 189, 190
compound object, 190
personal, 155
plural, 159
possessive, 157
reflexive, 158
relative, 195
singular, 159
subject, 155
punctuation, 202-211
apostrophe, 151, 157, 207
colons, 208, 294
comma, 142, 144, 145, 146, 153, 204-206
after interjections, 193
appositives and clauses, 205
direct address, 205
direct quotations, 205
in letters, 206
interrupters, 205
introducing a sentence, 204
places, dates, and titles, 206
separating items, 204
dashes, 210
exclamation mark, 139, 193, 203
hyphens, 152, 209
italics, 208, 290
missing, 146
parentheses, 210
period, 139, 202
practice, 211

question mark, 139, 203
quotation marks, 205, 207
semi-colon, 144, 146-147, 209
underlining, 208
sentences, 138-147
clauses, 143
dependent, 143, 145
subordinating
conjunctions, 145, 146-147
independent, 143, 144, 145
complete, 138, 146-147
complex, 145
compound, 144, 145, 146
conjunctions in, 192
declarative, 139
direct objects in, 166
exclamatory, 139
fragments, 146-147
imperative, 139, 141
indirect objects in, 166
interrogative, 139, 140, 160
phrases, 143
predicates, 136, 140, 143, 164
adjectives, 164
complete, 140
compound, 142
nouns, 164
simple, 141, 143
two or more, 144
run-ons, 146-147
simple, 138, 139, 141, 143, 192
subject, 136, 140, 143, 155, 160,
163, 176
active and passive
verbs, 167
complete, 140
compound, 142, 177
pronoun as, 155
simple, 141, 142, 143
two or more, 144
verb agreement, 176-177
types of, 139
verbs, 152, 162-178, 181, 196
action, 162, 163, 165,
166, 167

active voice, 167
agreement, with subject, 176-177
as adjectives, 181
direct objects, 165, 166
forms, 152, 175, 177, 196
verbals, 196
verbal phrases, 168, 176, 196-197
gerunds/gerund phrases, 196-197
infinitives/infinitive
phrases, 196-197
participial phrase, 196-197
Graphic organizers
cause and effect, 80
charts, 41, 50
K-W-L, 41
classification, 50
cluster maps, 8, 45
diagrams, 8, 51, 52, 80
Venn, 8, 52, 80
for comparison/contrast, 8, 80
graphs
bar, 121
circle, 122
line, 122
maps, 8, 53
organizing methods, 80
outlining, 49
problem and solution, 53, 80
story pyramid, 45
Graphs
bar, 121
circle, 122
line, 122
pictograph, 122
Group discussions, 7, 47, 73-74
Guide letters, 114-115

Haiku, 61
Hard news, 255
Helping verbs, 168, 171, 176
How-to guide, model, 272-273
Hyphens, 152, 209

Ideas, developing, 8, 10
ie, ei, 241

Idioms, 223, 231
Imagery, 65
Imperative sentences, 139
Importance, order of, 80, 254, 256
Indefinite article, 184
Indefinite pronouns, 159
Independent clauses, 194
Indexes, 112
Indirect object, 165, 166
Infinitive, 196-197
Infinitive phrases, 196-197
Information
evaluating, 23, 34, 39
gathering, 71, 88-101
organizing, 80
patterns
cause/effect, 48, 51
classification, 48, 50
compare/contrast, 48, 52
main idea, 48, 49
problem/solution, 48, 53
processing, 82
sources of, 23, 28
strategies, 49, 50, 51, 52, 53
synthesizing, 23
Informative writing, 256-257
Intensive pronouns, 158
Interjections, 193
Internal rhyme, 64
Internet, 123
Interrogative pronouns, 160
Interrogative sentences, 139, 140, 160
Interview
conducting, 84
requesting, 83
subject of, 83
techniques for, 83-84
tips for, 83
transcripts, 84
Interview, model, 278-279
Introduction, in writing, 251, 254,
256, 258, 260, 261, 264, 266, 267,
270, 272, 276, 286
Irregular adjectives, 182
Irregular adverbs, 187

Irregular verbs, 173-174
Italics, 208, 290

Journal partner, 31
Journal writing
  dialog journal, 31
  response journal, 37
  to understand, 22
  writer's journal, 24-31

Key, of map, 118-119
Key words, 110
K-W-L chart, 41
K-W-L strategy, 41

Least, **in comparisons using**
  adjectives, 182-183, 186
Less, **in comparisons using**
  adjectives, 182-183, 186
Letters
  business, model, 294-295
  capitalization in, 188, 199
  friendly, model, 296-297
  personal, 296-297
Library
  arrangement of, 106-110
  catalog of, 105, 109, 110
  computers in, 105, 110
  sources and services in, 110-120
Library research, 105-122
Line graph, 127
Linking verbs, 163, 164
Listening
  attentive, 72, 73-76, 80, 81,
  254-255, 260-261, 282-283
  considerate, 74
  critical, 82
    for bandwagon technique, 82
    for slanted facts, 82
    for faulty reasoning, 82
    to testimonials, 82
  debates, 85-87
  discussions, one-on-one, 72
  focused, 72, 73, 74, 75-76,

77-80, 81, 82, 83-85, 254-
255, 260-261, 282-283
  group discussions, 73-74
  interviews, 83-84
  speeches, 80-81
Literature, reading, 54, 56-
57, 58-59, 60-61, 62-63,
64-65, 66-67. *See also*
Fiction, Nonfiction, Poetry.
Logic evaluating, 39
ly **ending,** 179

Magazines, 13, 116-117
Main idea and supporting details,
  organizing by, 48, 49, 80, 251,
262-263,
Mapping, 8, 53
Maps
  atlas, 118
  elements of
    grid, 119
    index, 119
    legend, 119
    scale, 119
  historical, 118
  political, 118
  road, 118
Memoirs, 274-275
Metaphor, 58, 65
Meter, 64

Narrative writing
  beginning/middle/end, 16
  characters, 16
  problem and solution, 16
  setting, 16
  time order in, 16
  types of, 16
Negatives, double, 187
News article, model, 254-255
Newspaper
  article, 254-255
  headline, 254
  lead in, 254

locating in library, 116-117
  submitting to, 13
  writing for, 13
Nonfiction
  information patterns
    cause/effect, 48, 51
    classification, 48, 50
    compare/contrast, 48, 52
    main idea/supporting
    details, 48, 49
    problem/solution, 48, 53
Notetaking, 45, 126-127
  abbreviating, 127
  bibliography card, 127
  by mapping, 45
  labeling notes, 126
  organizing, 127
  paraphrasing/summarizing, 127
  recording quotes, 127
Nouns
  abstract, 149
  appositives, 153
    appositive phrase, 153
  as direct object, 165, 166
  as indirect object, 166
  clauses, 195
  collective, 152
  common, 148
  compound, 152
    hyphenated, 152
  concrete, 149
  object of preposition, 189
    compound object, 190
  plural, 150, 151
    exceptions, 150, 151
    possessive, 151
  predicate, 164
  proper, 148
  singular, 150, 151
  using with verbs, 152
  verbs as, 196-197

Object
  compound, 190

direct, 166
indirect, 166
of preposition, 160, 189, 190
pronouns, 190
Observational report, model, 260-261
On-line service, 123
Opinions and facts, evaluating, 23, 251, 254-255, 258-259, 266-267
Oral communication
debates, 70, 85-87
discussions, 72, 73-74
interviews, 70, 83-84
presentations, 75-87
speech, 77-81
strategies and techniques, 76, 77, 80-81, 82
using appropriate language, 72, 76, 81. *See also* Speaking.
Order
of details, 80
of importance, 81
time order, 8, 16, 264, 276
Outlining, 49
Overgeneralization, 39

Pantomime, 67
Paragraphs
closing, 255, 261, 269, 283, 294
introductory, 254, 256, 260, 264, 266, 268, 270, 272, 276, 278, 286, 292, 294
secondary information, 256, 268
Participial phrases, 196-197
Participles, 169, 173, 175, 196-197
Partner work, 7, 12, 31, 35, 47
Parts of speech
adjectives, 178-185, 191, 196-197
adverbs, 178-180, 186-187, 191, 196-197
conjunctions, 142, 144, 146, 147, 192
interjections, 193
nouns, 148-149, 150-151, 152, 153, 165, 166, 195, 196-197

prepositions, 160, 188-190, 190-191
pronouns, 154-159, 160-161, 189, 195
verbs, 152, 162-178, 196-197
Passive voice, 167
Past progressive, 171
Past participle, 169, 173, 175, 196
Past perfect tense, 172
Past tense, 169, 170, 173
Patterns of information, 48-53
Perfect tenses, 170, 172
Periodicals, 116-117
Personal connection to reading, 36-37
Personal narratives
endings for, 292-293
leads for, 292-293
model, 292-293
reading, 15, 16
Personal pronouns, 155
Personification, 58, 65
Persuasion
critical listening, 82
critical reading, 39
tips for, 81
types of, 15, 19, 21, 82
uses for, 81, 82
Persuasive techniques
bandwagon, 82
faulty reasoning, 82
slanted facts, 82
testimonials, 82
Persuasive writing
audience understanding, 19
author's purpose, 43
conclusions, 251, 259
editorial, model, 258-259
essay, model, 251-252
order of argument, 19
point of view, 19
specific reasons, 251
stating topic, 251
types of, 19, 21
use of facts, 19
use of influence, 19, 21
Photography, 71, 95

Pictograph, 122
Placement
of adjectives, 181
Plays, 66-67
Playwright, 67
Plot
climax, 57
conflict, 57
falling action, 57
rising action, 57
sequence of events, 57
Plurals, noun, 150-151
Poem, model, 288-289
Poetry
ballad, 61
basics, 60, 288-289
devices, 64-65, 288-289
figurative language, 65, 288
imagery, 288
metaphor, 65
personification, 65
simile, 65
forms, 55, 61-63
free verse, 55, 63
haiku, 55, 61
meter, 64
narrative, 288
reading, 60-65
repetition, 65
alliteration, 65
refrain, 65
rhyme, 64
end rhyme, 64
internal rhyme, 64
rhyme scheme, 64, 288
rhythm, 64
sonnet, 55, 61
stanza, 289
techniques, 64-65
villanelle, 61-62
writing model, 288-289
Point of view, 38, 58,
Possessive nouns, 151
Possessive pronouns, 157
Predicates, 136, 140, 142-144,

164, 181
Predicting strategy, 41
Predrafting, 2, 4-8
Prefixes, 226-227, 229
Preposition
common, 188
compound, 188
compound object, 190
object of, 160, 189, 190
object pronoun, 190
Prepositional phrases
as adjectives and adverbs, 191
using, 189-190
using before indirect object, 166
Present participle,
169, 171, 175, 196
Present perfect tense, 172
Present tense, 169, 170
Previewing reading, 40
Prewriting, 2, 4-8
brainstorming, 5, 7
choosing a topic, 5
exploring a topic, 5
focusing a topic, 5
freewriting, 7
ideas, 4
planning, 4-7
Principal parts of verbs, 169
Problem and solution, model,
270-271
Problem and solution,
48, 53, 56-57, 80
Problem resolution, 48, 53, 56-57, 80
Progressive verb forms, 171
Pronouns
antecedents, 154, 156,
158, 159
agreement, 156
gender, 156, 159
neuter, 156
number, 156
as indirect object, 166
as object of verb, 155
as subject of sentence, 155

demonstrative, 160, 161
indefinite, 159
intensive, 158
interrogative, 160
object of preposition, 155,
189, 190
compound object, 190
personal, 155
plural, 159
possessive, 157
reflexive, 158
relative, 195
singular, 159
subject, 155
Proofreading, 12
Proofreading marks, 12
Propaganda, 100-101
Proper adjectives, 185
Proper nouns, 148
Props, in plays, 67
Protagonist, 66
PROTO strategy, 131
Publishing
do a reading, 13
draw a cartoon, 13
give a performance, 13
make an anthology, 13
submit to a magazine, 13
write for a newspaper, 13
Punctuation
apostrophe, 151, 107, 207
colons, 208
comma, 105, 142, 144-146,
153, 204
appositives and clauses, 105
direct address, 105
direct quotations, 105
in letters, 105
interrupters, 105
dashes, 210
places, dates, titles, 105
exclamation mark, 139,
193, 203
hyphens, 152, 209

italics, 208
missing, 146
parenthesis, 210
period, 139, 202
practice, 211
question mark, 139, 203
quotation marks, 205, 207
semi-colon, 144, 146-147, 209
underlining, 208
Purpose
author's, 20-21, 43
categories of, 20-21
choosing, 20-21
clear, 20-21
content of writing, 20
for writing
to describe, 21
to entertain, 21
to explain, 21
to learn, 22-23
to analyze, 22
to evaluate, 22
to synthesize, 23
to understand, 22
to persuade, 21
to reflect, 20
in style of writing, 20-21
in tone of writing, 20-21
main, 20-21

Question marks, usage, 139, 203
Questions, asking, 36, 42, 79
Quotation marks, usage, 205, 207
Quotations, 83, 84, 105, 205, 207

Readers' Guide to Periodical
Literature, 116-117
Reading
aloud, 9, 12, 63, 64
for information, 48-53
group, 37
literature
drama, 66-67
fiction, 56-59

poetry, 60-65
methods
PROTO, 131
SQ-3R, 44
nonfiction, 48-53
cause/effect, 48, 51
classification, 48, 50
compare/contrast, 48, 52
main idea/supporting
details, 48, 49
problem/solution, 48, 53
strategic, 34-47
active, 34, 36-37, 38-39, 40-41,
42-43, 46-47
after, 35, 46-47
before, 35, 40-41
critical, 34, 38-39
during, 35, 42-43
summarizing, 46
Reference Sources, 17, 113-115,
116-117, 118, 119, 120
library, 105-122
almanacs, 120
atlases, 118
dictionary, 113, 224, 234-235
encyclopedia, 113, 114-115
maps, 118-119
periodicals, 107, 116-117
thesaurus, 113, 223, 236-237
Reflecting, 3, 14
Reflective writing, 20, 43
Reflexive pronouns, 158
Refrain, 65
Related words, 222, 223, 224-225,
226-229, 230, 231, 232-233,
234-235
Relative pronouns, 195
Repetition, 61, 65
Research, 5, 22, 106, 107, 110-120,
121, 123, 126-127.
Research report, model,
science, 262-263
social studies, 264-265
Resolution, plot, 57
Response journal, 37

Revising, 2, 10-11
Rhetorical questions, 79
Rhyme, 64
Rhyme scheme, 64, 288
Rhythm, in poetry, 64
Rising action, 57
Root words, 226, 229
Run-on sentences, 146-147

Scenes, 67
Scenery, 67
Script, 66, 290-291
Script, model, 290-291
Seeing
creative, 90
critical, 98-99, 100-101
reading visual images, 71, 88
advertising, 71, 100-101
cartoons, 71, 97
colors, 91, 93, 94, 95
depth, 92, 93, 94, 95
illustration, 71, 96
introduction to art, 71, 90
lines, 92, 93, 94, 95
paintings and drawings, 71, 91-93
photography, 71, 95
sculpture, 71, 94
shapes, 92, 93, 94, 95
symbols, 71, 89
television, 71, 98-99
visual clues, 89
Semicolon, usage, 144, 146-147, 209
Sentences
clauses, 143
dependent, 143, 145
subordinating conjunctions, 145,
146-147
independent, 143, 144, 145
conjunctions in, 192
complete, 138, 146-147
complex, 145
compound, 144-146
declarative, 139
direct objects in, 166
exclamatory, 139

fragments, 146-147
imperative, 139, 141
indirect objects in, 166
interrogative, 139, 140, 160
phrases, 143
predicates, 136, 140, 143, 164
adjectives, 164
complete, 140
compound, 142
nouns, 164
simple, 141, 143
two or more, 144
run-ons, 146-147
simple, 138, 139, 141, 143, 192
subject, 136, 140, 143, 160, 163, 176
active and passive verbs, 167
complete, 140
compound, 142, 177
pronoun, 155
simple, 141, 142, 143
two or more, 144
verb agreement, 176-177
types of, 139
Setting, 56, 274, 286, 290
Similarities and differences, 8, 22,
48, 51, 52, 80, 262-263, 266-267
Simile, 58, 65
Simple sentences, 138, 139, 141,
143, 192
Singular verb, 152, 175, 177
Slang, 72
Slanted-facts technique, 82
Sonnet, 61
Speaking
discussions, 72, 73-74
group discussions, 73-74
guidelines for, 74
key rules for, 74
tips for, 73
one-on-one discussions, 72
oral presentations, 75-87
debates, 70, 85-87
formal, 85
guidelines for, 86
judges, 85

moderator, 85
rebuttal, 85
strategies, 87
interviews, 70, 83-84
making a transcript, 84
preparation for, 83
strategies , 83-84
using tape recorders, 83
speeches, 77-81
making, 78
body, 78-79
conclusion, 78-79
introduction, 78-79
purposes
to inform, 80
to persuade, 81
strategies, 80-81
techniques for, 76, 82
persuasive, 82
tips for, 77
to varied audiences, 76, 78, 81, 82
using appropriate
language, 72, 76, 81 .

Speeches
making, 78
body, 78-79
conclusion, 79
introduction, 78-79
purposes
to inform, 80
to persuade, 81
strategies, 80-81
Spelling
bugs, 246-247
rules, 241-245
adding endings, 242
adding *s* and *es*, 242
nouns ending in *f*, 242
words ending in *ch, s,*
sh, ss, x, z, 242
words ending in *ff*, 242
words ending in *y*, 242-243
adding prefixes, 245
adding suffixes, 244

doubling letters to form
endings, 143
homophones, 245
irregular nouns, 243
words with *ie* and *ei*, 241
strategies, 238-240
dictionary, 239
spelling dictionary, 239
memory aids, 240
spell checkers, 240
SQ-3R Plan, 44
Stanza, 289
Story, model, 286-287
Storytelling, 287, 293
Stage directions, 66, 290-291
Story pyramid, 45
Strategies
after reading, 46-47
before reading, 40-41
critical reading, 38-39
critical writing, 22-23
descriptive writing, 17
during reading, 42-43
expository writing, 18
first draft, 9
information patterns, 48-53
narrative writing, 20
persuasive writing, 21
predicting, (K-W-L), 41
previewing, 40
prewriting, 4-8
proofreading, 12
reading, 38-39
revising, 10-11
test-taking, 132-133
vocabulary, 224-237
Study skills, 102-122
computer resources
CD ROM drives, 123
computer commands, 125
computer components, 124
computer terms, 124-125
Internet, 123
library computer catalog, 105, 110

key words, 110
visual aids, 121-122
bar graph, 121
circle graph, 122
line graphs, 122
tables and charts, 121
library resources, using, 105-122
audiocassette resources, 123
audiovisual resources, 108, 121,
123
call numbers, 105
card catalog, 109
computer resources, 105, 110,
121-122
Dewey Decimal System, 106-107
for research, 105-122
Library of Congress, 106
organization of, 106, 107, 109,
113-118, 120, 121
alphabetical, 106, 109
fiction, 106
nonfiction, 106
reference room, 17, 113-120
almanacs, 120
atlases, 118
dictionary, 113
encyclopedia, 113, 114-115
maps, 118-119
periodicals, 107, 116-117
thesaurus, 113
visual aids, 121
parts of a book, 111-112
bibliography, 112
copyright page, 111-112
glossary, 112
index, 112
table of contents, 111-112
title page, 111-112
note-taking, 126-127
outlining, 128
study strategies, 123-131
assignment notebook, 129
checklist, 130
reading method, 131

PROTO, 131
SQ-3R, 33-34
taking research notes, 126-127
test taking strategies, 132-133
visual aids, 121
Style, 11, 20, 293
Subject, 136, 140, 143, 155, 160, 163, 176
agreement with verbs, 175, 176-177
pronoun, 155
Subordinate clauses, 192, 194
Subordinating conjunctions, 145, 192, 194
Suffixes, 226-228, 229
Summarizing, 48, 267, 269, 282-283
Summary, model, 282-283
Superlative form
of adjective, 182-183
of adverb, 186-187
Supporting details, 48, 49, 80, 251, 262-263
Symbols, 71
Synonyms, 236-237
Synthesizing, 23

Table of contents, 111-112
Tenses, verb, 17, 169-175, 196-197
Testimonials technique, 82
Test-taking strategies, 132-133
Theme, 57
Thesaurus, 223, 236-237
antonym, 237
definition, 237
entry word, 237
example sentence, 237
part-of-speech label, 237
Third-person point of view, 58
Time
managing, 129
order, 8, 16, 264, 276
organization by, 80
restrictions, 74
Time order, 8, 16, 80, 264, 276
Titles, of works, 201
Tone, 252, 256, 260, 291, 293, 296

Topic
choosing, 5
exploring, 5, 9
narrowing, 80
specific, 18
understanding, 87

Underlining, 208

Venn diagram, 8, 52, 80
Verbs
action, 162, 163, 165, 166, 167
active voice, 167
agreement, with subject, 176-177
as adjectives, 181
direct objects, 165, 166
forms, 152, 175, 177, 196
base, 196
plural, 152, 175, 177
singular, 152, 175, 177
helping, 168, 171, 176
indirect objects, 166
intransitive, 165
irregular, 173-174
linking, 163, 164, 181
main, 168, 169
modifiers, 179-180, 191
object of, 155, 160
participles, 169, 171
passive voice, 167
phrase, 168, 176
plural, 152, 175, 177
predicate nouns and adjectives, 164
principal parts of, 169
progressive, 171
pronouns as, 155
singular, 152, 175, 177
subject-verb agreement, 175, 176-177
tenses
future, 17
participles, 169, 173, 175, 196-197
past, 169, 170, 173
past participle, 169, 173, 175, 196
past progressive, 171

perfect, 170, 172
future perfect 172
past perfect, 172
present perfect, 172
present, 169, 170
present participle, 169, 171, 175,196
present progressive, 171
transitive, 165
verbals, 196
verbal phrases, 168, 176, 196-197
Villanelle, 61, 62
Visual Aids, 121-122
Visual clues, 89
Visual details, 261
Vocabulary strategies
connotation, 235
context clues, 222, 224-225
comparisons, 224
definitions, 224
examples, 224
general context, 225
synonyms, 224
dictionary, using, 224, 234-235
definitions, 235
entry word, 234, 235
entomology, 235
example sentence, 235
guide word, 235
inflected forms, 235
part-of-speech label, 235
respelling, 235
etymology, 223, 232-234, 235
acronyms, 233
blended words, 233
clipped words, 233
eponyms, 233
figurative language, 58, 60, 65
avoiding, 273
homophones and homographs, 222, 223, 230, 245
idioms, 223, 231
thesaurus, using, 223, 236-237
antonym, 237
definition, 237

entry word, 237
example sentence, 237
part-of-speech label, 237
synonyms, 236-237
word parts, 222, 226-229
bases, 226, 229
prefixes, 226-228, 229
suffixes, 226-228, 229
Voice, writer's, 293

Who, what, when, where, why, 254,
256, 270
Who, whom, 160
Word origins, 223, 232-233, 234, 235
Writer's journal, 24-31
computer as, 25
dialog journals, 31
for ideas, 27-28
kinds of entries
learning notes, 28
personal thoughts and
experiences, 27
reading reactions, 29
privacy and, 25
tips for getting started, 30
using, 24-31
Writing
analyzing, 22-23
conclusions, 253, 255, 261, 263,

265, 267, 269, 277, 281, 283
evaluating, 22-23
introductions in, 251, 254, 256, 258,
260, 264, 266, 267, 270, 272,
276, 286
models
autobiography, 274-275
biography, 276-277
book review, 284-285
business letter, 294-295
cause/effect, 268-269
character sketch, 280-281
compare/contrast, 266-267
descriptive essay, 252-253
editorial, 258-259
feature article, 256-257
friendly letter, 296-297
how-to guide, 272-273
interview, 278-279
news article, 254-255
observational report, 260-261
personal narrative, 292-293
persuasive essay, 251
poem, 288-289
problem/solution, 270-271
research report, 262-263, 264-265
science, 262-263
social studies, 264-265
script, 290-291

story, 286-287
summary, 282-283
process
drafting, 2, 9
editing, 3
freewriting, 7
prewriting, 2, 4-8
proofreading, 12
publishing, 3, 13
reflecting, 3, 14
revising, 2, 10-11
purposes, 20-23
to analyze, 22
to describe, 21
to entertain, 21
to evaluate, 23
to explain, 20
to learn, 22
to persuade, 21
to reflect, 20
to synthesize, 23
to understand, 22
synthesizing, 22-23
types of
descriptive, 15, 17
expository, 15, 18
narrative, 15, 17
persuasive, 15
Writing folder, 4-5

Illustration credits
Part 1: Tim Lewis xiv-1, 2, 15, 20, 24; Joel Snyder 2, 3, 14, 21, 22, 23, 30 ; BB&K (tech art) 2-3, 8, 15, 20, 21; Robin Jareaux 5, 7, 11, 13, 26. **Part 2:** Nicolas Vial 32-33, 34, 35, 36, 48, 54; BB&K (tech art) 34, 35, 45, 46, 48, 51, 52, 53, 54, 55; Robin Jareaux 38, 42, 66. **Part 3:** Mark Bixby 68-69, 70, 79; Joel Snyder 70, 71, 78, 79 (top), 84, 85, 86, 88; BB&K (tech art) 70, 71, 89, 92, 101; Robin Jareaux 73, 76, 77, 81, 98; Rémy Simard 90, 91. **Part 4:** Julia Talcott 102-103, 104; BB&K (tech art) 104, 106, 109, 110, 114, 118, 118a, 118b, 119, 120, 121, 122a, 122b, 122c, 126, 127; Robin Jareaux 107, 116, 117, 133; Rémy Simard 111, 124. **Part 5:** John Jinks 134-135, 136 (left); BB&K (tech art) 136, 137, 148; Franklin Hammond 136, 137 (spots); Robin Jareaux 161, 163, 169, 185, 187, 190, 206, 211; Rémy Simard 199, 200a, 200b, 201a, 201b. **Part 6:** Kaz Aizawa 220-221, 222, 223, 226, 227, 229, 230, 238 (left), 244; BB&K (tech art) 222, 223, 234, 236; Rémy Simard 225, 246, 247; Chuck Gonzales 231, 238 (bottom), 245; Joel Snyder 237. **Part 7:** Valerie Marsella 248-250 (spread), 250 (strip); Chuck Gonzales 248, 250 (spots), 257, 263, 265, 267, 269, 270, 273, 274, 279, 282, 287, 291, 292; Valerie Marsella 298 (strip); Chuck Gonzales (spot); Rémy Simard 299, 300, 301, 303, 304, 305, 306, 307.

Photography credits
All photographs are by the Macmillan/McGraw-Hill School Division (MMSD) except as noted below.

Part 1: UPI/Bettmann 16; Sandra Dos Passos/Bruce Coleman Inc. 17; Helen Iranyi 24; Susanne Moss 24; Lori Adamski Peek/Tony Stone Images 25. **Part 2:** National Gallery, Prague/Art Resource, NY 60; Museum of Art, Cleveland/Superstock 62. **Part 3:** Musée D'Orsay, Paris/Giraudon/Art Resource, NY 93T; Art Resource, NY 93M; State Museum of Russia, St. Petersburg/Art Resource, NY 93B; Tate Gallery, London/Art Resource, NY 94T; B. Roland/The Image Works 94B; Lorraine O'Grady 95T; © Joel Sternfeld, Courtesy PaceWildensteinMacGill, NY 95B. **Part 5:** Phyllis Greenberg/Comstock 138L; Bob Daemmrich/Animals Animals 139; Focus on Sports 154L; Universal Pictures Inc./Photofest 160; David Stoecklein/Stock Market 162B; Bill Lea 168; Stephen Frisch/Stock Boston 178L; Larry Kolvoord/The Image Works 180; Elisabeth Zuckerman/PhotoEdit 188; Kenneth Garrett/WestLight 194B; Grant Faint/The Image Bank 196L. **Part 7:** Phil Shermeister/Photographers Aspen 255; Lauren Arce 281; Tim Davis/Photo Researchers Inc. 297.